Gotham's War within a War

Gotham's War within a War

Policing and the Birth of Law-and-Order Liberalism in World War II–Era New York City

Emily M. Brooks

The University of North Carolina Press CHAPEL HILL

© 2023 Emily M. Brooks

Set in Merope Basic by Westchester Publishing Services
Manufactured in the United States of America

Library of Congress Cataloging-in-Publication Data
Names: Brooks, Emily M., author.
Title: Gotham's war within a war : policing and the birth of law-and-order
    liberalism in World War II-era New York City / Emily M. Brooks.
Other titles: Policing and the birth of law-and-order liberalism in World War II-
    era New York City | Justice, power, and politics.
Description: Chapel Hill : The University of North Carolina Press, 2023. |
    Series: Justice, power, and politics | Includes bibliographical references
    and index.
Identifiers: LCCN 2023029874 | ISBN 9781469676586 (cloth ; alk. paper) |
    ISBN 9781469676593 (pbk. ; alk. paper) | ISBN 9781469676609 (ebook)
Subjects: LCSH: New York (N.Y.). Police Department—History. |
    Law enforcement—New York (State)—New York—History—20th century. |
    Police-community relations—New York (State)—New York—History—
    20th century. | Criminal behavior, Prediction of—New York (State)—
    New York—History—20th century. | BISAC: HISTORY / United States /
    20th Century | POLITICAL SCIENCE / Public Policy / Social Policy
Classification: LCC HV8148.N5 B76 2023 | DDC 363.209747—dc23/
    eng/20230721
LC record available at https://lccn.loc.gov/2023029874

Cover photos: *Top*, Fiorello La Guardia saluting policemen with Harvey Gibson
(Manuscript and Archives Division, New York Public Library); *bottom*, police
on 5th Avenue and 51st Street, ca. 1940 (unknown [x2010.11.4741], Museum
of the City of New York).

For my father, Jeffrey P. Brooks,
who was born in wartime New York City
and who taught me to view the past and future
with imagination and hope

Contents

Acknowledgments

I am delighted to be able to thank many institutions and people for their support over the course of this long project. The Martin E. Segal Dissertation Fellowship for the Study of the History of New York at the Graduate Center of the City University of New York provided support for me to finish the earlier draft of this project. Funding from the Mellon/American Council of Learned Societies Community College Faculty Fellowship enabled me to cut back on teaching to work on my manuscript. The National Endowment for the Humanities Long-Term Fellowship at the New York Public Library's Center for Research in the Humanities allowed me to complete the final stages of archival research and devote extensive time to writing. Thank you to Melanie Locay for support during the fellowship. I presented parts of this book as a member of the New-York Historical Society's Center for Women's History Early Career Workshop and received helpful feedback. Thank you to the *Journal of Urban History* and *Labor History* for permitting the reprinting of work that originally appeared as articles in those journals. Chapter 2 is derived in part from my article "Coercive Patriotism: Gender, Militarism, and Auxiliary Police in New York City during World War II," *Labor History* (November 23, 2022), copyright Taylor & Francis, available online: http:// www.tandfonline.com/ 10.1080/0023656X.2022.2147912. Chapter 5 is derived in part from the following article: "'Rumor, Vicious Innuendo, and False Reports': Policing Black Soldiers in Wartime Staten Island," *Journal of Urban History* 47, no. 5 (2020): 1032–49, copyright © 2020 (Emily Brooks), https://doi.org/10.1177/009614421999001.

I would like to thank the wonderful team at the University of North Carolina Press. I am honored to publish this book in the incomparable Justice, Power, and Politics series and extremely grateful to series editors Heather Ann Thompson and Rhonda Y. Williams for their support. My editors Brandon Proia and Dawn Durante provided invaluable guidance as I completed this manuscript. Brandon's support carried me through particularly difficult stages of the project. He fought for my work even when he did not have to, and I will always be grateful. Dawn came on toward the end of the project but embraced it fully and helped me get through the finishing stages. Thank you to the two anonymous readers who read my early sample chapter and then the entire manuscript. Their reports were extremely generous and improved the manuscript immensely.

The labor of many archivists was essential to this project. This book could not have been written without the work of the staffs at the Manuscripts and Archives Division at the New York Public Library; the New York City Municipal Archives, especially Rossy Mendez; the Manuscripts and Archives Division at John Jay College Library, particularly Ellen Belcher; the Schomburg Center for Research in Black Culture at the New York Public Library, particularly Barrye Brown; the Manuscript Division of the Library of Congress; the Social Welfare History Archives at the University of Minnesota; the National Archives at College Park; the Center for Jewish History; and the Columbia University Center for Oral History. The Carl Van Vechten Trust generously granted me permission to reprint an image to which they hold the rights. The Women's Prison Association graciously allowed me access to their organization's closed case files. I have tried to treat the women's stories that I found in those files with as much care as possible.

Many mentors, teachers, and colleagues provided insight and guidance that enriched this project. I am very grateful that I had the opportunity to learn from Khalil Gibran Muhammad, whose clarity as a scholar and a teacher is unparalleled. Joshua Freeman and Michael Rawson provided rigorous and encouraging criticism on how to connect the project to urban histories. Clarence Taylor gave invaluable comments related to histories of police brutality against Black New Yorkers. Joan Scott supported and pushed the project for years, strengthening it at every step of the way and helping me to see gender working in the processes I explored. Naomi Murakawa's sharp insights on the history of the carceral state made the manuscript clearer and smarter, and her guidance throughout the process of writing was essential. David Nasaw has championed my work since my first day of graduate school. He enthusiastically encouraged me, while always pushing for my writing to be clearer and my research stronger. His guidance and support helped make this book a reality. I could not have asked for a better teacher, adviser, or mentor. Thank you for everything.

I would also like to thank the many colleagues and friends who provided support for me or this project over the last ten years. Thank you to Larry May and Elaine Tyler May for your encouragement. Thank you to Karen Miller for asking the smartest and most political questions when reading and for being a great dinner host. Thank you to Ann Gray Fischer for improving chapter 6 with your generous and essential insights and for your advice throughout the writing process. Thank you to Hugh Ryan for sharing your thoughts on histories of women's imprisonment in New York and on primary sources. Matthew Guariglia exchanged ideas with me as we both completed our projects on policing in New York City, and this manuscript is stronger for it. Ean Oesterle and Katie Uva sustained me throughout this project, encouraging me and reading drafts when I felt stuck. The manuscript is smarter and clearer because of their comments. Thank you to Laura Fink for your support throughout this project. Sarah Litvin, Arinn Amer, and Jeanne Gutierrez provided invaluable feedback at our writing workshop lunch meetings. Thank you to Jessie Kindig for the witching, cocktails, and company. Kimberly Bloom-Feshbach, Joel Feingold, Ruth Baron, Erik Wallenberg, Edna Bonhomme, Jesse Zarley, Baird Campbell, Shifra Goldenberg, and Kallie Dale-Ramos provided feedback, friendship, and encouragement. Sarah Olle and Suma Chandrasekaran supported me through every crisis, every success, and every regular day. They heard more about 1930s and 1940s New York City than they probably ever wanted to.

I was extremely lucky to begin a new job at the New York Public Library's Center for Educators and Schools at the end of this project. I am grateful for the interest and encouragement of my new colleagues and for the ability to contribute to an essential institution that serves the public of New York City.

I would never have been able to complete this project without the support of my family. Thank you to the Zills for your encouragement of my work. Thank you, in particular, to Karen Zill for being such a loving granny and for providing essential childcare throughout the COVID-19 daycare closures. Thank you to my sister, Lizzy Brooks, for boosting me through the lows and celebrating the highs with me. Thank you to my mother, Karen Brooks, for believing in me for all these years, for showing me how to get things done, and for being Zelda's first childcare provider. We would not have gotten through 2020 without you. My father, Jeffrey Brooks, has been my number one supporter all my life. He showed me that reading, writing, and teaching history could be meaningful, creative, and fun. This book is for him. Finally, to my z's: Zach Zill has believed in this project since it began. Thank you for always pushing for it to be better and for always knowing I'd finish it. Zelda Brooks was born toward the end of this project. She made everything harder and so much more fun. Thank you.

Gotham's War within a War

Introduction

"I have always been in favor of strict enforcement of the morals laws. Corruption in police departments generally begins through alliances between police and morals laws violators."[1] So declared former New York City police commissioner Lewis Valentine in his 1947 autobiography. The book, introduced by the man who appointed Valentine commissioner, Mayor Fiorello La Guardia, and tellingly entitled *Night Stick*, included sensational anecdotes from the law enforcement leader's life, as well as clear articulations of his beliefs about how policing should work and the roles that police officers should play in city life. Though *Night Stick* was published after Valentine's death in 1946, its publication and positive reception reflected his prominence in discussions about policing in the United States. The book detailed his thirty-one years in the New York City Police Department before he was named police commissioner by La Guardia, his tenure as police commissioner, his subsequent period as an adviser for the popular radio show *Gangbusters*, and his experience overseeing the reorganization of civilian policing in U.S.-occupied Japan. The *New York Times* review of the book stated that though "the late Commissioner Valentine has labeled it an autobiography . . . it is more the history of the metropolitan Police Department he did so much to revitalize during his eleven-year tenure."[2]

Valentine's eleven-year stint as commissioner, from 1934 to 1945, was also the tenure of New York City's most famous reform mayor, La Guardia, and a period of crisis and change in American governance. La Guardia came into power in 1934 on the heels of a city-hall-shattering corruption investigation that called into question many long-held truths about how the government of Gotham, as New York City was colloquially known, should run. The Tammany Democratic faction that was discredited in these investigations had controlled city politics for much of the previous eighty years. Tammany mayors relied on NYPD officers to grant favors, protect allies, punish challenges, and improve the Democratic faction's chances at the ballot when overseeing elections. Additionally, police department appointments were granted to low-level party members, who then often extorted bribes or kickbacks from proprietors working in the underground economy, many of which then flowed upstream to powerful Tammany players.[3] Energetic,

1

progressive, and irascible, La Guardia barreled into office in 1934 with a new vision for how city government could function and the role of the police department within city life. After a brief experiment with another commissioner, he tapped Valentine to bring his vision to life. As Valentine's statement about morals laws policing illustrates, the pair believed that police corruption and permissive approaches to crimes of vice or morality that included prostitution (as sex work was known), juvenile delinquency, gambling, and disorderly conduct were the primary problems with policing in New York. La Guardia, Valentine, and their supporters contended that these crimes "endanger[ed] public morality" and proved "a disgrace to the people of the City of New York," while also enabling police corruption through payoffs and extortion.[4]

Following their assumption of office, La Guardia and Valentine crafted a new model of liberal law-and-order policing.[5] Rejecting the machine patronage system that their administration had replaced, the duo divorced the police department from partisan politics. "Police work is now a profession," La Guardia informed NYPD members, in which officers were "given a chance to do good work without political or any other kind of interference."[6] Professional officers were expected to enforce the law aggressively and uniformly to all city residents alike—to remain unswayed by partisan allegiance or bribes. Valentine and La Guardia—or the Little Flower, as he was sometimes known, based on the English translation of his first name—also positioned the NYPD as committed to hiring officers and policing the city without regard to racial hierarchy. Valentine proclaimed to the New York Urban League, an organization devoted to Black advancement, that his office was "willing and eager to work with any groups in the community willing to assist him in recruiting [Black] candidates for the police force with the necessary physical and mental equipment for the work."[7] As this quotation suggests, however, racist ideas about the capabilities of Black people and associations between criminality and Black communities structured policing under Valentine and La Guardia. The leaders interwove these racist conceptions with ideas about gender, sexuality, class, and morality and packaged them together under the concepts of "order" and "security."

Establishing an orderly and safe city was important to the administrators for a number of different reasons, one of which involved the city government's relationship to finance and investment. Though an avid fighter for the city's public sphere, La Guardia had a keen awareness of the role that actual and metaphorical investment in the city from finance and business could play in its governance. On his first day in office, he set about trying to close the city's budget deficit to restore the value of municipal bonds.[8] For La Guardia, however, a "scowling defender of the public interest," in the words of historian Mason Williams, the more important justification behind his commitment to expanding police power was the improvement he believed it would bring to the public lives of New Yorkers.[9] To the mayor and his police commissioner, sex workers, juvenile delinquents, gamblers, and disorderly persons were impediments to equitable access to public space and public resources. What their ideology overlooked, however, was the way that these criminal categories, whose definitions were entirely reliant on social hierarchies, created their own landscape of inequality. *Gotham's War within a War* tracks the emergence of this law-and-order liberalism, which was crafted in response to municipal corruption and a diversifying population and which profited greatly from the militarism and nationalism that accompanied the nation's mobilization for World War II.

New York City's changing racial demographics were central to the mayor and police commissioner's view of crime and order. From 1930 to 1950 the city's Black population more than doubled and grew from 4.7 percent to 9 percent of the city's total population.[10] These new residents came from the American South and, to a lesser extent, from the Caribbean.[11] The city's Puerto Rican population had also increased during the 1920s following the severe restriction of immigration from Europe. Though migration decreased significantly during the war, about 61,500 Puerto Ricans called New York City home in 1940.[12] The city's white officials, and many white Gothamites, viewed the new residents with extreme unease. Signs stating "No Dogs, No Negroes, and No Spanish" marked apartment buildings and advertised the city's racial hierarchy.[13]

La Guardia and Valentine worked to establish their vision of order and security throughout the 1930s, but met with resistance from the city's growing Black population, led by Black women, as well as from other criminalized groups including working-class women across races and young people. The mobilization for World War II shifted the terrain of this municipal contest; offenses previously categorized as challenges to urban order became threats to national security. During the mobilization, the prevention of Black uprisings or labor unrest and the preservation of the health and morality of enlisted white men who traveled through the city became even sharper priorities for the municipal leaders. In a landscape of an expanded and militarized state and constricted space for civil liberties, La Guardia and Valentine were able to fully realize a policing regime of municipal law-and-order liberalism that they had been pushing since 1934. As the mayor declared in the fall of 1940, he had "the heat turned on gambling and vice for some time, [and] this was no time to let down."[14]

Gotham, the duo knew, would play a central role in shipping out men and supplies were the United States to enter the conflict.[15] La Guardia worried that the city's role in transportation networks and its cultural significance would render it a possible target for air strikes or submarine attacks, despite its geographic protections and the fuel limitations of existing bombers. While such an external attack proved a slim possibility, Valentine and La Guardia knew well the internal threats that certainly lurked on the city's streets and in its harbors, bars, and theaters. On the eve of war, they redoubled their campaigns against such evils as juvenile delinquency, prostitution, gambling, and disorderly entertainment; this time with the protection of enlisted soldiers and sailors, wartime peace in the city, and national security in mind.

The increased importance of such efforts during the war, the municipal leaders argued, required the reorganization and expansion of the NYPD's anti-vice efforts, which now were an essential component of national security. They formed an auxiliary police force of over 7,000, raised the quotas for women in the NYPD, created a new National Defense Squad to suppress vice, organized community groups to monitor youth, and tried to prevent patrolmen from retiring during the war. The pair would also consistently link the civic sacrifices of soldiers and sailors to those of patrolmen, seeking to build connections between policing in New York City and the national war mobilization. In their efforts, Valentine and La Guardia would receive assistance from the city's Health Department, state and federal agencies, and the military, all of whom participated in shaping the policing landscape of wartime New York City.

So-called vice or morals laws policing proved particularly reflective of political shifts like the mobilization for war. This police activity was usually driven solely by law enforcement policy and discretion, rather than initiated by a civilian complainant. The legal and policy definitions of vice crimes or offenses purported to describe behavior, but were so general that they relied heavily on police discretion and surveillance of people with criminalized identities.[16] "General Instructions for Plainclothesmen" in the NYPD's 1940 manual noted, "Testimony given by an arresting officer that he had a female defendant under observation for ten or fifteen minutes; that during that time she covered but a short space of ground; that she spoke to or endeavored to attract the attention of several men, and that the police officer knew her to be a prostitute, will warrant a conviction."[17] These directives illustrate the extent to which discretion and the perceived identities of surveilled residents influenced police behavior. Further, we can see that gender and sexuality, along with race and class, were central to how police understood and interpreted the criminal categories that La Guardia and Valentine encouraged them to enforce with new vigor. The mobilization for World War II heightened the gendered divisions of citizenship and the role of gender in policing New York City. When NYPD officers policed for juvenile delinquency, gambling, and disorderly conduct, Valentine and La Guardia directed them to similarly use visual markers of race, class, and sexuality and consider them in conjunction with the city's geography to make judgments about criminality.

La Guardia and Valentine's new paradigm for policing did not escape local criticism and resistance. Their tenure was, in fact, bookended by two mass uprisings in Harlem driven partly by frustration with racist policing. Through the 1930s and 1940s, Black New Yorkers, youth, and working-class women across races individually and collectively resisted the heightened surveillance and criminalization that the mayor and police commissioner sought to introduce. During these years, ending racially targeted police brutality and harassment was a central civil rights demand for both newly arrived and long-established Black New Yorkers.[18] When the federal Office of Facts and Figures interviewed over 1,000 Black residents in New York about their opinions on the war and their status in American life in spring 1942, only 2 percent answered "police" when asked, "Who would a Negro go to around here if he couldn't get his rights?" For comparison, "Nobody—Cynical 'Who, indeed?'" was the response from 4 percent of respondents.[19] Women in Harlem, led by activists like novelist and reporter Ann Petry, criticized police practices that they felt labeled Black women as prostitutes and boycotted newspapers that disseminated these stereotypes. Incarcerated women petitioned city magistrates for retrials, calling their indefinite detention unjust. Young girls launched a daring nighttime escape from a Brooklyn reformatory. Burlesque performers picketed city hall after La Guardia's commissioner of licenses shuttered their theaters. Parents complained of the treatment their children met at the hands of NYPD officers. In many of these instances of resistance, New Yorkers connected their criticism to the ongoing war being fought in the name of democracy and freedom. When faced with police repression, they asked, in the words of one Long Island father, "Is this the freedom we are all working so hard for?"[20]

These protests did not fall on sympathetic ears. The city's leadership prioritized maintaining urban order and protecting the health and security of enlisted men, particularly white enlisted men, over respecting the civil, social, and sexual liberties of New Yorkers. Furthermore, the space for criticism of NYPD policies narrowed in the wartime political landscape. Politicians at the local and national levels, as well as many New Yorkers, adopted a framework of coercive patriotism in which any challenge to state authorities or the war mobilization was selfish, dangerous, and anti-American.[21] This perspective justified heightened surveillance and criminalization of sexually profiled women and girls, who were depicted as venereal disease carriers; led La Guardia to send letters to men deferred from military service telling them that they needed to volunteer for the city's new auxiliary policing agency or face the possible revocation of their deferral; drove neighbors to inform on each other for supposedly inappropriate use of resources or gambling practices; and broadly led to increased surveillance and criminalization of targeted populations throughout the city.[22] This book argues that La Guardia and Valentine crafted a new model of liberal law-and-order policing in New York City in the 1930s. It contends that this vision of policing thrived during the militarized moment of World War II when the space for criticism shrank and the NYPD received ideological and material support from the federal government.

New York City was not just any urban landscape. It was and remains the nation's largest city, as well as a cultural and financial center. As the head of the recently formed U.S. Conference of Mayors for almost his entire eleven years in office, the leader of the largest city in the country, and a well-known former congressional representative with sway in Washington, La Guardia exerted influence beyond New York City's five boroughs. Valentine was also a nationally recognized leader. His savvy awareness of the city's racial politics and his strain of seemingly unbiased yet harsh anti-vice policing distinguished him from many of his counterparts. When the governor of Maryland wanted to integrate the Baltimore Police Department in 1938, he looked to New York.[23] Unlike the police commissioner of Detroit, Valentine was celebrated for the way the NYPD handled an uprising in Harlem in 1943, even in some of the city's African American papers.[24] When General Douglas MacArthur sought a law enforcement expert to oversee the reorganization of the police force in occupied Japan, he requested Valentine "by name."[25] By the end of the war, there was no better representative of American municipal policing than the NYPD's Lewis Valentine, and other cities sought to follow his lead.[26]

Gotham's War within a War's interrogation of mid-twentieth-century liberal policing connects and enriches three branches of the growing subfield of histories of policing in the United States. The first branch considers the role of race and gender in structuring police power. Because of the United States' history of race-based enslavement and the racist criminalization of Black Americans that followed the abolition of slavery, racism on the part of police and resistance by Black Americans are at the center of much historiography on policing. Historians have shown that northern urban America was a generative site for this policing and resistance; Gotham proves no exception.[27] Scholars of African American history have explored the experiences of Black women in relation to police, and although much of the historiography on policing centers Black men, a number of historians have begun to consider how gender works with race, class, sexuality, nationality, and other forms of identity to structure police power.[28]

The second strand considers the way that the activities of the police intersect with city politics and liberal ideology.[29] Historians and scholars have begun to consider these interconnected themes but have not done so in La Guardia's New York City, which was one of the most long-running and influential municipal administrations in the United States in the twentieth century. By exploring policing in mid-twentieth-century New York City, *Gotham's War within a War* provides a missing link in histories of policing between studies of the late nineteenth century and Progressive Era, when police departments were small and reform generally came from outside government, and the post–World War II turn toward "urban crisis" and mass incarceration.

The book also enriches understandings of liberalism and urban politics by unearthing an essential, yet overlooked, component of La Guardia's influential administration. Despite his short stature, La Guardia casts a long shadow in New York City's history. Multiple biographers frame his life as emblematic of the city's trajectory into the "modern" twentieth century.[30] Yet the Little Flower's approach to policing and crime, one of the most modern and enduring aspects of his administration, has not been a focus of these works. Furthermore, Valentine, the man with whom La Guardia crafted his policing praxis and who led the NYPD for by far the longest term in the twentieth century, has merited even less discussion from scholars.[31] Historians have missed how central police reform was to La Guardia's larger urban vision and how formative his politics were to liberal visions of policing more broadly.

Finally, the third historiographical subfield that this book engages with is histories that explore policing from perspectives of militarism and military mobilizations. *Gotham's War within a War* considers the interconnections between militarism and policing by examining how World War II changed policing in New York City. It places studies of the World War II home front in conversation with histories of policing, therefore reframing how we see the impact of the war on American society and on the trajectory of policing in the United States.[32] During the war, in cities across the United States urban leaders were considering how to increase surveillance and maintain control over criminalized populations. Though the particulars varied in accordance with the city's demographic makeup and its role in military mobilizations and wartime production, municipal administrators across the country shared common goals. From Orlando, Florida, to Long Beach, California, coalitions of city officials, military administrators, police officers, and even Immigration and Naturalization Service agents worked to control populations they viewed as threats to urban order or the wartime mobilization. Depending on the city, these threats included Black migrants, Japanese Americans, sexually profiled women, Mexican American "zoot suiters" and "pachucas," Chinese sailors, and enlisted men on leave. As Aaron Hiltner argues, the war ushered in "a wave of urban militarization" that rippled through many urban systems, including policing.[33] *Gotham's War within a War* shows that the wartime obsession with gendered policing explored at the federal level by women's historians also affected municipal policing. This new history of wartime policing enriches understandings of the relationship between military mobilization and domestic policing. Though modern activists often reference the collaborative relationship between the military and domestic police departments today and scholars have highlighted how this relationship expanded after the Vietnam War, the longer histories of these intertwined branches of violent state power remain less well explored.[34]

The chapters that follow explore how La Guardia and Valentine sought to build their liberal policing regime and how New Yorkers resisted. Chapter 1 provides a political prehistory of policing in New York City in the years before La Guardia and Valentine took office. It explicates the way that policing functioned under Tammany and how the Little Flower and his police commissioner formed their conception of policing partly in reaction to the Tammany order. Chapter 2 explores La Guardia and Valentine's ideology of policing. It examines the ways they sought to change the police department and how the NYPD fit into La Guardia's larger vision for city administration as well as how the war intervened in these plans. Chapter 3 examines the NYPD's campaigns against prostitution. It considers how prostitution policing functioned under Tammany and how La Guardia responded to that. It explores how the city's Health Department collaborated with the NYPD to surveil, arrest, and incarcerate sexually profiled women and how these powers expanded with the mobilization for war. It examines the way that this policing was racialized and how Black women resisted criminalization. Chapter 4 looks at the construction of juvenile delinquency. It examines how youth policing had developed as a concept throughout the early twentieth century and the ways that gender and race dictated how officers conceived of and looked for delinquency. It explores the way anxiety about juvenile delinquency increased during the war and how these anxieties bolstered policing and surveillance, as well as how youth and their parents resisted. Chapter 5 considers the racialized ways that men were policed for gambling, as well as how service in the military influenced NYPD officers' interactions with men. It looks at how gendered conceptions of citizenship changed for men during the war and how those changes affected policing. It examines how NYPD officers were both directed not to "bother" enlisted men and sent in droves to police Black soldiers stationed on Staten Island. It centers wartime masculinity and coercive patriotism. Chapter 6 looks at the policing of nightlife in Harlem. It examines the NYPD's networks for surveilling leisure spaces and how the neighborhood was criminalized. It considers how residents resisted this criminalization throughout the 1930s and how it intensified during the war, with interracial socializing and the Savoy Ballroom as particular targets. Together these chapters present a new picture of 1930s and 1940s New York City, an altered perspective on the impact of World War II on American life, and a surprising origin story for the nonpartisan, deeply discriminatory form of policing that we know so well today.

CHAPTER ONE

A Political History of Policing in Pre-1930s New York City

Contemporary popular discourse in the United States understands urban policing solely through a lens of crime. This formulation fundamentally misconstrues the history of policing in U.S. cities and the relationships between police departments and municipal governments. Broader discussions about the roles that police play in American life are distorted by an expectation that when we talk about police, we are talking about crime, and when we talk about crime, we must talk about police.

The history of policing in New York City shows that policing is better understood not as a response to crime but as an expression of the political priorities of governing elites. These priorities generally involved efforts by members of this group to maintain political, economic, or social control. The process of writing laws, enforcing them, and creating criminal categories has always been a reflection of the priorities of governing institutions. Historian Kelly Lytle Hernandez describes human caging in Los Angeles as a practice embraced by those with political and cultural power to "resolve social tensions and reach political objectives."[1] The history of policing in New York City flows from the motivations of the city's ruling powers; from the West India Company's attempts to expand European settlement and exert power over neighboring Lenape communities, to English colonial administrators' efforts to prevent fires and quash uprisings of enslaved New Yorkers, to campaigns by revolutionists to punish disloyalty, to efforts by the occupying British to maintain an orderly class of soldiers, to ruling elites' endeavors to smash nascent industrial working people's movements, to the Tammany Democratic machine's attempts to solicit votes and distribute jobs, to Fiorello La Guardia's campaign to establish a nonpartisan regime of "law-and-order," politics drove policing in New York City. These efforts were not always successful, and what constituted the work of policing was also produced by the needs and desires of patrolmen themselves. Despite these caveats, the political motivations of the city's leadership were at the core of policing and law enforcement throughout the city's history. This chapter will briefly trace this political history of policing in New York City. It will demonstrate how efforts to enforce laws and maintain order were inextricable from the political motivations of ruling factions.

The model of policing that exists in the United States today can be traced to elite efforts to encourage investment and preserve order in an expanding and increasingly divided nineteenth-century Gotham. This model has roots that can be followed to earlier law enforcement projects in the city, including the organized patrols, vigilante groups, and town criers responsible for controlling enslaved people in public space throughout the eighteenth century, the night watch that vacillated between military and civilian control depending on colonial leadership's assessments of the risks of war with imperial rivals, and the West India Company's military commanders who selectively enforced the colony's laws in order to maintain a strong force of soldiers available for essential labor.[2] These law enforcement projects served the changing goals of New Amsterdam and then New York's leadership. As postrevolutionary New York became more densely populated and diverse into the nineteenth century, elites in the city began to push for a larger and more organized police force to protect their property, create a stable environment for investment, and control the city's poor.

"First of All We Will Expect Attention to a Municipal Police": Creating Professional Police in Nineteenth-Century New York

In the years after the American Revolution and into the nineteenth century, the city's population grew immensely, spiking from 200,000 in 1830 to 500,000 in 1850.[3] Because of its geographic advantages and size, Gotham was a hub in the nation's emerging capitalist economy.[4] New York State played a pivotal role in the movement of goods and people between the East Coast and the middle of the country, particularly after the 1825 completion of the Erie Canal. New York City's manufacturing and shipping industries attracted workers from the surrounding regions as well as large numbers of immigrants, particularly from Germany and Ireland. In addition to drawing workers to its streets and tenements, New York City housed many headquarters of those profiting from the nation's economic changes. Wealthy merchants, manufacturers, financiers, and shipping magnates all had economic and personal interests in the city that they were working to position as the "London of the New World."[5] Many of these merchants and financiers built their fortunes on financing or trading with Southern enslavers.[6] Early nineteenth-century Gotham, therefore, was home to a growing mass of workers and an emerging elite class, two groups whose economic interests were in conflict. Despite these combustible demographic shifts, the city continued to be policed by a small, poorly paid group consisting of night watchmen and a police force of sixteen elected constables and roughly sixty mayor-appointed marshals.[7]

Riots, protests, mass meetings, and crime threatened to destabilize the city's emerging class of elites. Though this class would become more united and self-conscious only later in the nineteenth century, it possessed disproportionate political control in the city in this earlier period as well.[8] Historian Lisa Keller notes that in the late 1830s, "three-quarters of the City Council consisted of merchants, businessmen, attorneys, and professionals, 15 percent were retailers, and only 10 percent were artisans."[9] For these middle- and upper-class councilmen, mass disruptions like the 1836 stonemason riot in opposition to New York University's use of prison labor, the 1837 flour riot, attacks on brothels, theater riots, and large meetings and protests by laborers and artisans undermined the city's appeal as a base for business and finance.[10] Additionally, antislavery organizing and vigilance groups who protected Black New Yorkers from being sent into slavery deterred Southern enslavers from traveling into the city. Constables and marshals formed part of what abolitionist David Ruggles called "the New York Kidnapping Club," a group that captured Black New Yorkers on behalf of Southern enslavers, as Jonathan Wells documents.[11] The overlapping motivations of supporting slavery to facilitate ties with enslavers' capital and maintaining social, economic, and political stability to preserve profits and attract investment more broadly set policing priorities during this period.

The desire for greater stability further impelled the city's political leadership to create a professional "day and night police" in 1845. Under the administration of Mayor James Harper, the owner of a publishing house and a reformer who had gained both Whig and Democratic support during his campaign, city council proposed legislation for a new system of municipal policing. The new force was modeled partly on the Metropolitan Police force created in London in 1829, which itself was modeled on British counterinsurgency campaigns in occupied Ireland, showing the colonial roots of municipal policing.[12] Elite New Yorkers admired the success of the Metropolitan Police in maintaining order and protecting the persons and property of the wealthy. The London correspondent for New York's second-largest circulation paper, the *Atlas*, declared in March 1844, "The *police system* in London day and night is admirable. No stranger need fear traversing the streets at any hour; his person is safe."[13] Gotham's new police bill replaced the existing patchwork departments of night watch, marshals, street inspectors, fire wardens, bell ringers, day police officers, Sunday officers, poll officers, inspectors of omnibuses, dock masters, and other urban services with a unified police force about 800 strong charged with preventing disorder and crime and overseen by a mayor-appointed chief of police.[14] Editors at the Democratic *New York Herald*, the city's largest circulation paper, shared their hopes for city council's priorities following the November 1844 election. "First of all we will expect attention to a municipal police. . . . We now want a good police more than ever."[15] In 1844, admirers of London's Metropolitan Police got their wish as the city created its own municipal police department.

Although the professional police force was intended to stabilize the city for business, from its inception it was clear that its provision of a new slate of municipal jobs constituted an important intervention in the city's partisan politics and economic landscape. "The new city Police law will furnish places for five hundred officers under the corporation," the *New York Herald* proclaimed of an early draft of the new police bill. Editors framed the force as a jobs program, continuing, "There are about five thousand hungry applicants. What will be done with the 4500? Can you answer that, Mayor Harper?"[16]

These hungry applicants included the city's growing Irish population who were fleeing famine and would, over the course of the next ten years, make up over 25 percent of the city's population.[17] Tammany Hall, the powerful Manhattan faction of the Democratic Party that regularly controlled city hall, welcomed Irish immigrants into the fold, providing them access to government jobs, including in the new police force.[18] Members of the new police force were appointed to fixed terms by the aldermen of the wards they were to patrol, imbedding them within the city's partisan political system. This structure allowed officers to operate with more individual discretion and granted political parties greater control than in the system of policing in London after which the NYPD had first been modeled.[19]

The department was further centralized and moved under the control of the mayor in the early 1850s. It became a central node in Democratic mayor Fernando Wood's mid-1850s machine. Wood took, in the words of Terry Golway, an "inordinate interest" in staffing the New York Police Department, and his opponents accused him of favoring Democrats.[20] The mayor was also a virulent racist. He sought to destroy the free Black community of Seneca Village in the construction of Central Park, and he was a fierce supporter of the slave South during the Civil War, even going so far as to advocate that New York City secede from the Union.[21] Wood's manipulations of the police department and his antipathy toward Black New Yorkers were interwoven: he wielded police power against the city's Black population, while also excluding them from a central node of the most powerful political entity of the city, thereby shoring up power in other communities. Wood further used the police to strengthen his political advantage by encouraging the Municipal Police Department not to enforce an 1857 temperance law, which was opposed by his supporters.[22]

Because of this connection to Democratic political power, Republican reformers, who wielded a strong hand in state politics but struggled to assert control in Gotham, took aim at the police department in 1857. The Metropolitan Police Act of that year created police forces for Brooklyn and for Queens, Westchester, and Staten Island (which were not yet part of New York City), as well as a second Manhattan-based force known as the Metropolitans. Governor-appointed commissioners oversaw the new departments.[23] For a brief period, the Wood-controlled municipal police continued to operate and the city housed two opposing police agencies—one loyal to the Republicans and one to the Democrats. A court order disbanded the Municipals after a few months of this chaotic situation, however, and control of the police department stayed in Albany until 1870 when the Tammany Tweed Ring created a new city charter.[24] The competition between the two parties over who could control policing in New York illustrates that policing was affected by partisan shifts in power, but also that both parties recognized the police department itself as a tool to strengthen party control.

On Gotham's streets, the police department had a powerful, if unpredictable, impact on residents, particularly those whose presence in public space proved problematic for city elites. Changes in gender relations and attitudes toward female sexuality led middle-class reformers and city officials to devote new attention to sex work and policing working-class and poor women in the 1850s. This new priority was then reflected in the work of the police department. In 1855, members of the police department aided Dr. William Sanger in an investigation into prostitution that resulted in an influential report titled *History of Prostitution*. Between 1850 and 1860, the number of women incarcerated for vagrancy, the statutory offense that included prostitution, more than doubled. From 1849 to 1860, imprisonments for keeping disorderly houses increased by more than five times.[25] These dramatic increases in imprisonment, which one historian has suggested were accompanied by a decrease in prostitution in proportion to the city's population, indicate the relatively new municipal police department was turning significant attention to policing women's sexuality and poor women in public space.[26] Police attention was unpredictable and politicized, however; officers sometimes underrepresented the amount of prostitution in an effort to weaken criticism of their political allies.[27] Both the new attention to policing poor women and the episodic efforts to underplay the popularity of prostitution in the city reflected the relationship between the priorities of political elites and policing.

The mid-nineteenth-century municipal police department, however, did not always carry out the priorities of city elites. The department proved particularly inept when it came to episodes of mass violence in the city. In 1857, the Dead Rabbits and Bowery Boys rioted in the streets, killing twelve and injuring three times that. During the fighting, the Metropolitans failed "even to protect themselves from the fury of the mobs," according to the *New York Herald*.[28] Six years later, in July 1863, the city descended into the worst episode of mass violence in its history, the Draft Riots.[29] The rioters targeted military and government buildings before turning against Black people and spaces associated with them. Though resistance to the class privilege written into the Conscription Act of 1863 was the catalyst for violence, rioters were influenced by the widespread proslavery and anti-Black political traditions in the city. They were encouraged to violence by antiwar newspaper editors and Democratic Party leaders.[30] At least one hundred Black New Yorkers were killed in the violence, hundreds were wounded, and thousands were driven from their homes. Junius C. Morel, a journalist, educator, and political leader in the Black community of Weeksville in Brooklyn, described the events as a "fearful volcano of fire, blood, death, lamentation and wo" in which "no black person could show their heads but what they were hunted like wolves."[31] In Manhattan, outnumbered police officers failed to halt well-armed rioters and sometimes became the target of violence themselves. In the wake of the riots, many Black New Yorkers fled the city permanently.[32] For Gotham's political elite, the Draft Riots illustrated the insufficient state of the city's current policing apparatus and reaffirmed the necessity of a force capable of protecting property and ensuring stability.[33] Following further violence in 1871 when parading Catholic Orangemen were attacked and National Guard troops protecting the group fired into crowds, the city's police board won the passage of a law regulating all processions excluding funerals and military parades. The new law expanded police power and restricted New Yorkers' right to gather publicly for any reason.

Policing Greater New York

The years between the Draft Riots and the turn of the twentieth century saw a nationwide economic crisis and the emergence of a growing labor movement. In this context, strikes and labor unrest became an increasing part of the city's public life. Between 1881 and 1900 an estimated 962,470 workers in New York City went on strike. As the enforcers of the status quo, protectors of property, and regulators of public space, police played a central role in restricting this activism. Employers paid local police for additional support, as piano factory owner William Steinway did in 1883, and hired their own detectives.[34] In 1886 hundreds of thousands of workers struck as part of a Knights of Labor action, including trolley car conductors, piano makers, and furniture makers in Manhattan. Historian Sven Beckert notes that "policemen during these months had escorted strikebreakers to work, had clubbed workers who tried to keep trolleys from running, and had used conspiracy laws to undermine the workers' most powerful weapon in the competitive local economy, the boycott."[35] In the 1880s and 1890s, employers organized within and across industries and turned with increasing frequency to police in their efforts to quash the power of labor.[36]

In addition to keeping the streets orderly during mass uprisings, the police also performed regular neighborhood patrols. On these patrols their duties were, according to a 1905 police manual, "to preserve the peace, prevent crime, detect and arrest offenders, and enforce all laws and ordinances." How officers interpreted this mandate depended on the priorities of the department and city leadership. Officers on patrol were trained to view themselves as "street level-bureaucrats," accountable to the department rather than the neighborhood.[37] Despite this perspective, officers established their own relationships with the communities they patrolled. These relationships emerged out of desires for company and entertainment, but also material needs that officers faced on the job, such as the need to relieve themselves, find shelter, and eat. Officers were closest, according to historian Christopher Thale, with "those people who were best organized, had the most resources, and felt the most solidarity with the police."[38] In most neighborhoods this group consisted of property owners, who desired police protection from threats to their property and who had the ability to provide patrolmen with comfort that proved valuable while on patrol. By establishing these day-to-day affinities with the most elite and conservative elements in a neighborhood, patrolmen participated in building the politics and political influence of the police department as a whole.[39]

Members of the city's police department felt the least responsibility toward and connection to Black New Yorkers. The antipathy and disregard that police officers and officials exhibited toward Black New Yorkers were rooted in the virulent racism that was widespread among white New Yorkers in the early twentieth century. This racism also fostered a perception on the part of Tammany Hall that Black New Yorkers were not an important part of their constituency, or an economic power in the city.[40] Harlem Democratic Party organizer J. Raymond Jones reflected on the relationship between Black Democrats and the party in the early twentieth century in a memoir published in the 1980s, from which historian Matthew Vaz quotes: "Tammany leadership did not take us seriously, but we were serious."[41] By the 1890s, Tammany Hall had cemented its control as the city's most powerful political player. At both the local and national levels, Democrats did not see Black voters as an important part of their constituency, instead identifying them with Republicans. New York Democrats, for example, decried the Republican efforts of the 1890s to strengthen federal oversight of local elections in an effort to combat suppression of Black voters. Democrats dubbed this effort "the Force Bill," and Democratic papers ran articles proclaiming, "No Force Bill! No Negro Domination."[42]

Democratic opposition to the federal election bill was one example of the intense partisan conflicts that structured political life at the end of the nineteenth century and within which campaigns to reform the NYPD emerged. As Daniel Czitrom argues, Republican opponents of Tammany, who styled themselves as good government reformers, were partisan actors as well.[43] The 1894 Lexow Committee, which highlighted such brutalities as the "Clubber Brigade" and inaugurated a roughly every-twenty-year-cycle of police investigations and reform, was partly the result of conflict between the Albany-based Republicans and Gotham's Democrats.[44] Following the investigations, a reform administration took power in 1894, naming Theodore Roosevelt head of the police commission. Like many reformers who would follow him, Roosevelt was primarily concerned with police corruption and the department's connections to the Democratic machine.[45] The Lexow Committee investigation, which was the culmination of efforts by Reverend Charles Parkhurst and his allies to make public life conform to their conceptions of morality, was a precursor to more widespread reform campaigns that grew in the early twentieth century. Following in Parkhurst's footsteps, these reformers were often critical of the Democrat-controlled police department, while also engaging in campaigns of surveillance and policing that themselves stemmed from anxiety about the behavior of the city's growing Black and immigrant communities. In 1898, the five boroughs of Brooklyn, the Bronx, Manhattan, Staten Island, and Queens were consolidated into the city of Greater New York and all of the boroughs' police department were combined into the larger New York Police Department. This newly expanded department now oversaw a massive landmass across multiple boroughs and a population that included growing numbers of immigrants from southern and eastern Europe and increasing numbers of African American migrants from the U.S. South.

In the early twentieth century, Gotham's growing Black population worked to resist violence from white mobs and police officers, as well as criminalization and surveillance from police and progressive reformers like Parkhurst. Between 1890 and 1900, Gotham's Black population increased from 36,183 to 60,666, more than half of whom lived in Manhattan.[46] Many city leaders viewed Black New Yorkers as outsiders who had no right to city resources. The municipal police department would not hire its first Black officer until 1911 and would continue to discriminate against Black members and reject Black applicants for decades.[47] Aspiring Black firefighters faced similar forms of exclusion and discrimination.[48] Even Black storeowners, homeowners, and businessmen—the community members whom police officers most identified with in other communities—would struggle to have their demands met by the police department.

Poor and working-class Black men, women, and children experienced violence and criminalization from the police department at the same time as they were regularly attacked by white mobs from whom the police provided no protection. In the summer of 1900, May Enoch was the victim of such treatment when a white police officer attempted to assault her. Her partner, Arthur Harris, intervened to protect her and a fight ensued. The officer died from wounds sustained in the fight. When word spread through the city that a white police officer had been killed by a Black man, white mobs, including policemen, raged through the city attacking Black New Yorkers.[49] In the wake of the violence, as historian Cheryl Hicks shows, Enoch spoke about the particular challenges that Black women faced in the city as victims of intersecting racist and sexist violence and criminalization. Police accounts, newspaper reports, and even some Black community leaders framed Enoch as a "bad" woman who bore partial responsibility for the attack.[50]

Though they did not launch a robust and unapologetic defense of Enoch, Black community leaders were outraged at the rampant violence and misconduct displayed by the police during the riot. Black ministers, doctors, lawyers, and businesspeople founded the Citizen's Protective League and retained a lawyer to demand accountability and recompense from the department. Despite widespread appeal among Black New Yorkers, months of organizing, and an investigation into the department's actions during the riot, the group was only able to wring a special order from the police commissioner to officers to be "courteous" to New Yorkers. After this affront, a number of Black political leaders came out against Tammany, whom they saw as accepting and enabling police misconduct, in the next mayoral election, proclaiming, "Our battle cry is 'Remember the Riot.'"[51]

In the years after the 1900 racist attacks, many Black Manhattanites migrated to Harlem, where they worked to protect themselves and build community. Historian Shannon King demonstrates the diversity of approaches that Harlemites took to police violence and criminality during the early twentieth century, including legalism and armed self-defense.[52] Harlem became the biggest Black community in the city and an internationally known hub for Black culture and politics. Because of the neighborhood's significance for Black New Yorkers and the racism among white Gothamites that led many of them to associate Black people with crime and entertainment, Harlem became a site for intense surveillance by the city's police department and the private police associations that middle-class white New Yorkers were beginning to form during these years.

The city beyond the boundaries of Harlem was also changing in the early twentieth century. Growing numbers of immigrants from southern and eastern Europe arrived in the city, joining and leading a burgeoning movement for industrial workers' rights. African Americans migrated from the U.S. South seeking greater job opportunities, more political inclusion, and escapes from oppressive white violence. Gender and sexual barriers were disrupted as young women carved out new social and economic freedoms. In the face of these changes, middle-class activists or reformers formed organizations including the Committee of Fifteen, the Committee of Fourteen, the Colored Auxiliary of the Committee of Fourteen, the People's Institute, and the National Civic Federation. Members of these groups saw a city rife with immorality, corruption, and inefficiency. For these groups, historian Jennifer Fronc has noted, "the problems they perceived, such as prostitution, gambling, race mixing, juvenile delinquency, and radical political movements, represented the failure of government both to police behavior and to provide services to the city's working-class, immigrant, and African American populations."[53] Through private policing societies, these groups sought to gather information about and assert their own perceptions of order over these communities, activities that included working to racially segregate the city's leisure landscape in direct violation of the state's Civil Rights Act of 1873.[54]

Reform activists depicted the city's police department as unwilling and unable to control the changing social and sexual mores, but NYPD members were also surveilling working-class, immigrant, and Black communities, sometimes using the same undercover techniques as their volunteer counter-parts. Policewomen in the NYPD performed critical work penetrating femi-nized immigrant spaces to criminalize and police working-class women's sexuality and reproduction.[55] The police department was also a target of re-form itself during these years. Advocates for police reform came from both outside and within the profession. Police officials and criminologists pushed to incorporate knowledge gained by the U.S. military in colonial incursions in the American West and the Philippines into policing in the United States, particularly through centralization, professionalization, and the adoption of counterinsurgency practices.[56] The entrance of the United States into an-other military conflict in 1917 would also produce significant developments in policing in New York City.

Following the United States' declaration of war on Germany in the spring of 1917, the nation's domestic policing apparatus grew and its goals shifted. Though the war was fought abroad, official and voluntary policing groups proliferated at home. Americans across the country joined or found them-selves the subjects of thousands of voluntary associations devoted to polic-ing the behavior of civilians.[57] In preparation for the war, New York City police commissioner Arthur Woods mobilized the Citizens' Home Defense League, a force of "fit men . . . training to be able to preserve law and or-der in the city" more than 20,000 strong.[58] Additionally, preexisting private associations, such as the American Social Hygiene Association, received new authority from the federal government to surveil and police.

The federal government created the Commission on Training Camp Ac-tivities, which was devoted to preventing enlisted men from engaging in sex with sexually suspicious women. Though providing chaste entertainment for soldiers was part of the group's official purview, policing women became its dominating purpose, and this purpose was overseen by a member of the pri-vate anti-vice organization the American Social Hygiene Association.[59] The Commission on Training Camp Activities then led a drive to shutter red-light districts in cities including San Antonio, El Paso, Montgomery, and, most infamously, New Orleans.[60] These federal efforts joined those of local health officials and vice squads to spur mass arrests of women as suspected prosti-tutes and venereal disease carriers.[61] Historian Elizabeth Clement argues that many of the policies that the federal government encouraged states to adopt to repress prostitution during the war had already been embraced in New York City, including expanding incarceration facilities for women and reject-ing fines in favor of mandatory imprisonment.[62] The city's police power, however, was further expanded during the war, bolstered by a 1918 state law that granted the Health Department the right to examine men and women (but mostly women) against their will if they were suspected or accused of having a sexually transmitted infection. With prostitution reframed as a threat to the nation during war, the NYPD became increasingly aggressive in anti-prostitution policing. It engaged in more undercover work and used anonymous informants at higher rates than in prewar years, and judges became more accepting of these tactics in the courtroom.[63] Wartime exigencies, therefore, served to justify and intensify prewar policing strategies and to heighten surveillance and incarceration of populations conceived of as vectors of disorder and disease. Many of these dynamics would reemerge during World War II, when the mobilization for the war again amplified the importance of policing civilians at home.

Police and City Politics in Post–World War I Gotham

For much of the early twentieth century, control of Gotham's police department and city government bounced between the Tammany Democratic faction and short-lived coalitions that united to challenge the municipal powerhouse. The city's Democratic Party was organized into county districts, but Manhattan's Tammany Hall faction, sometimes known as the Tammany Tiger, was the most powerful force in city politics. The Tiger appealed to working-class white New Yorkers, particularly European immigrants and their descendants. As many historians have shown, Tammany maintained power through a neighborhood- and ethnicity-based network that provided New Yorkers with food, coal, jobs, and other necessities in return for votes.[64] The faction was also notoriously corrupt; graft, patronage, and election fraud, though not unique to the Tiger, were regular mechanisms through which the group functioned. Periodically, Democrats who sought to undercut Tammany's influence would join with the city's beleaguered Republicans to mount a "fusion" campaign against the Tiger. The city's police department was a key source of power for Tammany. The Democratic faction provided NYPD jobs for party members, who then owed their employment to the organization and granted favors for party elites. Furthermore, policemen supervised city elections, placing them in a position to solidify Tammany power at the polls. Aware of the role that the NYPD played in the Tiger's political network, reformers often focused on the police department in anti-Tammany campaigns.

The NYPD in the early 1920s was led and shaped by Police Commissioner Richard Enright. Mayor John Hylan appointed Enright in January 1918, and the commissioner's seven-year term was the longest in the twentieth century until Lewis Valentine held the position for eleven years. Enright replaced Arthur Woods, a reformer who had introduced a number of European practices into the department, including increased formal instruction and training for officers, heightened reliance on photographic and written records, and Fordist time-management techniques.[65] The putatively nonpartisan but decidedly anti-Tammany *New York Times* fretted of Enright's ascension that "the admirable work of Arthur Woods in the department is to be undone with some present speed."[66] Enright was embraced by Tammany and the uniformed NYPD membership alike. Members of the uniformed force celebrated the new commissioner for his willingness to publicly share rank-and-file criticism of NYPD brass and for his campaign against legislation that would have barred dismissed policemen from appealing the decision.[67] He was also quick-witted and charismatic; one department member who had served as a patrolman under Enright recalled that the commissioner could "wake up . . . in the middle of the night, out of a sound sleep, and give a speech extemporaneously that . . . 999 out of 1000 would give a pretty penny to be able to speak."[68]

Enright reshaped the police department in ways that enabled corruption and prioritized improving the day-to-day experience of uniformed officers. He created a citywide Special Service Squad responsible for enforcing prohibitions on vice, including liquor. This squad, a former patrolman remembered, was designated by "special shields" and possessed significant power within the department.[69] The commissioner also changed the department's organization to allow members more time off (thirty-six hours off every six days as opposed to every nine days). When describing the rationale for this change, the commissioner stated that he sought to make policing "a white man's job."[70] Enright reversed this reorganization in 1920, but his explanation for the increase in time off, combined with his regular support for workplace protections for the uniformed force, revealed much about his approach to the job of policing. To Enright, part of the value of the police department was its provision of desirable jobs for working-class white men. For patrolmen and the European immigrant communities from which many of them hailed, membership in or proximity to the police department was a means of gaining increased access to powerful institutions in the city and the country, as well as a path to financial security.[71]

While proximity to the NYPD provided advantages for some communities, many Gothamites felt little connection to the officers who patrolled their neighborhoods. In December 1922, the NYPD consisted of 11,837 members,

10,326 of whom were patrolmen.[72] Most patrolmen lived outside the neighborhoods they patrolled and were relocated to new precincts roughly every two years. Furthermore, officers did not always patrol the same posts even during their time in one precinct and generally cycled through at least a few different assignments. As historian Christopher Thale notes of NYPD members in the early twentieth century, "Though an officer's position as patrolman in the NYPD was remarkably stable, his connection with a particular work place was not, whether under machine or reform regimes."[73]

Much of the population on a patrolman's beat, therefore, particularly those who did not own property, had no personal relationship with individual officers, and many viewed representatives of the NYPD with suspicion or antipathy.[74] Negative depictions of police officers, in fact, appeared regularly in the city's newspapers. Cartoons making fun of the department were common and so incensed Commissioner Enright that he excoriated the press in the NYPD's annual reports and even included reprints of the offending cartoons.[75] Enright argued that, in addition to suffering attacks from the press, the department's authority had been "emasculated and diminished" while "the City has grown enormously in population, [sic] there are a dozen or more races comprised in the bulk of the population, [and] the transient criminal is far more numerous and dangerous."[76] According to Enright, the department faced assaults on all sides from criminals, journalists, and racially diverse residents.

For many city residents, the police themselves were a regular source of violence and crime. The nation's introduction of alcohol prohibition, first as a wartime measure and then as a constitutional amendment, unfolded during Enright's term as police commissioner and brought with it new opportunities for corruption and brutality. Though violence and corruption had always been central to policing in Gotham, during the 1920s NYPD members became increasingly embedded in the city's illicit economies.[77] In patterns that would later come to light through the investigations of Samuel Seabury, officers framed women for prostitution arrests, demanded protection payments from illegally operating speakeasies, beat residents on the streets for disregarding police authority, and tortured arrestees at station houses to extract confessions.[78] After hearing evidence related to a police raid and assault in March 1922, City Magistrate Joseph Corrigan declared that he had "never seen conditions so bad among policemen as in the past few months" and scolded that "the police are running rough-shod over the rights of the people."[79]

Members of the NYPD engaged in targeted brutality, as well as indiscriminate violence. The practice of torturing confessions out of arrestees, popularly known as the third degree, became particularly widespread in New York after a change in the state's Code of Criminal Procedure in 1881 loosened restrictions on self-incrimination, according to historian Marilynn Johnson.[80] By the end of the 1920s, violent police practices like the third degree attracted national attention, in part due to President Herbert Hoover's creation of the National Commission on Law Observance and Enforcement. The commission's report on violence and criminality in police departments, *Lawlessness in Law Enforcement,* named the NYPD one of the departments with the most egregious third-degree violations out of departments investigated in fifteen cities.[81]

No demographic of the city felt the detective's nightstick or the patrolman's boot more regularly than Black New Yorkers. Gothamites of all races faced violence from police officers on the streets and in station houses, but the NYPD had a particular history and practice of viciousness against Black residents.[82] The 1930 records of the Voluntary Defenders Committee, an organization that assisted poor defendants in felony cases, would show that among its clients who reported experiencing third-degree assaults, Black complainants appeared at a rate of over seven times their representation in the population of the city.[83] During the early 1920s, activists, journalists, and community leaders in Harlem regularly criticized the department's policy of beating confessions out of arrestees and harassing Black New Yorkers.[84] Historian LaShawn Harris has detailed how Harlem's newspapers, particularly the *New York Age,* publicized information to assist women in guarding themselves against false arrest and physical and sexual assault at the hands of police informants, patrolmen, and undercover officers.[85] In 1922, the case of Luther Boddy, who shot two white NYPD officers in Harlem after surviving years of police beatings, gained widespread media attention. The *Amsterdam News* later wrote of the case that "no local incident has been more widely discussed."[86]

Police brutality in the 1920s was fueled in part by intensifying surveillance over Harlem. Historians have argued that surveillance over Harlem's sexual and leisure landscapes increased during Prohibition both by the NYPD and by white and Black reformers who worked with the police through private groups like the Committee of Fourteen and the Urban League.[87] This heightened surveillance followed what Shannon King describes as the "expansion of white control over commercial entertainment" in the neighborhood that emerged with Prohibition.[88] For Black working-class men, historian Douglas Flowe contends, Black-run saloons in the pre-Prohibition era had served as "material and architectural sites of potential power."[89] Black men could find financial, sexual, and social autonomy in such spaces, free from white surveillance or intrusion. A Prohibition-led infusion of white capital and patrons into Harlem disrupted these establishments and brought with it heightened policing.

With widespread attention to police brutality in the Black press and intensified white attention toward Harlem, the NYPD launched a public relations campaign in the pages of the city's Black newspapers in the fall of 1925.[90] The department's effort to influence the opinions of Black New Yorkers was most transparent in an article published in the *Amsterdam News*. E. E. Hart, who was employed by the NYPD, penned an article to run in the Black daily extolling the opportunities that Commissioner Enright had supposedly bestowed on Black New Yorkers.[91] The author proclaimed that the commissioner had "provided for the colored people the protection they had sometimes lacked" and therefore "was the first city official to give them their place in the sun."[92] The appearance of Hart's article and the effusive praise that he lavished on the police commissioner indicate the NYPD's concern with Black New Yorkers' attitude toward the police. Claims like Hart's were not commonly expressed in the pages of the Republican-leaning *Amsterdam News*, which tended to be critical of city Democrats and regularly reported on police brutality. Many Black activists, in fact, associated Enright and Tammany with police corruption and brutality. This view, however, was not uniform among Black New Yorkers.

In the early to mid-twentieth century, Black New Yorkers' allegiance to the Republican Party was in flux, particularly at the local level. As the party of the Union army, the Republican Party had received the majority of Black political support since the Civil War. Decades into the twentieth century, however, Black voters were questioning this commitment, since Republicans regularly failed to deliver on important national issues like anti-lynching legislation and voter disenfranchisement. In the 1910s and 1920s, some Black Gothamites in Manhattan and Brooklyn were turning toward Tammany, while leftist Black women like Grace Campbell worked for political advancement in the Socialist Party. Both the main political parties began running Black male candidates for office semiregularly in majority-Black districts in recognition of the need to court Black voters by the late 1910s.[93] In the 1920s, both local Republican and Democratic organizations were considering how to appeal to Black voters.

During these years, Black and white supporters of Tammany were losing interest in Mayor Hylan and coalescing around another well-known and flamboyant politician.[94] Tammany backed Jimmy Walker, a longtime player in state politics and a man-about-town, to run against the flagging Brook-lynite in the 1925 mayoral election. Walker had led the Democrats in the state senate, where he served for ten years following six in the state assembly.[95] He was a skilled and popular politician. He had the backing of Governor Al Smith and a reputation as an enthusiastic supporter of the city's legal and illegal entertainment industries. Walker easily beat Hylan in the primary and went on to win the general election by one of the largest margins in the city's history, positioning Tammany to be "more firmly intrenched [sic] than ever" in the city.[96]

Once in office, Walker proved a colorful mayor. From his suits to his salary, he lived large, changing the former multiple times a day and doubling the latter while in office. As Michael Lerner argues, the new mayor was a "constant defender of working-class leisure and entertainment," which endeared him to much of the city's population.[97] Under Walker and Smith, the city's working-class European immigrant population, particularly the Irish, saw themselves reflected in city and state government.[98] As mayor, Walker expanded the city's park system and created a department of sanitation. New Yorkers, however, identified his administration most with his embrace of Gotham's nightlife and with corruption that solidified Tammany's power in the city.[99]

Upon entering office, Walker replaced Enright with a series of police commissioners who were close to him and acceptable, though not ideal, for Tammany. Tiger officials had come to feel that the former commissioner was getting too big for his britches. "Enright thinks he is running the city, even going so far as to ignore letters from Tammany leaders," members of the organization complained.[100] Enright, in fact, would run against Walker as an independent candidate in the 1929 election.[101] The commissioners who followed Enright served briefly and did not overshadow the mayor.

Walker, memorialized as "the night mayor" in an eponymous Broadway show, directed commissioners to extend leniency to the city's licit and illicit entertainment industries.[102] The night mayor vehemently opposed alcohol prohibition and directed the NYPD against enforcing it in the city. Under Walker's relaxed approach to regulating Gotham's nightlife, the city entered a heyday of drag balls hosted by lesbians, gay men, and crossdressing, transgender, and genderqueer New Yorkers.[103] These balls and the city's night revelers more broadly did not escape police interference completely; Walker oversaw the enactment of the Cabaret Law of 1926, which required venues with music, food, and dancing to obtain a license and to close at three o'clock in the morning.[104] The Cabaret Law was loosely enforced, but it expanded the city's ability to regulate and surveil nightlife venues and their employees.[105] The night mayor's overall leniency toward the city's entertainment venues, however, and his enthusiastic opposition to prohibition were widely appreciated among New Yorkers.

Walker's leniency toward policing entertainment endeared him to residents, but his opponents in the mayoral election of 1929 hit the mayor hard on policing issues. He faced off for reelection against idiosyncratic Republican Fusion candidate Fiorello H. La Guardia, the Socialist Party's Norman Thomas, and former police commissioner Richard Enright of the newly formed Square Deal party.[106] During the campaign, Walker's police commissioner, Grover Whalen, came under intense criticism. "By word and deed he has encouraged the lawlessness of the Police Department against the constitutional rights of citizens," Thomas railed against the commissioner.[107] When La Guardia accepted the Republican Party nomination, he informed his audience that "one of the meanest sources of graft in the entire city is that developed in the Police Department in its so-called 'regulation of labor disputes.'"[108] The pro–La Guardia Harlem Citizens' Welfare Committee queried, "Why has Mayor Walker permitted the inhuman, brutal and heinous treatment inflicted on Negroes by members of the police department under his control?"[109] Even Enright claimed that the NYPD failed to make arrests after the murder of Arnold Rothstein in order to hide the fact that police and city officials had profited from financial arrangements with the slain gangster. According to *Times* journalist J. A. Hagerty, revelations connected to the Rothstein murder proved "the most serious menace to the re-election of Mayor Walker and the success of Tammany in the city election."[110]

The most serious menace to Walker's reelection chances, however, was not very serious. Despite the criticism, the mayor was popular. He had the support of Tammany as well as of various other labor and European ethnic associations and he received limited but meaningful support among Black New Yorkers.[111] Walker took the election in a "Tammany tidal wave" by a record plurality of almost 500,000 votes. The *Brooklyn Daily Eagle* labeled the election a "smashing victory on all political fronts with the exception of Queens" for the Democratic machine.[112] La Guardia, whom the *Eagle* dubbed "the worst beaten Republican nominee for Mayor in years," failed to carry a single assembly district in the city.[113]

Despite Tammany's sweep, not everyone in the city was marching to the Democrats' drum. The Socialist Party celebrated its highest-ever recorded vote in a municipal election (overtaking the previous 1917 peak) and planned to build on the vote to expand the party's base.[114] Republicans won some important victories, notably in Harlem's Nineteenth and Twenty-First State Assembly Districts, where Francis E. Rivers and Lamar Perkins, who were both Black, triumphed after running campaigns that emphasized the importance of Black representation for the neighborhood.[115] Though Rivers and Perkins won, Black Republican Hubert Delaney's effort to represent Harlem in Congress failed. A number of Black papers contended that the effort was undermined by Tammany operators who tore down Delaney banners and mobilized white children to parade down the streets of white areas of Washington Heights in blackface carrying banners reading, "Do You Want to See a Negro Elected to Congress?"[116] Reflecting on the election, the *Amsterdam News* presciently wrote of La Guardia, "No man could have done more than he to shake off the octopus that has settled itself upon New York City. His work may yet bear fruit. After another four years of the Walker administration the believers in good government may get together and in their accumulated disgust sweep Fiorello La Guardia, or one like him, into the Mayor's seat."[117]

From the Night Mayor to the Little Flower

The *Amsterdam News* was right; during Walker's second term, violent conflicts between the NYPD and protesters, as well as rampant corruption, discredited his administration. The first months of 1930 were a challenging time in city life. Unemployment in the city was up among unskilled laborers as well as in most of the city's skilled manufacturing industries.[118] In the context of a growing economic crisis, unemployed New Yorkers, Communists, and labor radicals increased their presence on the city's streets. Commissioner Whalen established a pattern of using violence against leftist protesters, which Walker's subsequent commissioners continued to varying degrees.[119]

By the summer of 1930, the stories of rampant corruption, police violence, and unemployment in New York City were becoming inconvenient for Democratic governor Franklin Delano Roosevelt, who was up for reelection in November. Roosevelt needed support from city voters as well as upstate Republicans to win another term, and Republicans on the board of aldermen were publicly pressuring the governor to investigate corruption in the city. In August, Roosevelt and justices in the Appellate Division of the New York State Supreme Court appointed Samuel Seabury to investigate corruption in the city's magistrates' courts. Seabury, or the Judge, as he was known by many in his personal circle, was a wealthy anti-Tammany Democrat with a reputation for painstaking conscientiousness.[120] Seabury's investigation into the magistrates' courts bore enough fruit to feed Republican calls for wider anti-corruption investigations, one of which would ultimately lead to Walker's resignation.

During the course of the investigations, the Judge's team of lawyers interviewed over a thousand witnesses and examined financial and legal records connected to the courts. Seabury then held public hearings where he highlighted witness testimony and generated press attention.[121] Early in the hearings, the investigators uncovered evidence of rampant police corruption. Witnesses testified about the NYPD's practice of framing women for prostitution arrests and extorting money from them to avoid imprisonment. Police informant Chile Acuna detailed his role in the practice (which he claimed netted him about $150 a week) and named twenty-eight vice-squad policemen in the audience who had used his services. Seabury's team inspected the finances of more than a hundred patrolmen, serving blanket subpoenas to 2,000 banks and brokerage houses. This campaign revealed a pattern of NYPD members banking sums of money significantly larger than their annual salaries, the provenance of which they could not convincingly explain. Magistrates were also implicated in the scheme to frame women. Others were shown to have paid for their appointments or to have performed favors for Tammany after their appointment. The public responded to these revelations with outrage. Governor Roosevelt pardoned six women who were on parole after serving sentences for prostitution, and Police Commissioner Edward Mulrooney suspended all NYPD members named by Acuna.[122] These revelations had a significant but problematic impact on anti-prostitution policing, which will be explored in chapter 3.

In the midst of the investigation into the magistrates' courts, the murder of a witness planning to provide evidence to Seabury drove Roosevelt to direct the Judge to look into the office of the district attorney of New York County. Seabury's examination of the DA's office revealed significant evidence of racketeering and corruption, but ultimately the investigator judged the DA incompetent, not corrupt. Relations between Roosevelt and Tammany continued to sour, however, and the evidence of incompetence in the DA's office whet the palates of Republicans eager to hunt down more proof of Democratic corruption. In March 1931, Roosevelt approved an investigation into the city government itself. The investigation lasted a year and a half and involved over 2,000 interviews. Research into Walker's finances revealed numerous corrupt connections, including a deal with a front company, the Equitable Coach Company. The company was backed by a group of politicians and businessmen seeking to receive a franchise from the city board of estimate to control all surface transportation in the city. In exchange for the franchise, which the company won despite owning no buses at all, Walker received letters of credit against which he withdrew thousands of dollars. After collecting evidence of Walker's financial malfeasance, Seabury encouraged Roosevelt to remove the mayor.

Walker's popularity, however, posed complications for the governor. Roosevelt was working on gaining support to win the 1932 Democratic presidential nomination, but he needed both pro-Tammany backers of Al Smith and anti-Tammany Democratic camps to join behind him. After clinching the nomination, the governor began removal proceedings against Walker, who ultimately resigned before he could be removed. Even after resigning, Walker remained popular, and the Tammany candidate, John P. O'Brien, easily won a 1932 special mayoral election.[123] Board of aldermen president and anti-Tammany Democrat Joseph McKee, however, received an unprecedented 137,538 write-in votes, illustrating that Tammany was losing support even if oppositional forces had not yet united into a viable challenge.[124]

Those forces would coalesce in the election of 1933. For fusionists, three possible candidates emerged. The first was General John F. O'Ryan, who had served as commander of the Twenty-Seventh Division during World War I and was considered an independent, but conservative, Democrat. Next came master municipal manipulator Robert Moses, a Republican schooled under the unlikely tutelage of Tammany's Al Smith. Finally, there was Fiorello La Guardia, the son of a Jewish mother and Italian father, a former congressman representing East Harlem, and a wet progressive Republican. La Guardia, who won his seat in Congress as an independent, had a reputation as a principled, hardworking vote-getter who supported progressive social legislation. With Seabury's insistence, La Guardia gained the backing of the fusionists. O'Ryan agreed to support La Guardia, and in return he would be named first police commissioner in the new administration.[125] In the general election, La Guardia faced Mayor O'Brien and Joseph McKee, who was running on the Recovery Party ticket, which had been backed by Democratic leaders Edward J. Flynn of the Bronx and James A. Farley, who was secretary and chairman of the state Democratic committee as well as chairman of the Democratic National Committee.[126]

La Guardia and his supporters positioned his candidacy as a shift of monumental importance in the political life of the city. At a rally in Madison Square Garden five days before the voters went to the polls, Seabury spoke of the "new era in municipal government" that would be ushered in by the

Little Flower's election. "When we drive out the gangster and the racketeer, industry will be freed from the tolls and extortions now levied upon it," the Judge proclaimed in near-biblical terms, "and the profits of industry will go where they belong—to the workers and employers, and not to political leaders and their gangster friends."[127] On November 7, La Guardia beat both opponents by about 300,000 votes, chasing Tammany from city hall for the first time in sixteen years.

CHAPTER TWO

The War Is On!

Policing Practice and Ideology in a Reform NYPD

"The Fusion administration is now in charge of our city," Fiorello La Guardia triumphantly declared upon his swearing in. "Our theory of municipal government is an experiment," he continued, "to try to show that a nonpartisan, nonpolitical local government is possible, and, if we succeed, I am sure success in other cities is possible."[1] The new mayor was sworn into office in investigator and former judge Samuel Seabury's home, demonstrating the political closeness between the two men.[2]

The reform ideology that La Guardia brought to his office was deeply influenced by Seabury and other anti-Tammany reformers. According to the mayor's 1948 posthumous autobiography, as a child little Fiorello, then living in Arizona, followed anti-corruption investigations against Tammany Democrats in the national press. La Guardia recalled developing a deep resentment against Tammany, which grew into "almost an obsession," coupled with a belief that "good people could eliminate bad people from public office."[3] The image of a young boy devouring the details of good government campaigns after he finishes the funny pages strains credulity, but La Guardia's former teachers remembered him as unusually bright and interested in politics and law from an early age.[4] Furthermore, the inclusion of the anecdote in La Guardia's autobiography illustrates the author's wish to emphasize his early and enduring commitment to New York City's oppositional politics. La Guardia's belief in the importance of clean government was further cemented when his father died after eating unsanitary meat in the army while he had malaria, a death that his son attributed to "the work of crooked Army contractors."[5] In the pages that follow, we will consider the ideological and institutional systems that La Guardia and Lewis Valentine crafted to police New York City and how the duo reshaped these systems as the nation mobilized for war.

To the new mayor, the primary ill that could be visited on urban citizens was government corruption. In his eyes, a city government that operated without political favors would be one that treated all residents fairly. The police department, La Guardia believed, had a central role to play in establishing and maintaining good government. Administrators needed to purge dishonest police officers from the ranks of the NYPD and then rely on a strong police presence to rid the city of the crime and disorder that corrupt government had nurtured. If honest administrators could remove the fetters of favoritism and corruption, the theory went, the city government would engage equitably with Gothamites as individuals, dispensing justice uniformly to all residents. As La Guardia stated in his swearing-in remarks, the primary aim of his ambition was to prove that "nonpartisan, nonpolitical local government is possible."[6] His administration succeeded in this goal and American urban governance since has been deeply influenced by his vision. But the nonpolitical local government that he crafted relied on other modes of hierarchy and differentiation in which policing played a central role.

According to La Guardia's worldview, a large, aggressive, nonpartisan police department was an essential component of municipal order and safety. The new mayor contended that residents needed such a force to "clean this town of gangsters and racketeers," thereby protecting the rights of Gotham's law-abiding citizens.[7] La Guardia was not unfamiliar with problems of police abuses, but he believed that such misconduct stemmed from corruption and political interference in the apolitical realm of order and crime enforcement. Similarly, he viewed low-level crimes of vice or morality solely through the lens of government corruption and organized crime. La Guardia later reflected of his time in the mayor's office, "The suppression of commercialized vice during my administration as Mayor was more efficient than at any previous time. We just did not tolerate police corruption and were determined to wipe it out."[8]

Throughout his administration, La Guardia equated vice with police corruption, which impeded his ability to conceive of how anti-vice policing justified violent and disruptive incursions into the lives of New Yorkers. In his autobiography, the Little Flower reflected revealingly on his experience working as an interpreter in the city's night court (or court of prostitution) in the 1910s. He wrote compassionately about the young immigrant women he met through this work and blamed their arrest and prosecution on the lack of living wages for women and the "professional procurers who exploit these unfortunate girls." He demonstrated, however, little compunction about the violence of the state in this process, remarking dispassionately of the women, "If any of them had been here less than five years, warrants were issued and upon proper proof they were deported."[9] Ultimately, he believed that much urban crime would decrease "provided there is increasing economic security, and provided enforcement agencies keep after the professional procurers."[10] The mayor's approach to improved governance, therefore, rested on state investment in the twin pillars of an enhanced social safety net and an augmented law enforcement infrastructure.

In these views, La Guardia embodied the progressive branch of an emerging popular liberal ideology. Unlike adherents of nineteenth-century liberalism who embraced a doctrine of negative freedom from state interference for white men, mid-twentieth-century liberals saw a positive role for government in improving the lives of its citizens. Proponents of this perspective responded to unprecedented mass protest among unemployed and impoverished Americans and built on decades of labor, socialist, anarchist, and progressive organizing. Not all citizens benefited equally from these state interventions, however, as numerous historians of the New Deal have shown.[11] Furthermore, many leading liberals called for increased policing and surveillance as part of the government's expanded role in the life of its citizens. These demands, often framed as a "war against crime," justified expanding the punitive state at the municipal, state, and federal levels. During the early 1930s, President Franklin Delano Roosevelt significantly increased the purview and capacity of the Justice Department's Bureau of Investigation, which continued to grow under its new name, the Federal Bureau of Investigation.[12] In language similar to that embraced by La Guardia and Valentine, supporters argued that citizens needed government protection from violent and predatory criminals. The liberal policy makers of the 1930s crafted programs of increased economic security for some and enhanced surveillance for others with criminality supposedly marking the dividing line. But gender and race proved constitutive for how liberals understood concepts of both economic rights and criminality. Exponents of mid-twentieth-century liberalism, therefore, reshaped but preserved the inequalities along lines of gender and race that political scientists like Charles Mills argue have proved a foundational component of liberalism since its inception.[13]

La Guardia and his administrators were further influenced by early twentieth-century theories developed to categorize and quantify racialized criminality. These theories fueled acceptance among white liberals of a program of racial management that combined heavy policing with limited opportunities for individual advancement in municipal government. During this period, intellectuals and policy makers produced a conception of Blackness that was uniquely tied to criminality, while the identities of European immigrants were "decriminalized," as historian Khalil Gibran Muhammad has shown. The year of La Guardia's election was also the first year the FBI-produced Uniform Crime Reports began publishing arrest statistics by race. Before La Guardia left office, the racial categories would be simplified to describe arrestees as "members of the white and Negro races."[14] In New York City, as long as police officers were not lining their own pockets or performing political favors, La Guardia saw their presence as bringing safety and order to high-crime Black and interracial neighborhoods struggling with criminogenic "cultural" problems. Focusing on crime and disorder became a way for elites to voice anxieties about the city's increasingly interracial population, changing sexual and gender norms, and class conflict, while the admittance of small numbers of (mostly) white women and Black men to the police department insulated city leadership from accusations of discrimination. Discussions of crime, therefore, became central to the way the system of racial hierarchy that scholars have dubbed "the Jim Crow North" functioned in New York City in this particular historical moment.[15]

Like government corruption, in La Guardia's worldview, racial injustice stemmed from the actions of self-interested or immoral individuals. His political orientation fit within a larger paradigm that historian Karen Miller has described as "Northern racial liberalism."[16] He was opposed to discrimination against individuals based on race and sometimes drafted rebukes to white New Yorkers who wrote to him complaining about their Black neighbors.[17] He acknowledged the need to incorporate Black leaders into city government, appointing the first African American woman judge to the city's domestic relations court in 1939.[18] He did not, however, offer programs to remedy the specific structural problems faced by nonwhite New Yorkers.[19] Historian Dominic Capeci states that in La Guardia's mind-set, "all residents would be treated fairly, but none—regardless of unique experiences—would be treated specially."[20]

This perspective contributed to a complex relationship between the mayor and Black political leaders and residents throughout the Little Flower's tenure.[21] Support for La Guardia was not uncommon among Black New Yorkers throughout the 1930s and early 1940s. In early 1942, in response to a question in a survey from the federal Office of Facts and Figures asking, "Who would a Negro go to around here if he couldn't get his rights?" 10 percent of the over 1,000 Black New Yorkers interviewed answered, Mayor La Guardia. Only city councilman Adam Clayton Powell Jr., one of the most influential men in Harlem, was named more frequently and, even then, by just 11 percent of respondents.[22] In the months following this survey, La Guardia's appeal among his Black constituents soured, partly due to his approach to policing and closing Harlem's Savoy Ballroom, which we will explore in chapter 6.[23] Criticism of La Guardia from Black New Yorkers became more intense over the course of his tenure, but the Little Flower came into office with a heavy reliance on policing as a response to problems of racial inequality. He appointed a police commissioner who shared his commitment to fighting police corruption but who possessed a more retrograde approach to policing Black New Yorkers and working-class women across races.

In Lewis Valentine, La Guardia found an efficient administrator whose deep antipathy for police corruption rivaled the mayor's own. Valentine was not La Guardia's first police commissioner; political compromises had required he name Major General John O'Ryan, his rival for the Fusion mayoral nomination, to the post. After less than a year, however, O'Ryan's aggressive campaigns against leftists and labor activists clashed with the mayor and led to the commissioner's resignation. To replace O'Ryan, La Guardia named Valentine, and the two would serve together for the next eleven years. At the time of his appointment, Valentine had been in the NYPD for thirty-one years and was the chief inspector of police, a position that oversaw all uniformed NYPD members.[24] He had experience at all levels of the department, while also being familiar enough with the latest trends in criminology to work academic references into his departmental addresses. Under Valentine, NYPD members were expected to conform to high standards of professionalism (he "seriously" objected to officers smoking while in their uniform).[25] The new commissioner was a strict enforcer who believed in a disciplined, well-ordered, and violent police force.

Valentine's experience in the department shaped his views about how it should function. He was born in Williamsburg, Brooklyn, and joined the NYPD in 1903.[26] After ten years in the department, he came to the attention of "Honest Dan" Costigan, an inspector who oversaw a confidential squad dedicated to uncovering police corruption created under Mayor John Mitchel's reform administration. Costigan named Valentine to the confidential squad, and the latter's time in the squad proved formative for the then-sergeant's ideas about policing. Later in life, Valentine fondly remembered launching "raid after raid upon brothels" protected by the police. Perhaps informed by this early experience, Valentine carried with him throughout his career a belief that surveilling and incarcerating sexually suspicious or "unwholesome" women was a central responsibility of the police department. He would become even more committed to this project and would gain support for it as the nation mobilized for war. In his earlier years on the force, however, the confidential squad was disbanded when Tammany retook the mayor's office and Valentine was subjected to a series of undesirable transfers.[27] After years of watching his career ebb and flow depending on the party in charge of city hall, Valentine claimed to have been preparing to retire when La Guardia tapped him as police commissioner.

Valentine brought a sophisticated ideology of policing into the commissioner's office. He believed in a two-pronged approach to law enforcement in which officers used brutality and harassment against "criminals" and courtesy toward "non-criminals." He often told department members that they were "selling service" and reminded them, "To the Public our slogan must always be 'At Your Service.'"[28] While the public deserved service, criminals were to be met with violence. In November 1934, shortly after his appointment, Valentine attracted attention from the press for directing NYPD members to beat arrestees in police custody. "Muss 'em up," he encouraged, "teach them to fear arrest." Elaborating on his approach, Valentine mused, "We want to be careful not to kill innocent people and we don't want to use brutality on others because of different political faiths, but with the killers, racketeers and gangsters—the sky is the limit." Here, the commissioner revealed a central tenet of his approach to policing: some residents were law-abiding and deserved respect, while others were criminals who should be met with repression and violence. La Guardia gave Valentine his full support in this approach, telling members of the Patrolmen's Benevolent Association, "The war is on, and you cannot expect that a police officer is going to stand up and be shot down by a cowardly crook without defending his own life." He also declared that "any crook" coming to Gotham should know that "we are going to drive him out by the use of force."[29]

To Commissioner Valentine, however, the dividing line between criminals and the public was not constituted through evidence of criminal activity. For example, Valentine ordered NYPD members to drive sexually profiled women from the streets using laws against loitering and vagrancy "if it was too difficult to get conclusive evidence of prostitution." He also reminded officers, however, not to arrest "innocent women" or to repeat the "unsavory conduct" revealed in the Seabury investigations.[30] To the commissioner, race, ethnicity, gender, class, and physical ability proved powerful interconnected markers of character and criminality; Dan Costigan, Valentine's NYPD mentor, was a "powerfully built and rugged Irishman" from whom the commissioner learned that "an honest, tough and alert cop was the first requisite of good law enforcement." Gangsters like "Two-Gun" Francis Crowley were "undersized, under-chinned, [and] under-witted."[31] Valentine further demonstrated his racialized beliefs on crime and character in his description of nineteenth-century Williamsburg, where his parents grew up. "Dutch traits made for an honest, preserving way of life," before "the Irish, German, Italian, and Jewish immigrants began swarming across the river."[32]

Valentine believed that Black New Yorkers, in particular, required special attention from the police department. At a conference in June 1943, when contemplating the possibility of Black uprisings or racial unrest, the commissioner articulated his discomfort with the fact that Black New Yorkers were becoming an increasing proportion of the city's population. In his comments about what he described as the "negro [sic] problem," Valentine discussed the possibility of racial conflict in the city as a threat that Black residents carried with them. "We are all concerned by the possibility of disorder anywhere," he informed his audience, and he provided aggressive policing of Black New Yorkers as the solution.[33] During the war, when racial conflict could affect the morale of the troops or impede wartime production, the commissioner believed racially targeted policing proved more important than ever. The war effort, therefore, presented both an alibi and a rationale to aggressively police the increasingly interracial city.

The Structure and Organization of the NYPD in the 1930s

Valentine's commitment to policing vice was reflected in the NYPD's organization. The department's command system was divided into boroughs, divisions, precincts, and posts. Division commanders bore particular responsibility for the enforcement of "laws relating to public morals, gambling, and intoxicating liquors."[34] Undercover or plainclothes officers working in details out of the offices of the borough or division commanders were central to the NYPD's regulation of morals laws, though any member of the department could make an arrest for such a violation.[35] After a morals arrest, borough or division commanders could designate the location in which the arrest occurred a "raided premise" and assign a patrolman from the Raided Premises Squad to monitor the venue.[36] Officers of the Raided Premises Squad were required to record information about the location at the close of each tour of duty. This information was then filed in the precinct in which the establishment was located and formed the basis of applications for warrants, summary arrests, or "other action as the circumstances may require."[37]

Valentine's racialized and gendered conceptions of criminality further informed his organization of the NYPD. The commissioner believed that women, particularly white women, proved important assets to the police department. These women could rely on their sexualized or maternal femininity to enhance their surveillance and undercover work. They were expected to play important roles in policing other women and children as well as to work with policemen in undercover operations when necessary. As Mary Sullivan, director of the 147 women in the NYPD in 1935, stated, "Policewomen are increasing rapidly because of their proven worth to the department."[38] Valentine demonstrated his commitment to women's role in the NYPD by issuing new regulations requiring policewomen to carry guns. The new requirements, however, were not intended to undermine women's distinct position. Policewomen were required to carry .32-caliber guns, which were smaller than the .38s carried by their male colleagues.[39] In 1943 policewomen were issued purses with compartments for their weapons as well as for makeup kits. "Use your gun as you would your lipstick—only when you need it," La Guardia instructed the policewomen as they received the bags.[40] During the war, white women's feminized position in the department became increasingly valuable as the city and NYPD sought to expand surveillance over working-class and nonwhite women in the city.

Policewomen's positions within the department overlapped inextricably with the policing of working-class and nonwhite women and children on the city's streets, a connection that had existed since the department began accepting women in the Progressive Era. Reformers in the late nineteenth century called for police departments to appoint "police matrons" to oversee female arrestees and reduce abuses from male guards. Roles for women in police departments expanded along with calls to regulate and criminalize the new social and sexual liberties of young working-class women in urban centers at the turn of the twentieth century.[41] Reformers and law enforcement officials conceived of white middle-class women in police departments as using their feminine properties to assist and protect disorderly or criminal women and children. As Samuel Walker has argued, the inclusion of women in police departments also coincided with and gained support from a push to expand the roles of police officers as "social reformers."[42] This drive occurred within the larger Progressive Era movements for state expansion and professionalization. Reformers believed that policewomen could soften and improve police departments' impact on the women and children they policed. The "social reform" model of policing that criminologists, reformers, and police chiefs associated with female officers, however, also expanded the reach of police departments, particularly over working-class and nonwhite communities.

The NYPD coordinated the work of policewomen through the Women's Bureau, overseen by the commanding officer of the Juvenile Aid Bureau

(JAB).[43] The Women's Bureau was first formed in 1926, following a brief post–World War I experiment with a women's precinct.[44] Mary Sullivan directed the bureau from its formation in 1926 until her retirement in 1946 and described its members as "ranging from blondes . . . to whitehaired, motherly souls."[45] Women also played important roles in the JAB, which had been formed in 1930 to coordinate and expand the surveillance of young New Yorkers and which will be discussed in chapter 4. By 1940, the JAB included a staff of 213 who worked in the main office at NYPD Headquarters at 240 Centre Street or in one of its thirteen field units spread out around the city.[46] The formation of the JAB was influenced by a growing movement among social workers, criminologists, and law enforcement officials who argued that monitoring children was an essential component of "crime prevention."[47]

The drive to include women in projects of "social reform" did not include Black women on an equal basis. Throughout the Progressive Era, Black women in New York had engaged in reform efforts, including in the criminal justice sphere, forming their own organizations or auxiliary groups. Those who sought to work in or with white institutions, however, often experienced racism or exclusion themselves.[48] Black women and girls received disproportionate attention from the police, but during the war years the NYPD included only a handful of Black policewomen (six in 1945, up from two in 1929), and there is no evidence that the department employed any Puerto Rican women.[49] African American women in the department likely experienced challenges unknown to their white peers. In the 1990s, historian Andrew Darien interviewed Black women who had served in the NYPD. The interviewees commented that, during their tenure, supervisors had often assigned tasks associated with femininity to their white counterparts, while Black women received more dangerous assignments.[50] For Valentine, white women had a special role to play in monitoring the increasing female misbehavior that emerged during the war.

While the commissioner valued white women for their supposedly feminine properties, he also believed that Black men could play an important, but circumscribed, role in the NYPD. The hiring of more Black police officers and promotion of those on the force had been a regular, though not universal, demand of Black New Yorkers protesting police harassment and brutality throughout the late nineteenth and early twentieth century.[51] Valentine and other high-ranking NYPD officials claimed that they were open to these demands, but never followed through in practice.[52] The *Amsterdam News* noted in the fall of 1943 that people were "constantly asking for an explanation as to why there are no Negro patrolmen and high-ups on duty throughout the most 'democratic' city in the world."[53] Annual NYPD reports do not consistently document exact numbers of Black NYPD members, but in 1942 the *Amsterdam News* reported that the entire police force included only 131 Black members of all genders.[54] These members were almost all men. In 1944, Valentine put the number of Black NYPD members at 200.[55] If Valentine's statement was correct, African Americans made up roughly 1 percent of the police department and 6 percent of the city's population. Edward S. Lewis, executive secretary of the Urban League of New York City, accurately argued that based on the city's demographics, African Americans should constitute 1,000 members of the department.[56]

Furthermore, Black members of the NYPD experienced racism and discrimination on the job. The NYPD placed most Black officers in precincts in Harlem or Bedford-Stuyvesant and excluded Black department members from the Detective Bureau and Police Headquarters.[57] Rank-and-file members of the department and residents in Harlem and Bedford-Stuyvesant observed that white officers found guilty of being drunk on the job were sometimes assigned to precincts in these neighborhoods, though Valentine denied this practice.[58] Samuel J. Battle, the NYPD's first Black officer, remembered getting the "silent treatment" and death threats when he first entered the department and noted that it was after his transfer to Harlem in 1913 that white officers stopped harassing him. He reflected on the role that Black officers played in the highly racialized department, remarking that his white colleagues had realized "they needed me as much as I needed them and sometimes more."[59]

Although NYPD leaders acknowledged the role Black officers could play in policing the racialized city, African Americans in the department were regularly passed over for promotions. Frustration with discrimination led Black members of Harlem's Twenty-Eighth Precinct to form a fraternal organization known as the Guardians in 1943, which included Puerto Rican officers as well. The Guardians were not officially recognized until 1949, and Darien argues that recruitment was difficult because participants feared punishment from their superiors.[60] After the war, the number of Black members in the NYPD increased to 564, but the department still included only six Black sergeants and one Black captain in 1953.[61] A clear assumption that white New Yorkers possessed particular rights in relation to the police department that did not extend to their Black peers undergirded the NYPD's internal and external practices. Despite Valentine's resistance to hiring more Black officers and the racist restrictions he placed on those who did get hired, the perception that his department was open to qualified African Americans was an important part of his law-and-order liberalism.

The career and support of Battle played a significant role in Valentine's ability to present this image. After being named the department's first Black sergeant in 1926, Battle became its first Black lieutenant in January 1935.[62] The lieutenant got along well with Valentine and considered La Guardia "the greatest mayor New York City has ever had."[63] He used his unique position to try to calm protesters during the Harlem uprisings of 1935 and 1943 and participated in public hearings that followed the 1935 conflict. He represented the NYPD in Baltimore when the Maryland governor wanted to integrate the police force, and he accompanied La Guardia to Philadelphia in uniform when the mayor was invited to speak at the NAACP's annual convention in 1940. In 1941, La Guardia named Battle the city's first Black parole commissioner. Though Battle felt conflicted about leaving the police force, he believed he had a responsibility to accept the new position, and he spoke publicly about policing and racism throughout the war. He worked with the Urban League to prepare African Americans to take the police exam, and he served as a lieutenant colonel in the City Patrol Corps. After racial violence broke out in Detroit in June 1943, Battle assisted La Guardia and Valentine in crafting a plan to enforce police restraint in the event of a similar conflict in New York. He then advised and assisted the duo when an uprising broke out in Harlem.[64] Battle played an important role in structuring Valentine and La Guardia's policies and intervening in debates about policing during his time in the department and as parole commissioner.

In addition to promoting a small number of Black men like Battle and white women, Valentine also sought to create more positive relations between nonwhite New Yorkers and the NYPD through the department's community policing and anti-delinquency campaigns, including the Police Athletic League (PAL). Throughout the 1930s, the department relied on these programs to increase surveillance over Black and working-class youth across races and to cultivate positive associations with the NYPD among these heavily policed populations. During the war, city and police officials used PAL programs and centers to engage young people in the war effort and to project a vision of racially inclusive citizenship at a time when many Black, progressive, and Communist New Yorkers were criticizing the department for police brutality and racist policing. In April 1939, the department's official magazine touted that the PAL "brings into every-day contact children of all races, creeds and colors, and does much to promote comradeship among them."[65] During the war, the NYPD would expand these projects and try to use them to support the military effort as well as the police department. In a 1943 article about juvenile delinquency in the *Brooklyn Daily Eagle*, Valentine described the importance of the PAL and its ideal contribution to the war effort. The article included a letter from former PAL member Eddie Moe, now serving in the U.S. Navy, in which the writer declared that it was through the PAL that he learned "how to behave [him]self." Valentine said of Moe's letter, "There can be no greater tribute."[66]

Throughout the 1930s, the NYPD under Valentine and La Guardia launched campaigns against prostitution, juvenile delinquency, gambling, and disorderly establishments, which will be discussed in the chapters that follow. These campaigns met with varying degrees of success, but they all gained momentum and institutional support as the nation began mobilizing for a possible entrance into the growing global conflicts in Europe and Asia.

Expanding the Wartime Policing Apparatus

In New York City in late 1939 and early 1940, as in much of the rest of the country, "all talk was of war."[67] One of the questions on the municipal civil service exam required for promotion to lieutenant asked respondents, "In what ways may the situation created by the repeal of the United States Neutrality Act affect the work of the Police Department?"[68] In the summer and fall of 1940, Congress debated the Selective Training and Service Act, and officials and citizens alike worried about global instability. In this precarious global context, federal, state, and municipal politicians created new agencies to police domestic populations during a possible mobilization for war.

The city's Health Department worked closely with the NYPD to meet these wartime challenges. Article 17B of the Public Health Law granted the Health Department the authority to detain and perform venereal tests on any person suspected of having a venereal disease, which included any woman arrested for prostitution.[69] This provision dated from World War I. In the interwar period it fell out of use, but it remained on the books. It was revived in the mid-1930s, an event that I will discuss in chapter 3, and became a central component of the city's policing networks during the war. The Health Department joined in the project of wartime policing, sharing with the NYPD descriptions of almost exclusively female venereal disease "contacts" as well as the locations in which men met them and using the broad power granted to it through Article 17B to justify the imprisonment and testing of such women. At a September 1944 conference on controlling venereal diseases, Commissioner Valentine, always a supporter of corralling "unwholesome" women, discussed how this public health policy could be used to "force in" a woman: "She has been acquitted of the criminal charge, but she is forced in under the Public Health Law into one of our hospitals, particularly Bellevue, and detained there until released by the physicians."[70]

La Guardia, Valentine, and Health Commissioner Ernest Stebbins found support for their programs in Governors Herbert Lehman and Thomas Dewey. Lehman, who believed that, "in this period of national emergency, the strength of law enforcement may become as important as the strength of our army and navy," expanded the state police.[71] The governor also successfully pushed for the creation of a wartime state guard in case National Guard members were called into federal service.[72] At its high point, the state guard's ranks included about 18,000 members.[73] The state guard and state police, however, did not play a central role in policing in New York City. The former were only activated a handful of times during the war, and the latter included about half as many officers as the city's NYPD.[74] Members of the state guard were called to "stand by" during an uprising in Harlem in August 1943 but were never deployed.[75] Governor Dewey, a former prosecutor, proved an ally after his election in 1942. Policing operations in New York City, however, were primarily in the hands of La Guardia and Valentine.

New York City's expansion of anti-vice policing developed in tandem with the enlargement of federal wartime policing powers. The dangers of prostitution and venereal disease were a cause of particular concern for many federal officials, who sought to protect the moral and physical health of the men they believed would be necessary to populate an American military and wartime industrial production. Congress appropriated $3,000,000 for 1938–39 and $5,000,000 for 1939–40 to assist states in combatting syphilis and gonorrhea for the first time since 1922.[76] In the spring of 1939, representatives of the U.S. Army, the U.S. Navy, the Federal Security Agency, and the American Social Hygiene Association, a private anti-vice association based in New York City, met in Washington and formulated what became known as the Eight-Point Agreement.[77] The agreement articulated a collaborative relationship between federal, municipal, and military agencies in the shared goals of repressing prostitution and preventing enlisted men from contracting venereal diseases. It stated that "the probable source" of venereal disease infection of military or naval personnel must be reported to state or local health authorities. The agreement further articulated that local police bore responsibility for the repression of prostitution and control of "recalcitrant infected persons."[78] Federal assistance for the incarceration of such recalcitrant persons was provided during the war through the 1941 Lanham Act, which funded clinics and detention centers where women who tested positive for venereal diseases were imprisoned.[79]

Though the Eight-Point Agreement was written in gender-neutral language, participants were undoubtedly aware that policing prostitution meant policing women. The federal infrastructure for monitoring sexually profiled women increased further in 1941 when Paul McNutt, the head of the Federal Security Agency, created a new division focused on combatting wartime sexual threats. The Social Protection Division (SPD) was, in the words of its employees, focused exclusively on "sex delinquency, from excessive promiscuity to commercialized prostitution."[80] Throughout the war, the SPD supported local law enforcement agencies through participating in joint conferences and producing propaganda alerting Americans to the sexual threats lurking in their midst. Congress further bolstered the punitive power of federal anti-prostitution efforts by passing the May Act in June 1941, which rendered prostitution near military establishments a federal crime. The act authorized the secretaries of war and the navy to call on the FBI to intervene to control prostitution in such areas. The May Act was only invoked twice during the war and was never needed in New York, where Valentine and La Guardia had already embraced its guiding principles. The May Act's passage as well as the Eight-Point Agreement and the creation of the SPD, however, all signaled the federal government's increased interest in monitoring problematic women.

In addition to the municipal and federal actors, the military played a role in monitoring the social and sexual activities of its members and civilians. The army adopted a more lenient policy toward men engaging in heterosexual sex during World War II than had been in practice during World War I. Distributing condoms, providing prophylaxis stations, and, beginning in early 1942, accepting men who tested positive for venereal diseases all became official policy.[81] This acceptance, however, did not extend to sexually active women, whether in the military or out of it. Similar practices were never applied to women in the Women's Army Corps, who were aggressively monitored for any sexual activity and often depicted as prostitutes or lesbians.[82] Military police officers and members of the Navy Shore Patrol monitored sailors and soldiers, while military officials worked with representatives from the NYPD and the Health Department.

In New York City, Major General Thomas A. Terry oversaw the army's operations. Terry had graduated from West Point in 1908 and commanded what was known as the Second Army Corps Area and later the Second Service Command from its headquarters on Governors Island.[83] The area included New York, New Jersey, and Delaware. As leader of the Second Service Command, Terry bore responsibility for troops stationed in or passing through his district and oversaw medical military facilities. He and his staff worked closely with Commissioner Valentine and New York health commissioner Stebbins to identify and monitor sexually threatening women. Representatives from the Second Service Command attended meetings with the two municipal commissioners to discuss prostitution and venereal diseases in New York City. Military officials regularly sent the NYPD detailed lists describing women from whom enlisted men claimed they had contracted venereal diseases and the locations of these illicit encounters.[84] The city's Health Department, the police department, and army and navy administrators used this information to create a record of venues in which men met female "contacts" from whom they claimed to have contracted venereal diseases.

This gendered system, however, relied on a number of assumptions, which constituted part of how what Allan Brandt describes as the "'social constructions' of venereal disease" functioned in this historical moment.[85] Central to how officials thought about and shaped venereal disease policy was the idea that any venereal infection identified in a serviceman had been contracted from a recent female "contact." With assistance from these federal, military, and public health officials, La Guardia and Valentine prepared to finally banish vice from the city limits. Though they appreciated the interagency cooperation and assistance, the pair worried about the NYPD's ability to handle a wartime increase in immorality and to protect enlisted men in the event of a war.

La Guardia, Valentine, and other NYPD officials fought to preserve the ranks of the department before the United States officially entered the war. The mayor argued that any peacetime conscription act should exclude police officers because of their essential role in protecting American cities. Members of the NYPD agreed. At the New York State Police Conference in August 1940, Patrolman Joseph Burkard, head of the Patrolmen's Benevolent Association, introduced a resolution proposing the exclusion of policemen from conscription because of their role as "the first line in home defense."[86] "The maintenance of law and order in our large cities," La Guardia declared in December 1940, "is one of the most important functions of our National Defense Program."[87] The mayor argued that police officers received all the training necessary in their positions as law enforcement and were needed in the city until the federal government declared war.[88]

Despite this advocacy, when Roosevelt signed the Selective Service and Training Act into law on September 16, 1940, it included no blanket exclusions for police officers. Officers could be granted individual exemptions based on their perceived expertise, but this practice was at the discretion of the draft board. During the war, NYPD ranks fell to more than 3,000 below the 18,790 department members allocated in the budget quota.[89] Though the department's numbers decreased, Valentine devoted expanded resources for the officers who remained to monitor and prevent vice.

The NYPD Goes to War

Policing New York City became even more important to municipal officials after Japan attacked the U.S. airfields at Pearl Harbor on December 7, 1941, and the United States declared war on Japan and Germany. Gotham's officials stepped up their efforts to place the city "on immediate war footing." La Guardia formed the War Emergency Board, which included Valentine, the fire commissioner, the commissioner of public works, and the deputy commissioner of hospitals, and more than 500,000 New Yorkers volunteered to contribute to civilian defense activities.[90] Valentine assigned additional patrolmen to the waterfront, communication centers, power plants, and defense industry sites. He also directed commanding officers to inform their patrolmen to devote extra attention to public utilities, bridges, tunnels, shipyards, defense manufacturing plants, and other sites related to defense production and mobility around the city. Patrolmen delivered the first news of the Pearl Harbor attack to many sailors and soldiers. NYPD officers assisted members of the FBI in arresting between 2,000 and 2,500 Japanese Americans and immigrants. Officers and FBI agents raided Japanese restaurants around the city and grabbed people in their homes. Agents directed Japanese American New Yorkers to pack a suitcase before transporting the prisoners to Ellis Island while federal authorities evaluated their "status."[91] In the police department's internal magazine, *Spring 3100*, Valentine reminded department members that since "modern warfare is no longer a matter of remote battlefields," officers faced a "grave" responsibility.[92]

In order to appropriately protect New York City from the dangers of modern warfare, La Guardia created an auxiliary police force of unpaid uniformed volunteers known as the City Patrol Corps in January 1942. The mayor conceived of the corps as an organization created to "supplement and assist the City Police in every proper and effective way possible."[93] He explained the importance of this new agency to the public, proclaiming, "In time of stress, particularly war-time, the responsibility of the Police Department is very great."[94] The initial stated aim of the City Patrol Corps was to prevent sabotage at key infrastructure points and to provide NYPD backup at parades and special events. Veterans made up a significant proportion of its earliest volunteers and leaders.[95] These ranks quickly expanded, however, to 7,125 volunteers in 1942, a significant addition to the 17,582 members on the NYPD payroll in December of that year.[96] The high rates of enrollment are not surprising given that the mayor sent the following letter threatening to revoke the deferrals of men who refused to participate in the City Patrol Corps:

> Dear Registrant: you have been temporarily deferred from duty with the armed forces by your local draft board and placed in deferred classification 3-A. This temporary deferment does not entirely relieve you of your civilian responsibilities and patriotic duties to your country. The City Patrol Corps of the City of New York is now engaged in enrolling men to the duty of guarding places vital to the war effort, which are considered sensitive and vulnerable to sabotage. New York City needs able-bodied men for this service. You owe it to yourself, your family and your neighbors to come forward and assist the local authorities protecting your city. If you fail to apply for enrollment with the City Patrol Corps your defense status with the protective forces of the city will be reported to the local draft board.[97]

As the war progressed, the responsibilities of City Patrol Corps members shifted. Rather than patrolling vulnerable points around the city, members became responsible for the regular police work of monitoring civilians. The leader of the corps stated that Gotham's organization was the only wartime police auxiliary to "perform police duties daily."[98] This appears to be a bit of an exaggeration, as auxiliary agencies did do police work informally in other municipalities during the war, but the degree to which New York's City Patrol Corps became officially embedded within the NYPD was unusual.[99] The head of the City Patrol Corps noted in his final report on the force that by early 1944, the commanders of City Patrol Corps companies around the city had "been ordered to establish the closest and most cooperative liaison possible with police precinct captains, and give them the help wanted."[100] The mayor supported this transition and encouraged New Yorkers who wrote to him with concerns about crime and delinquency to join the new agency.[101] Volunteers took orders from NYPD precinct captains, acting as armed adjuncts to the department. Though the head of the City Patrol Corps initially planned to arm volunteers with only nightsticks, he found that "the general attitude of the men was 'no gun, not important.'"[102] The NYPD provided both general training for all members of the corps in skills like the use of firearms and specialized courses for selected volunteers who then moved into leadership roles in their companies. The *Amsterdam News* commented in an article discussing the City Patrol Corps and the NYPD that "just about the only difference between the two is that CPs volunteer their service."[103] The regional director of the Office of Civilian Defense commented approvingly that City Patrol Corps volunteers were "cloaked with police authority."[104]

Members of the City Patrol Corps worked with NYPD precincts to monitor young people, suspicious women, and New Yorkers of color during the war. In the Bronx, patrol corps members surveilled concerts and dances at Poe Park with NYPD members and walked beats in the Hunts Point and Longwood neighborhoods.[105] Volunteers monitored Times Square in the evenings together with regular members of the police force.[106] The headquarters of the City Patrol Corps Division in Queens reported that its members proved "instrumental in the apprehension of 21 juvenile delinquents" over the course of its operation (June 1, 1942, to August 31, 1945) and noted, "It is probable that many other incidents of minor nature have occurred in which the members of Queens division played an active part, reported or unreported, which are not included in the above [report]."[107] Harold Kay, an African American lieutenant of the corps in charge of recruiting in the Jamaica area of Queens, declared that "juvenile delinquency and petty complaints . . . diminish in a neighborhood covered by the Patrol Corps."[108] African American members of the corps formed part of the 1,500 Black civilian volunteers who joined the NYPD in patrolling Harlem during the uprising of August 1943, which will be discussed in more detail in chapter 6.[109] Their deployment, which the Harlem-based *People's Voice* described as "superlative," was partly a strategic move to prevent further confrontations between primarily white NYPD officers and Black residents angered by police brutality and racial discrimination.[110] Divisions around the city assisted in policing for juvenile delinquency, but the 600 members of the Women's Division of the City Patrol Corps were seen as bearing a special responsibility for this task. The leadership of the patrol corps and the NYPD structured the work of female corps members around gendered responsibilities of policing children and young women. Female volunteers assisted with clerical work, the provision of snacks to male corps members, motor transport, and addressing "the problem of juvenile delinquency brought on by the war."[111]

Though official policy of the patrol corps encouraged the volunteers to avoid making arrests, in practice many violated this provision. The record of injuries reported by members of the City Patrol Corps indicate that volunteers performed arrests and engaged in routine police work. Dominic Albino of Brooklyn's A Unit sprained his ankle and pulled muscles in his stomach while "attempting to subdue a number of ruffians on [his] post." Albert Capodici, who patrolled in Richmond's B Unit, sustained a scrape on the shin while pursing four boys he suspected of stealing lumber. One of the children threw a stone at the volunteer, hitting him in the leg. Two other volunteers reported injuries to their hands while attempting to make arrests, and another fell down while "attempting to subdue a disorderly person."[112] Patrol corps volunteers, like NYPD patrolmen, monitored and arrested New Yorkers for supposed criminal activity and, like their remunerated counterparts, met resistance.

In addition to the City Patrol Corps, the NYPD worked to expand wartime community surveillance through the creation of precinct coordinating councils.[113] Each of the city's eighty-one patrol precincts set up its own coordinating council of local business owners, residents, and religious leaders.[114] The stated objectives of these councils included aiding in "the prevention of delinquency and waywardness and the promotion of moral and physical welfare of the youth of the community."[115] Police officers and community members served on the committees, which sponsored discussions on topics including "the impact of war on youth" as well as recreational and athletic activities.[116]

In practice, the councils served multiple aims. They functioned as neighborhood community spaces that strove to provide positive recreational activities for young people, and participants often supported the councils as a way to reduce the justification for a large police presence in their neighborhoods. The councils also, however, worked directly with their local police precincts, expanding networks of youth surveillance and blurring distinctions between police and community supervision. For example, a coordinating council near the Brooklyn neighborhood of Crown Heights hosted athletic tournaments for youth. NYPD members in the Seventy-Seventh Precinct participated in the games, and the winning children received shirts labeled "PAL" and "77."[117] Through the coordinating councils and the City Patrol Corps, New York City and the NYPD augmented police power during the war.

Wartime concern about rising rates of criminality among children and women meant that female members of the NYPD became increasingly important in the city's policing systems, though in gendered and racialized positions. Valentine believed that the increasing criminality of young women during the war necessitated a particular feminine type of policing, which expanded the small foothold women had gained in the department by the late 1930s. The department raised the budget quota for policewomen from

166 to 184 in July 1942, and again from 184 to 190 in February 1943, where it remained throughout the rest of the 1940s.[118] In February 1942, the City College Division of Public Service Training began its first course for the training of policewomen in its two years of existence. The relatively new division expanded the course, which had previously accepted aspiring policemen and firemen, because of the shortages of male laborers due to the draft.[119] The NYPD openings were almost exclusively for white women.[120]

In February 1944, *Spring 3100* introduced a column entitled "Strictly for the Girls!," which provides insight into the gendered and racialized framework that structured the roles of female NYPD members. The editors described the audience for this column as the department's 273 "feminine members," as well as the "mothers, wives, sisters, and even sweethearts of members of the force." The column would, editors declared, demonstrate that "'our girls'—both in the Department and at home—are ever in our thoughts."[121] The column included a mixture of recipes, advice, and topical information. The advice covered makeup tips and the updates included how war rationing might affect the production of girdles. One story in the column chronicles the transition of a young woman who marries and gains weight, growing "careless with her once luscious form." Authors described the young beauty's "creamy-white hue of smooth-textured skin," noting that she was "a sight to quicken the pulse of any man."[122] In this articulation, authors made explicit a theme that ran implicitly through the columns and through the NYPD's approach to both policewomen and policing young women: that the feminine qualities justifying women's presence in the department were predominantly the possession of white women. Through the introduction of the column, Valentine and other department officials acknowledged that white women had a role to play in the police department, and that this role proved increasingly important during the war. The title and content of "Strictly for the Girls!," as well as the rationale provided for introducing it, however, clearly illustrate the gendered parameters of these positions.

The wartime focus on the behavior of young women meant that policewomen's services were increasingly in demand and the space for them in the department expanded. The increased policing of teenage girls, however, restricted the social and sexual liberties of these young women and increased the vulnerability of girls of color. Dorothy Schulz has called policewomen of this era the "bridge generation" between the middle-class reformers who joined police departments in the Progressive Era and the working-class women who would follow them and become more fully integrated into departments.[123] Patrolwomen's advancement in the NYPD bore similarities to the experiences of women moving into other male-dominated fields of the civilian labor force during the war.[124] Women working in wartime manufacturing faced new economic opportunities, but found that gendered assumptions about their family responsibilities and position in society persisted.[125] Additionally, though the percentage of Black women engaged in industrial work increased from 6.5 percent to 18 percent during the war, many employers still resisted hiring Black women or restricted their workplace opportunities more than those of white women. For example, a survey performed by the United Auto Workers in April 1943 found that only 74 out of 280 employers that hired women in production work expressed willingness to hire Black women.[126]

The experiences of patrolwomen also paralleled those of women in the military, who faced fewer opportunities than their civilian counterparts to break out of traditionally feminine responsibilities of service and support work.[127] Although the positions of women in the military and the NYPD continued to be circumscribed by assumptions about women's capabilities and limitations, women were not pushed out of these professions after the war.[128] Women in the NYPD were more integral to the city's police department than their peers in other municipal police departments around the country, due to Valentine's belief in women's importance in anti-vice policing.[129] The commissioner embraced policewomen, arguing that they proved essential to combatting wartime female misbehavior and morals laws violations.

Valentine's commitment to enforcing the city's morals laws led him to create another new police division devoted to this task in January 1942. The commissioner established the Division of National Defense in the NYPD, charging its twenty members with suppressing gambling, prostitution, and other forms of "vice" in areas frequented by soldiers on leave. Valentine and La Guardia viewed the new division as part of the city's efforts to protect service men passing through its streets. These men, according to the commissioner and the mayor, could be entrapped or preyed on by gamblers, prostitutes, or juvenile delinquents and they needed protection from the venues that hosted such dangers.[130] From its headquarters on 300 Mulberry Street, members of the division set out to search for "gamblers, prostitutes, and criminals" who supposedly threatened the health of soldiers, sailors, and men on the home front.[131]

Commissioner Valentine oversaw the new squad directly with the assistance of Chief Inspector Louis F. Costuma. Costuma was a longtime department member, having joined the force in 1906. As a child, he had "loved a uniform," but his immigrant parents, Bernard Costuma, a cigar manufacturer, and Sara de Young, could not afford his dream of West Point and he only attended school through the eighth grade.[132] Costuma became chief inspector in 1939, after organizing the first Police Crime Prevention Bureau in 1929, which later became the Juvenile Aid Bureau.[133] Costuma's experience in the Police Crime Prevention Bureau prepared him well for his role suppressing gambling and other crimes of vice in the Division of National Defense. To Costuma, the city's policemen were "soldiers of the public safety who must fight for the most part alone."[134] Throughout the war years, members of the Division of National Defense patrolled the city on the lookout for prostitutes, gamblers, and juvenile delinquents. They focused particularly on Times Square and Harlem, where, officials argued, enlisted men went in search of young women and a good time.

The belief that policing New York City was as essential part of the nation's war mobilization undergirded the expansion of these various policing projects throughout the war years. The NYPD's internal magazine, *Spring 3100*, which Valentine served as the editor of, worked to strengthen connections between men serving in the NYPD and those in the military. *Spring 3100* published letters and articles written by police officers who were now serving in the armed forces.[135] In March 1943, the magazine began running a collection of such letters in every issue in a column entitled "Yes . . . Spring 3100 Does Get Around." The authors of such letters spoke of the thrill of reading descriptions of the NYPD's activities, and the connection that they felt with the department's members. In March 1943, Lieutenant Stanley Koutnick, who had worked as a patrolman in the 114th Precinct, wrote to the editor of *Spring 3100* from "somewhere in Africa." Koutnick stated of *Spring 3100*, "This excellent magazine serves as a bond between our buddies in the Department and we members serving in the armed forces of our country." The patrolman also noted that the publication "brings back many pleasant memories of our men in blue who are performing their duty at home just as we in khaki are doing abroad."[136] By sending *Spring 3100* to enlisted men like Koutnick and publishing their letters, Valentine and his subordinates maintained a personal connection with NYPD officers serving in the military. The editorial tone of *Spring 3100* and its celebration of both police officers and members of the military encouraged its audience to consider these jobs equally important to the war effort. At the close of the war, such connections would be used to encourage veterans to join the police department.

The landscape of wartime anti-vice policing proved a network of expanding and overlapping surveillance systems. Together this network enacted the robust urban law-and-order response that La Guardia and Valentine had sought to bring to Gotham since 1934. Federal agencies provided support and oversight in the form of the Social Protection Division and the FBI. NYPD bureaus expanded anti-vice policing through the newly formed Division of National Defense and the increased numbers of policewomen. Volunteer police officers patrolled the city through the City Patrol Corps, neighbors monitored each other through the precinct coordinating councils, and children volunteered for police supervision in the Police Athletic League. The chapters that follow will explore how this policing apparatus functioned to facilitate the arrest and surveillance of New Yorkers for prostitution, juvenile delinquency, gambling, and disorderly entertainment.

CHAPTER THREE

Another Form of Sabotage
The NYPD's Anti-prostitution Crusade

When investigator and former judge Samuel Seabury began probing into the city's magistrates' courts in 1930, one element of the larger corruption scandals dominated the press coverage: sex, or sex work to be exact. The press reported regularly on the public hearings, and Seabury played to his audience, informing journalists that he planned to save the city "from the low and sordid estate to which it has sunk."[1] False arrests and convictions for prostitution, as sex work was known at the time, quickly emerged as the most high-profile evidence of this "sordid estate."

Seabury solicited testimony from women who had been arrested for prostitution after being framed by police or police informants. The testimony highlighted changes in anti-prostitution policing that had been unfolding throughout the early twentieth century. As historian Timothy Gilfoyle argues, by the start of the 1920s, sex work had become "a clandestine, underground activity."[2] Throughout the following decade, as organized crime grew increasingly powerful in the city, anti-prostitution policing became more brutal, violent, and corrupt.[3] In the 1930 investigation, these police practices became public in sympathetic testimony from female arrestees. Journalists portrayed the women as victims of a network of predatory NYPD officers, judges, and gangsters. Under Seabury's critical lens, widely accepted NYPD and court practices, including arresting and convicting women based solely on evidence given by NYPD officers or paid informants, received new scrutiny in court and in the press.

The city's press was horrified at the revelations of police corruption wielded against women, many of whom were white, married, and employed. The front page of the *New York Times* proclaimed the hearings "a story of police corruption, of 'shakedowns' and 'frameups,'" in which innocent women sometimes fell victims of cash-thirsty detectives, bondsmen and lawyers."[4] The *New York Amsterdam News* deplored that the investigation revealed "the most nauseating practices in the history of city government," including the framing of "guiltless girls" for prostitution.[5] According to the *Brooklyn Daily Eagle*, Seabury and his special counsel, Isidor Kresel, "parted the curtains and revealed a shocking picture of conditions in the Women's Court in Manhattan."[6]

The picture of women's commercial and noncommercial sexual activity was in flux in the 1930s and 1940s. Throughout the early twentieth century, young urban working-class women embraced the practice of "treating" or engaging in sexual activities with male companions in exchange for expense-paid nights on the town.[7] These years saw the emergence of "sexual liberalism," John D'Emilio and Estelle Freedman contend, when sex began to be decoupled from procreation and accepted as a central part of personal expression, in and out of marriage.[8] By the mid-1930s, almost half of white American women engaged in premarital sex, and historian Amanda Littauer argues convincingly that during World War II rates of heterosexual premarital sex increased even further.[9] The birth control movement met success in the 1936 U.S. Court of Appeals decision to exempt contraceptives prescribed by physicians from the Comstock Law, and the use of contraception generally had increased. By the 1940s, sexual advice manuals for married couples recognized the importance of sex, and even of women's sexual fulfillment, while seeking to preserve men's authority in domestic relations.[10] Women were also moving into the workplace in increasing numbers. They participated in labor activism through Congress of Industrial Organizations auxiliaries and took jobs in New Deal–funded programs. Women's working patterns changed further with the mobilization for World War II.[11] Married women took jobs outside the home, and new industrial sectors of the workforce became temporarily open to women. For many, this shift represented a challenge to the idealized notion of a male breadwinner and soldier tied to a wife whose professional and civic responsibilities centered on the home. These sexual, economic, and social shifts rippled through anti-prostitution policing campaigns throughout the 1920s, the Depression, and the war years.

In 1930s New York City, the public revelations that NYPD members framed married, white, professional women disrupted anti-prostitution policing. Court magistrates became less inclined to convict women based solely on the word of arresting officers, and officers responded by arresting fewer women for prostitution. In 1931, prostitution arraignments in the women's court dropped precipitously from an average of 2,763 in the preceding five years to 513 in the first eleven months of the year. As investigators noted, this reduction reflected "the tightening of the checks upon police officers."[12]

The hearings discredited the administration of Mayor Jimmy Walker as well as the broader systems of NYPD administration and policing developed under Tammany city rule. They provided the opportunity for the election of

Fiorello La Guardia, who was determined to reform the police department away from the practices on display in Seabury's hearings. Lewis Valentine, the anti-Tammany cop and La Guardia's new police commissioner, became the city's standard-bearer for a new model of anti-prostitution policing. Valentine, like La Guardia, argued that the purpose of policing was to create an orderly city, not to enrich working-class officers or to shore up political control in the city. Women suspected of prostitution or promiscuity constituted a particular moral and sexual threat to the health of the city, according to Valentine and La Guardia.

These women, who rarely marched for their own freedoms and had less access to the press than their middle-class detractors, still managed to leave a record of their battle for social and sexual autonomy and their resistance to state violence. This chapter explores the state's attempts to control these women throughout La Guardia's and Valentine's tenures. In the process, it reveals the changing ideology of policing, the utility of the war mobilization for projects of surveillance, and glimpses of what scholar Saidiya Hartman describes as these women's "radical imagination and everyday anarchy."[13]

Seabury's investigations challenged the power of police officers to harass and extort women with access to financial and social capital. In response, Valentine and La Guardia crafted a new ideology of policing, in which professional and honest officers would protect all upstanding New Yorkers, regardless of race or class, from the prostitutes and criminals seeking to despoil their city. This fiction depended on the support of a small number of high-profile Black members of the NYPD, as well as on middle-class Black New Yorkers' opposition to working-class street activity. Despite claims of impartiality, Valentine encouraged NYPD members to rely on the racialized geography of the city as well as visual signifiers associated with distinctions of gender, race, class, and sexuality when identifying criminality. Though extorting women was prohibited, uniformed and plainclothes policemen could still arrest women for prostitution based on their appearance, and these officers could almost guarantee a conviction through their testimony alone.

The war mobilization injected new justifications into this gendered and racialized policing regime. Historian Anne Gray Fischer has argued that World War II–era anti-prostitution policing campaigns represent the most powerful and last wave of sexual policing that primarily targeted white women. Fischer also notes, however, in another context, that police in New York City were ahead of the rest of the nation when it came to systematically targeting Black women for policing. Because of La Guardia and Valentine's political perspectives on anti-vice policing, race, and municipal corruption, wartime anti-prostitution policing in New York was more focused on Black and Puerto Rican women and Black neighborhoods than in many other U.S. cities, setting Gotham ahead in policing trends that would soon become dominant across the country.[14]

The ideology that La Guardia and Valentine brought to their post-Seabury administration did not fundamentally challenge the ability of police officers to harass and arrest women they believed to be suspicious. In the years after the Seabury investigations, in fact, while arrests of white women for prostitution decreased, arrests of Black women increased significantly in terms of both absolute numbers and percentage of total prostitution arrests.[15] Hartman has written that in the early decades of the twentieth century, "prostitution was a charge levied to extract information, extort money, harass and abuse, and establish the boundaries of what a black woman could and could not do."[16] Under La Guardia and Valentine, these first two purposes of prostitution arrests faded in favor while the last two rose in importance.

Policing Prostitution under La Guardia and Valentine

Cracking down on prostitution was a priority for both La Guardia and Valentine, for whom working-class sexuality was immoral and street disorder a blight on the city's reputation. "The unrestrained operation of street prostitutes within a city will bring that city into bad repute," Valentine asserted at the U.S. Conference of Mayors in November 1936.[17] Valentine associated sex work with police corruption and positioned his department as attacking both. Corruption persisted despite his efforts, but the commissioner pushed an approach that replaced the haphazard and self-interested anti-prostitution policing of Tammany with rigorous surveilling of sexually profiled women, which included Black and Puerto Rican women across classes, working-class women across races, and young women, all of whom the city's political, law enforcement, and health officials construed as vectors of danger and disease.

During La Guardia's and Valentine's terms, magistrates, public health officers, and members of the NYPD used two primary modes of surveillance to monitor sexually dangerous women. The first was contact tracing, or following up on reports from the Health Department.[18] These reports were provided by men who tested positive for venereal diseases and named women with whom they had recently had sex. The Health Department collected records from the U.S. Army, the U.S. Navy, the U.S. Coast Guard, the U.S. Merchant Marines, and its own clinics, which it then forwarded to the NYPD.[19]

The second way to identify supposed prostitutes was to patrol the city looking for sexually profiled women, paying particular attention to Black or interracial neighborhoods and entertainment districts. Officials considered Black women and Puerto Rican women of all classes as well as working-class women across races particularly likely to engage in prostitution or to carry venereal diseases. These women, officials believed, required additional police attention. Officers applied this logic to their patrols, perceiving women in these groups as suspicious and dangerous, particularly if officers saw them alone or in an interracial couple. Most prostitution arrests were performed by plainclothes officers in the special service division of the NYPD, which included sixteen districts and a headquarters, with roughly fifteen officers assigned to each one.[20]

Female members of the NYPD also participated in this surveillance of suspected prostitutes. The police commissioner believed that female department members, who were almost exclusively white, were particularly qualified to surveil other women and children. In December 1935, the NYPD rolls included ninety-seven members under the title "policewoman" (who supervised female arrestees) and forty-nine listed as "patrolwoman" (the separate categories would be merged under the title "policewomen" in 1939).[21] *The Policewoman's Handbook*, a popular policing text published in 1933, advised policewomen that "the girl or woman who is a prostitute may sometimes be identified by her slow pace, or gait, and apparent lack of destination, by her dress, which is usually conspicuous and often out of place, by excessive make-up, etc. Her attitude often shows lack of interest in anything but her objective of securing a man. . . . Occasionally the young prostitute is very modestly and correctly dressed and may only be detected by her conduct."[22]

Under this supposedly unbiased regime, women were often criminalized because of *whom* officers perceived them to be, rather than anything they *did*. Poor women who had limited access to private spaces and whose clothing officers might read as disorderly were at increased risk of arrest, as were Black women and Puerto Rican women. In 1928, 2,379 white women and 1,039 Black women were arrested for prostitution; in 1932, these numbers were 817 white women and 1,245 Black women. In 1935, the author of a report on prostitution and the women's court commented on the dramatic changes in the racial breakdown of these arrest statistics: "It is hardly reasonable to suppose that so great a reformation could have taken place in the morals of white women as these figures would suggest or that there is so marked a difference between the races. Much more probable is the inference that the enforcing mechanism operate differently for white and Negro offenders."[23] This trend in overrepresentation of Black women arrested for prostitution continued, though with a reduced disparity, throughout first six months of 1934 when 861 white women were arrested and 671 Black women.[24] The author of the 1935 report noted that the high rates of arrest of Black women in 1928 and 1932 "suggest that the officers are not directing their efforts to those districts in which [prostitution] may be most prevalent, but are contenting themselves with the arrest of Negro women instead."[25] Under Valentine's watch, arrests for "Vagrancy, Prostitution" also increased overall — rising by 26 percent between 1934 and 1935 from 3,190 to 4,299.[26] The increase in overall arrests while the arrest of white women decreased demonstrates the growing racial disparity of post-Seabury reformed prostitution policing. Officers became more cautious about arresting women whom the courts, police higher-ups, and city officials might deem innocent, and more aggressive in targeting women whom these institutions labeled as dangerous.

The mayor's office and the NYPD set Gotham's anti-prostitution policies, but the courts and Health Department supported the city's carceral network. Women arrested for prostitution were processed through the women's court, housed on the second floor of an aging building on the corner of Sixth Avenue and Ninth Street in Manhattan.[27] "It is called the women's court," Magistrate Anna Kross commented on the name and function of the Sixth Avenue facility in 1938, but "it is really the court of criminal prostitution."[28] All women arrested in any borough for engaging in prostitution, being a wayward minor, running a disorderly house, or committing misdemeanor shoplifting came through the Sixth Avenue facility.[29] Though men were also arrested and charged with vagrancy, prostitution, or being a "street walker," such crimes constituted a much smaller proportion of male arrests and were processed in the magistrate's court in the district where the offense occurred.[30] Magistrates, who served as judges in the women's court, convicted the majority of women arraigned on prostitution charges and generally granted these women terms of three months or less at the House of Detention for Women, located at Tenth Street and Greenwich Avenue.[31]

Magistrates were mayoral appointees. Some magistrates, like Kross and Jonah Goldstein, had been active in progressive reform efforts. Kross was the first woman to be appointed a magistrate in New York City and was an immigrant from a working-class background.[32] She regularly argued that prostitution and female juvenile delinquency should be treated as medical and psychiatric problems, rather than issues of crime.[33] This approach, though less draconian than that of some of her counterparts, extended the state's power over women and girls by lowering the justifications necessary for intervention and extending the length of state surveillance, often indefinitely, under the guise of paternalistic support.

In 1935, Kross's contemporary Goldstein attracted press attention for announcing that he planned to hold all women charged with prostitution for forced venereal disease testing before trial.[34] Goldstein argued that his power to do so was found in Article 17B of the Public Health Law, which granted authority to the Health Department to detain and perform venereal tests on any person suspected on "reasonable grounds" of having a venereal disease. This description included any woman arrested for a prostitution charge.[35] Article 17B was a World War I–era incursion into women's social and sexual liberties, which would serve as important precedent during World War II.

The state legislature had passed Article 17B in 1918 as part of a nationwide campaign to protect soldiers from female sexuality during World War I. The War Department launched this campaign through the Commission on Training Camp Activities, which was charged with overseeing recreational activities for enlisted men. The commission's formal responsibilities were wide ranging, but at its center was what its leader, Raymond Fosdick, described as a "resounding battle" against prostitution and venereal diseases.[36] The Commission on Training Camp Activities and the Council of National Defense drafted municipal police departments and private anti-vice associations like the Committee of Fourteen into the battle against prostitution. The passage of Article 17B in New York was a clear example of the way World War I energized the state's capabilities of surveillance and incarceration in the name of morality and public health. Although Article 17B fell out of use after the war, it was not removed from the state's Public Health Law and was, therefore, available when Magistrate Goldstein sought to incarcerate and examine arrestees in 1935.

In the 1930s under La Guardia's administration, the city's Health Department revived the enforcement of Article 17B and the broader battle against sexually suspicious women and venereal diseases. La Guardia appointed Dr. John Rice as health commissioner in 1934. To Rice, venereal diseases were the "biggest single problem facing the Department of Health," and he quickly went to work attacking this challenge.[37] He increased the number of Health Department clinics that provided care for syphilis and gonorrhea, solicited a survey on sexually transmitted infections from the American Social Hygiene Association, sent a committee to observe syphilis treatment in Scandinavia and Britain, and established the Bureau of Social Hygiene inside the Health Department.[38]

Rice held legitimate concerns about venereal diseases. Syphilis and gonorrhea were relatively common (the U.S. Public Health Service released a study in May 1935 that placed the number of new infections of syphilis and gonorrhea nationwide in the previous year at 1,555,000) and carried serious and sometimes deadly consequences, particularly when untreated. Addressing this problem in the United States was made all the more difficult by the nation's lack of widespread free or affordable health care.[39] In this context, the health commissioner turned to carceral rather than health-oriented solutions and joined other city officials in relying on racist and misogynistic ideas to inform these solutions.

Incarcerating women arrested for prostitution was a central provision of the Health Department's campaign against venereal diseases. Women arrested for prostitution could be forcibly tested for syphilis and gonorrhea and imprisoned until labeled noninfectious. The Health Department used this process as a primary means of finding and treating sexually transmitted infections in New York's population, but the approach was deeply flawed. First, the small number of men who were arrested in connection with prostitution did not undergo testing for venereal disease. The Bureau of Social Hygiene assumed that these men would have contracted any infection at the time of arrest and therefore would not yet exhibit symptoms at the time of their arraignment. Physicians and nurses counseled these men about what to do if they experienced symptoms after returning home.[40]

Women, in contrast, were required to undergo both a physical examination and laboratory testing, but no medical consensus existed over how to use these tests to identify active cases of syphilis and gonorrhea. In April 1935, the chief of the Health Department's Division of Venereal Diseases commented on the problems this ambiguity posed in a letter to the Health Department's deputy commissioner. He noted that only 4 percent of the women the city's courts labeled as positive for gonorrhea received that judgment after gonococcus was identified in a smear at a laboratory. In other words, 96 percent of the women whom the court deemed to have infectious cases of gonorrhea received that label after a negative laboratory test, based on a physical examination and their personal history. The chief, rather defensively, argued, "The fact that we cannot demonstrate the gonococcus in some 60 to 70 percent of the cases under any condition does not, of course, rule out gonorrhea in them and does not permit us to state that they may not be sources of infection to others. In the examination we are taking the benefit of the doubt, but whether this would stand a test before a court is a question."[41]

Health Department officials framed women arrested for prostitution as "sources of infection to others," despite evidence to the contrary. In November 1935, a report produced by a committee at the New York Academy of Medicine for the Health Department acknowledged that prostitution accounted for "only a small fraction of the entire problem of venereal disease control."[42] Despite this acknowledgment, the authors recommended "strict enforcement" of the state's health statute, arguing that it would allow the state to forcibly imprison and treat suspicious women without ever having to bring them to trial.[43] The collaboration between the NYPD, the courts, and the Health Department, therefore, not only stripped women of due process but likely imprisoned many women who did not, in fact, have the infection for which they were forced to undergo treatment. A fiction of unbiased public health necessities performed similar ideological work to the facade of equitable policing, justifying a system completely reliant on gendered, racialized, and class-based perceptions of criminality and disease.

In addition to soliciting recommendations from the New York Academy of Medicine, the Health Department also created the internal Bureau of Social Hygiene in 1936, devoted to controlling sexually transmitted infections.[44] During the Progressive Era, John D. Rockefeller Jr. had funded a private organization by the same name.[45] In the years between the creations of the two Bureaus of Social Hygiene, primary responsibility for policing sexuality had migrated from private associations to state-backed law enforcement agencies.[46]

Women rounded up as part of this response were imprisoned in crowded conditions against their will and forced to undergo treatment before release. Before trial, they were held at the House of Detention until tests for syphilis and gonorrhea were completed. If the court labeled them positive, they were sent to Kingston Avenue Hospital for Communicable Diseases in Brooklyn, where they were required to accept treatment as a condition of regaining their freedom. This treatment usually lasted at least a month.[47] Under Valentine and La Guardia's watch, both prostitution arrests and the numbers of women incarcerated for treatment for sexually transmitted infections increased. The city began facing shortages of spaces to imprison these women, and in the summer of 1937 officials set up an auxiliary hospital at the Women's House of Detention where women were held before sentencing. In February 1938, a group of women held at the makeshift hospital protested their preconviction incarceration. The group refused to remain in the jail and demanded to be returned to court for sentencing. Those who had been labeled positive for syphilis or gonorrhea were sent to Kingston, while the majority won their release. When a second group of jailed women repeated the tactic shortly thereafter, the chief magistrate instructed sitting magistrates to sentence female arrestees to jail for 120 days to guard against this activism.[48] The prisoners' activism and the magistrate's response reveal a front in the ongoing battle between criminalized women and the state over women's autonomy.

Officials' conceptions of contagion centered on racist as well as sexist ideas, which can be seen clearly in their discussions of Puerto Rican migration to New York City. In the mid-1930s, La Guardia and his administrators wrote to federal officials expressing concern that "there is a substantially larger proportion of venereally infected persons in the insular possessions than on the Continent."[49] The deputy mayor reached out to the commissioner of welfare in the summer of 1938, strategizing as to how to prevent migrants from accessing public economic support, and he commented, "It appears that they bring a good deal of contagious disease."[50] Commissioner Rice reflected on the challenges posed to the state by the migration of people with venereal diseases across state lines. He noted that, though "we have been studying the Puerto Rican situation as it relates to venereal diseases for some time . . . the only method of enforcement that we can see is to examine all individuals coming from Puerto Rico at the point of entry."[51] Rice may have been referring to personal experience when he referenced "studying the Puerto Rican situation." In between getting his MD and becoming Gotham's commissioner of health, Rice traveled to Central America, Trinidad, and Puerto Rico working for the Rockefeller Foundation. The Rockefeller Foundation's projects varied widely in their scope, but the ethos of many employees relied on the idea that, according to scholar Laura Briggs, "the tropics were inhabited by dark people whose bodies were a wellspring of disease."[52] City officials brought this approach to their attitude toward Puerto Rican residents in New York City. Racialized conceptions of disease, criminality, and sexuality proved central to city officials' efforts to combat the spread of venereal diseases and prostitution.

Anti-Prostitution Policing in Harlem

The NYPD's anti-prostitution campaigns were a frequent topic of discussion and debate among Black New Yorkers throughout the 1930s. New York Age contributor Eric von Wilkinson set off a controversy in February 1935 when he shared his support of white police officers' practice of stopping interracial couples on the assumption that a woman in such a couple was a prostitute.[53] Von Wilkinson's piece provoked multiple responses in the *New York Age*. Ebenezer Ray reminded von Wilkinson that the profiling he described was "an infringement on somebody's constitutional rights." Ray went on to note that his colleague had "endowed a cop with the privilege of conceding that a woman is a prostitute after he has seen her walking the street. No legal statute endows a police officer with such a gift of conclusion."[54] Although Ray accurately noted that the policy von Wilkinson supported violated the law, von Wilkinson more closely described the way police officers enforced prohibitions on prostitution.

Disagreements over the acceptability and status of interracial relationships were not unusual in Black newspapers' discussions about prostitution and policing in 1930s and 1940s New York City. Sexual policing to protect and then arrest white women throughout the 1920s and 1930s justified police penetration into Black neighborhoods and segregationist logics throughout the urban North.[55] More broadly, discussions about interracial relationships were a component of press coverage of lynching and civil rights law, as well as the subject of personal and cultural debates.[56] While Black activists and residents denounced the NYPD for harassing interracial couples, some journalists also wrote negatively about interracial sex, often depicting white men in such relationships as exploiters or trafficking in misogynistic criticisms of Black women.[57] Other writers lambasted the disproportionate police attention devoted to prostitution and vice in Harlem. Writing in the *Amsterdam News* in the spring of 1935, Theophilus Lewis criticized what he described as "this comic opera war on vice" and argued that the police department's drive on prostitution and policy gambling "will not improve public morals. It will further degrade them."[58]

In the mid-1930s, Valentine launched new assaults against prostitution in Harlem, which the NYPD justified by depicting sex workers as outsiders in the community. This exclusionary rhetoric, combined with the criminalization of Black New Yorkers and of interracial sex, shaped the geography of anti-prostitution policing and the NYPD's approach to policing Black women. In the summer of 1937, after declaring "war on prostitution," Valentine launched a series of raids against female Harlemites.[59] The following summer, the NYPD again targeted women in Harlem, particularly Seventh Avenue between 110th and 125th Streets. "Colored girls are standing on street corners between 1:00 and 6:00 every morning advertising their wares to white men," an NYPD captain claimed. Patrolmen in Harlem's Twenty-Eighth Precinct received orders to pay particular attention to women on this stretch of street.[60]

As summer passed into fall, the NYPD added new resources for surveilling Harlem streets, assigning officers from other precincts to "special posts" devoted to "driving all prostitutes, pimps, and muggers out of the neighborhood."[61] Captain William A. Turk of the Twenty-Eighth Precinct proclaimed that officers were "arresting prostitutes, pimps, muggers, and degenerates, day and night." Despite this activity, Turk argued that prostitution continued in Harlem because "the community is being invaded by hordes of white men and Negroes from other cities."[62] This language mimicked some descriptions used by middle-class Black Harlemites who objected to working-class behavior that they viewed as disorderly by framing it as criminal and exogenous to the Harlem community. The NYPD capitalized on this framing to assume a position of responsiveness toward Black residents while racially targeting women in the neighborhood.

Black property owners in Harlem often supported these campaigns, despite the risks they themselves faced from police harassment. In November 1935, homeowners in the interracial West 118th Street Improvement Association worked with the police to engineer the arrest of Daisy Sievers and her husband, who were convicted of operating a handful of "bawdy houses" in the neighborhood. Members of the association testified against Sievers at her trial and sent a letter to Commissioner Valentine complaining that the NYPD was neglecting its duty in Harlem.[63] Grace Ward, a widow who ran a rooming house on West 126th Street, had made several complaints to police officers at the Twenty-Eighth Precinct about "questionable characters who parade up and down the street night and day." In October 1938, however, she found herself the target of police attention. According to Ward, an officer entered her home without identifying himself, a common practice in prostitution policing, and threatened her at gunpoint. The rooming-house owner's harrowing account illustrated the risks a heightened police presence could present to Harlem residents. Despite this attack, Ward continued to support increasing the NYPD's presence in Harlem and called on Valentine to prevent residents from being "molested by prostitutes and other underworld characters."[64]

Ward was not alone in her demand. Participants raised similar grievances in a meeting discussing crime and prostitution in lower Harlem at the New York Urban League in early October 1938. Attendees included members of the NYPD's Twenty-Eighth and Twenty-Third Precincts, the managing editor of the *Amsterdam News*, and the NYPD's highest-ranking Black officer, Lieutenant Samuel Battle. Participants at the meeting read letters from business owners and residents complaining about prostitution, robberies, mugging, and juvenile delinquency in the stretch from West 128th Street to 110th Street and Lenox to Eighth Avenues. In Brooklyn's Bedford-Stuyvesant, another large Black community in the city, the Fulton-Macon Civic Association similarly appealed to Valentine to prevent "hanging out" in front of neighborhood stores.[65] These appeals reflected the views of a cohort of Black New Yorkers, consisting mostly of members of the middle class, who wanted the NYPD to be more aggressive against prostitution in Black neighborhoods. Adherents to this strategy, which historian Shannon King describes as "legalism," called on city officials to change police practices in Black neighborhoods and worked to differentiate themselves from Black Gothamites whom they identified as criminal or disorderly.[66] When it came to working-class disorder on the streets of Harlem and Bedford-Stuyvesant, many Black property owners looked to the police as a solution. Undergirding this strategy was a complex relationship between Black property owners and the NYPD informed by the pull of racial solidarity against police victimization of Black people on the one hand and the pull of class solidarity against working-class disorderliness on the other.[67] Though legalistic campaigns were often led by members of the middle class, as LaShawn Harris argues, working-class Black New Yorkers held varied views on the underground economy and some participated in efforts to remove vice from Black neighborhoods.[68]

Valentine strategically fostered a perception that the NYPD was open to the concerns of Black New Yorkers and used it to the benefit of his department. He promoted Battle to the rank of lieutenant in 1935, making him the first Black lieutenant in the police department. The commissioner relied on Black department members, such as Battle and Sergeant Emanuel Kline, as emissaries to Black New York. The *New York Amsterdam News* described Battle as a "good will ambassador between the races," and Valentine sent Kline as his representative to "preach" against left-wing soapbox speakers in Harlem at the Metropolitan Baptist Church.[69] In response to demands that the NYPD hire more Black officers to better police Black neighborhoods and reduce discrimination within the department, Valentine claimed that he too was "very much disappointed that more [police department] examinations were not taken by Negro applicants," a posture that he would repeat throughout the 1940s.[70] When critics accused NYPD members of police brutality or of rounding up Black women in prostitution raids, Valentine pointed to Black NYPD members and to the demands of home and business owners as evidence that an unbiased force was responding to the needs of the community.

Home and business owners were not the only Black New Yorkers concerned with prostitution. Working-class Black Gothamites were most vulnerable to police harassment, but they had limited access to organizational and institutional modes for expressing their political perspectives. Left-wing activists and writers, however, tended to take a more class-based approach to discussions of prostitution. Journalists St. Clair Bourne and Marvel Cooke wrote a piece in the *Amsterdam News* in April 1939 that focused on the experience of "the lady of the night" rather than her middle-class detractors.[71] The authors argued that economic need drove women into prostitution, and they centered the employment and housing needs of Black women in their discussion. Cooke, who was a leading left-wing writer and thinker in the city, often wrote about Black women's experiences from a working-class perspective.[72] A similar concern with health and housing needs led fifty physicians practicing in Harlem and a group of Black social workers to collaborate with city agencies to propose alternative treatment for arrestees for prostitution. The group of doctors and social workers agreed to provide free social and medical services so that these women could receive treatment without incarceration. The *New York Times* noted that women who participated in this community-based approach were far more likely than their incarcerated peers to complete their treatment.[73] These important efforts at humanizing sex workers and improving their lives provided an alternative to the legalism of the West 118th Street Improvement Association. Even those who subscribed to this more compassionate approach, however, often missed the role that police officers played in producing the supposed problem of prostitution in Harlem by targeting Black women and the neighborhood.

Who were the women subjected to this police surveillance and criminalization? Women who were arrested for prostitution by the NYPD are not easy to find in the historical records. Because such crimes were misdemeanors, court records do not include trial transcripts or extensive information about the defendants. Prostitution arrests of ordinary women were not usually covered in newspapers or magazines. Those whose names can be found in the census records, however, were overwhelmingly working class or poor. They were women like Sarah, a married thirty-five-year-old African American manicurist who lived as a lodger in a building on Seventh Avenue. Sarah was unable to work at the time of the census and had been employed for only twenty-six weeks in 1939. She had completed eighth grade, listed her income for 1940 as $130, and noted that she had no other income sources.[74] Bernice, a twenty-six-year-old African American widow who had not attended college, was arrested on December 11, 1940, and sentenced to the House of Detention for Women.[75] Alice was arrested for vagrancy and prostitution in June 1940 and was convicted and sentenced to 120 days in the workhouse.

She was a white fifty-one-year-old woman who lived as a lodger on Dean Street in Brooklyn. Alice was a widow who had completed up to the sixth grade in school. In the census, she stated that she was not employed for pay but that she was looking for work, and that she had only worked twenty-six weeks in 1939. Her monthly rent was sixteen dollars and fifty cents.[76] Rosetta was a married domestic worker with a sixth-grade education struggling to find work. She had immigrated to New York City from the Virgin Islands and was arrested May 14, 1941.[77]

The extant sources suggest that women arrested for prostitution throughout the 1930s continued to be disproportionately Black. As Harris has argued, "Extreme poverty, sexual abuse and trauma, and the active pursuit of sexual desire and pleasure brought a diverse yet significant group of black women into sexual labor."[78] The significant disparity in arrests for prostitution between Black and white women and the NYPD's practices in Harlem indicate a pattern of targeting Black women and Black neighborhoods when making arrests for prostitution. Indeed, for some officials and officers, perceiving a woman as Black could itself be constitutive evidence of her engagement in prostitution. In a report on prostitution published by the Welfare Council of New York City in 1941, the author noted that in 1939 Black women had accounted for 54 percent of the arrests for prostitution, despite forming only 4.7 percent of the city's population. The author commented that she was "struck" by the gravity of the racial disparity in arrests, as was her counterpart in 1935.[79] Throughout the war years, Valentine and the federal Social Protection Division advocated for increasing the aggressive policing of African American women as a means of protecting white soldiers, ensuring that the disproportionately high arrest rate of Black women would continue.

Mobilizing against Prostitution in the Wartime City and Nation

The mobilization for World War II provided new justifications and injected new resources into La Guardia and Valentine's crusade against prostitution. The battle lines were redrawn and the municipal leaders framed prostitutes as not only a moral blight but a threat to national security; consequently, municipal efforts to police prostitution received additional backing from the U.S. military and federal government.[80] In 1939 and 1940, politicians, officials, journalists, and citizens across the country became increasingly concerned about the physical, moral, and sexual health of the American men who would be called on to staff the nation's military if the United States entered the growing global conflict.

According to political, health, military, and law enforcement officials, prostitutes and sexually active women presented threats to servicemen. Different branches of the American state adopted varied and contradictory approaches to this threat. Controlling sexual interactions between American soldiers and women in occupied nations was a priority for the American military throughout the war and served as a means of exerting U.S. diplomatic power abroad in the immediate postwar period.[81] Sexually active women existed at home too, however, and during the war mobilization they were moving out of the home in concerning ways. Women's labor and sexuality were mobilized in the service of the war, while also posing an ever-present threat to the men on whose shoulders the nation's warfighting machines were built, according to officials.[82] This insidious female peril could weaken American soldiers before they ever set foot on a ship or a battlefield. National arrest rates of women for morals offenses increased 95 percent between 1940 and 1944 in response to this supposed threat.[83]

New York served as a site for men shipping out to Europe and as a destination for sailors and soldiers on leave. Army officials stationed in the city sought to deter enlisted men from trysting with female Gothamites and pushed the NYPD to monitor the women of New York. Commissioner Valentine embraced the militarization of anti-prostitution policing, arguing that sexually active women engaged in acts of "sabotage" by putting men at risk of contracting sexually transmitted infections.[84] For Valentine and La Guardia, protecting enlisted men from promiscuous women and venereal disease was a municipal wartime duty, but this duty was not the only rationale for combatting prostitution. While military leaders' concern with prostitution began and ended with its impact on enlisted men, La Guardia and Valentine were also invested in projecting an image of New York City that conformed to their visions of order and morality. The wartime context proved hospitable to this vision.

In May 1939, representatives of state health departments met with members of the War and Navy Departments and the Federal Security Agency to discuss venereal disease control in the context of a likely military mobilization. The attendees produced what became known as the Eight-Point Agreement. The agreement articulated the collaborative commitment of federal, state, and local governments to monitoring and incarcerating women through anti-prostitution policing in order to curb the spread of venereal diseases. Point five of the agreement proclaimed that "recalcitrant infected persons" would be forcibly isolated until deemed noninfectious. In point six, participants agreed that "the local police department is responsible for the repression of commercialized and clandestine prostitution."[85] The Eight-Point Agreement signaled an escalation in the drive to monitor and control sexually threatening women. National policies like the Eight-Point Agreement and the Selective Service Act, which was passed in September 1940 and required men aged twenty-one to forty-five to register for a military draft, moved the protection of American servicemen to the center of national discourse. The federal Public Health Service launched new propaganda campaigns through posters, leaflets, and films intended to warn soldiers of the dangers of sex with suspicious women.[86] Supporters of this project, including Valentine and La Guardia, believed that with the health of the nation's future military strength at risk, surveilling and incarcerating women proved more important than ever. The NYPD, in turn, increased arrests for prostitution in New York City to 4,960 in 1940, a 23 percent increase over the annual average for the previous four years. Magistrates also convicted arrestees at higher rates than in previous years.[87]

As the mobilization for war brought more weight to anti-prostitution policing and discussions of venereal disease, officials' race and class perceptions of women structured the city's expansions of prewar policies. City Magistrate William Ringel wrote to Dr. Rice in March 1941 to discuss the "very difficult problems" of prostitution in New York City. Ringel expressed his alarm that "prostitutes are of all races, color and creeds" and that "many men draw no color lines in their dealings with prostitutes."[88] The changing racial makeup of Gotham's population unnerved many city officials, including Valentine and La Guardia, and some white residents. The possibility that these demographic changes might increase opportunities for white enlisted men to engage in sex with Black or Puerto Rican women proved particularly upsetting to these officials, who pathologized interracial relationships and associated nonwhite women with prostitution and sexually transmitted infections.

La Guardia enthusiastically supported efforts to protect enlisted men from prostitutes and backed the expansion of the federal government's power over sexually suspicious women. The mayor spoke in favor of the May Act, which made prostitution near military installations a federal crime, before the House Military Affairs Committee in March 1941. La Guardia suggested amendments to extend the bill's purview, arguing the act should also cover "loiterers" and owners of establishments "used for immoral purposes." At the conclusion of the mayor's testimony, Congressman John Costello of California made one final inquiry that conveyed the importance of municipal policing in the wartime campaigns against prostitution. "You are mayor of the largest city in the world," Costello remarked. "To make a program like this successful you would have to have local and State cooperation. What would you say in reference to that?" The mayor's succinct reply, "I think you will get it," signaled his own plans to step up anti-prostitution campaigns in New York City.[89]

The same month that the May Act became law, Congress passed the Lanham Act, another piece of legislation that structured the surveillance of women during the war. The Lanham Act amended the 1940 Defense Housing Act to provide funds for public facilities that were seeing expanded use during the war. Though the act is most well known for its role in providing housing and community facilities, as well as limited childcare services for working women, it also funded "public sanitary facilities," which functioned as auxiliary prisons where women arrested for prostitution or accused of carrying syphilis or gonorrhea could be incarcerated against their will for treatment.[90] Although funds for the facilities came through the Lanham Act and support for medical care was provided through the Public Health Service under the Venereal Disease Control Act of 1938, the centers tended to be overseen by state or municipal staff. Lanham Act funding, therefore, further expanded the collaboration between federal, state, and municipal entities in the wartime carceral state.

In New York City, Valentine directed city resources toward monitoring suspected prostitutes, who, he argued, now posed a danger to the nation's security. At a conference on civilian defense in February 1942, the commissioner demanded that prostitution receive "particular and sustained" attention, after recounting reports from the Department of Health that members of the military were contracting venereal diseases from prostitutes in New York City. He called on plainclothes officers to pay increased attention to the locations reported to the Health Department as sites where sailors and servicemen met prostitutes.[91]

The experience of one woman who was arrested in December 1941 provides a window into what this "particular and sustained" police attention could mean to the women of New York. Following her arrest, the woman stated that she was held for six hours for identification at the station house before being transferred to an unheated cell, and that she was provided with no blankets or food during her incarceration. She reported that she had contracted an upper respiratory condition as a result of her treatment. Rice, who relayed her complaint, remarked that though he did "not know the merits of her statement . . . she was suffering . . . and appeared ill at the time she called at this Department."[92]

Valentine worked to expand the NYPD's surveillance of women like the arrestee and to increase collaboration between the city's agencies and army officials stationed in Gotham. Valentine formed the Division of National Defense in the NYPD in February 1942. The *Brooklyn Daily Eagle* described the mission of the new division succinctly as the "protection of soldiers and sailors from prostitutes."[93] Shortly after its formation, officers in the division initiated large-scale vice raids in Harlem and midtown, arresting dozens of people for vagrancy and loitering near places of prostitution.[94] Members of this unit went on to arrest women in over one hundred hotels around the city by 1944.[95] Valentine was also in regular contact with the leaders of the army's Second Corps Area on Governors Island about prostitution and venereal diseases. Representatives from the Second Corps Area attended conferences organized by the NYPD commissioner to discuss the city's campaigns against venereal diseases and prostitution.[96] At these conferences, Valentine encouraged officers to report any bars harboring "lone women" to the Alcoholic Beverage Control Board.[97] Seeking to tackle this problem, the NYPD arrested over 800 people in May and June 1942 as part of its campaign against prostitution and vice.[98]

Though anti-prostitution policing was aimed at women, police raids in midtown sometimes caught up gay men. Theaters, particularly those on Forty-Second Street, were a destination for men seeking sexual encounters with other men in the city. Bud Robbins, who was stationed at the Chelsea Naval Hospital in Massachusetts during the war but visited New York City, remembered that "in the Times Square area, in the theater area, it was so easy to get picked up."[99] The writer and memoirist Donald Vining recorded the pickup patterns on display during his visit to the Park Theatre on Columbus Circle and Fifty-Ninth Street on November 17, 1942, for a showing of *Abe Lincoln in Illinois* and *Marseillaise*. Of the showing, he recounted, "The theatre had few people in it and half must have been homos on the make. I never saw so many men getting up and going to the john ten minutes after they came in, followed by other men with whom they subsequently left."[100] At another theater on Forty-Second Street, Vining was "amazed by the way men came in and left in about five minutes. The sailors were cleaned out of there by 8:30."[101] The city's health and police commissioners were alerted to gay encounters at the National Theater on Canal Street and Broadway after a young man who visited one of the city's social hygiene clinics described receiving his infection from another man at the theater. Commissioner Rice noted that according to "others in the community," this theater was known as "a place where questionable and undesirable men frequent."[102] The NYPD may have followed up by stationing an officer on the theater's premises, perhaps after labeling it a "raided premise." In January 1945, Vining reflected on a similar situation, recording, "There was a policeman by the Selwyn box office so I wasn't surprised to find no standees row. The added danger lends excitement to the chase, tho it makes service men rely more on service men since they're sure they're not detectives."[103] Men, however, were not the target of wartime anti-prostitution policing, and enlisted gay men were under the purview of the military police or the shore patrol, rather than the NYPD. As one gay GI recounted, "I have no one to answer to, as long as I behave myself during the week and stay out of the way of the MP's on weekends."[104] Gay men like Vining were not the explicit target of the wartime anti-prostitution campaigns, but an increased police presence in Times Square and heightened attention to the spread of venereal diseases created risks for gay New Yorkers.

Military officials did not rely solely on NYPD campaigns to prevent enlisted men from meeting up with women in the city. Soldiers on Governors Island received lectures advising them to avoid prostitutes and off-limits establishments, and army officials sent lists of "pick-up spots and brothels" to the health commissioner.[105] Major General Irving Phillipson wrote to La Guardia multiple times from Governors Island in the spring of 1942 complaining that the NYPD was not harsh enough against prostitution in the city, which he described as a "Mecca for soldiers and sailors on pass or furlough."[106] In August, Valentine again ordered high-ranking officers to ramp up their campaigns against prostitution after receiving complaints from army and navy officials about servicemen testing positive for venereal diseases. According to the *Brooklyn Daily Eagle*, vice squad members were directed to pick up "all known prostitutes immediately," and the NYPD, the Division of Alcoholic Beverage Control, and representatives from the army and navy planned to cooperate in the round-up.[107] These letters illustrate that the drive to crack down on women in New York City did not stem solely from Valentine and La Guardia's personal preferences. The Social Protection Division pushed for harsh policing, the May Act declared that the FBI could intervene in any locale in which policing proved too lenient, and the military commanders on Governors Island demanded aggressive enforcement. This wartime context provided a hospitable environment for La Guardia and Valentine's profiling campaigns to thrive.

The experience of one woman arrested and incarcerated for prostitution in 1942 reveals how the wartime focus on prostitution threatened women's autonomy, mobility, and safety. A social worker for the Women's Prison Association (WPA), a private philanthropic group, recounted the story of a woman who had resided at the WPA's facility for formerly incarcerated women, Hopper House, after serving time for prostitution. The former prisoner had secured employment outside the city and had intended to visit a friend before her departure. The social worker stated the woman left Hopper Home at seven in the evening and "before nine she was in the station house, having been arrested for loitering by the same officer who had arrested her the first time." The WPA employee argued that because of the timing and location of the arrest, the resident could not have been "plying her trade." Despite the protests of the social worker, the arrestee received a conviction and a three-month sentence.[108] NYPD policies of targeting women on the street severely limited the freedoms of women like the WPA client, who lacked economic advantages, who had been arrested before, or whom officers deemed "unwholesome" or suspicious.

A group of incarcerated women, perhaps including some arrestees grabbed in the roundups of May and June, launched a collective protest against their detention in the summer of 1942, reprising a tactic used by incarcerated women in 1938. These women had been "forced in," or incarcerated indefinitely under the power of the Health Department, and housed at the House of Detention. They presented the magistrates of the women's court with a petition protesting their unjust indefinite detention, declaring their right to receive finite sentences, and requesting to be returned to court for sentencing. The magistrates complied.[109] Through this act of resistance, these imprisoned women exerted control over their lives, asserted their right to a finite sentence, and challenged the authority of the court. Following their petition, magistrates closed down the House of Detention's hospital facility but continued to send women to Kingston Avenue Hospital and later opened a new facility at Bellevue to house "forced-in" women.

As the city's police and public health departments monitored more and more women, efficient collaboration between the two agencies became increasingly important. In the fall of 1942 under Health Commissioner Dr. Ernest Stebbins's oversight, Dr. Theodore Rosenthal, director of the Bureau of Social Hygiene, met with Inspector John W. Sutter from the Division of National Defense to discuss "time saving procedures in the transmission of information" between the health and police departments.[110] The pair decided that the Health Department would send "routine" notification letters to the police department about reported venereal disease cases and in return the police department would telephone the Bureau of Social Hygiene when officers located "individual cases." The Health Department would then force women in if "insufficient evidence for police action has been obtained." Rosenthal believed that these efforts would "speed up the entire machinery."[111] By early February 1943, Stebbins celebrated the efficacy of New York's programs in a message to Surgeon General Thomas Parran. Stebbins noted that the "intensive efforts" by the police department and Department of Health to suppress prostitution "has resulted in the apprehension of a constantly increasing number of persons charged with this offense."[112]

The campaigns against sexually targeted women and the drive to heavily police nonwhite New Yorkers reinforced each other. In June 1943, Valentine noted of the predominantly African American neighborhood of South Jamaica in Queens, "We have locked up so many women from there that we couldn't arraign them in the Women's Court, we had to charge them with disorderly conduct and take them to their District Court." He also noted that "every woman, whether exonerated or convicted is held, to determine whether she is infected with venereal disease." He applauded these efforts, remarking, "We are making progress."[113] The wartime focus on venereal disease provided justification for NYPD officers to monitor, arrest, and forcibly incarcerate Black and Puerto Rican women, who were already under intense surveillance because of the NYPD's association of nonwhite New Yorkers with urban disorder.

The contact reports used by New York City's Health Department reinforced a racialized narrative about venereal diseases. Between December 10 and December 29, 1943, the Health Department collected and shared with the NYPD 156 reports of venereal disease contacts. Men identified "colored" women as the supposed source of their infection in 60 percent of the records.[114] These reports, however, must be analyzed with caution. The members of the military and civilians interrogated about their sexual history were likely exposed to the widespread argument that venereal diseases were more common and manifested differently among African Americans than among whites.[115] Surgeon General Parran had argued in both his 1938 article in *Survey Graphic*, "No Defense for Any of Us," and his book *Shadow on the Land* that Black women remained infectious with syphilis longer than their white counterparts.[116] The alleged connection between African Americans and venereal disease was also promoted at a New York conference attended by 1,000 representatives from the army, navy, Public Health Service, and New York City Department of Health earlier in 1943. Attendees heard from one expert who argued that venereal diseases were being transmitted from African Americans to white civilians and soldiers.[117] Men reporting venereal disease "contacts," therefore, may have misdiagnosed the source of their infection based on these racist assumptions. Alternatively, some men may have deliberately named a fictitious source to protect an actual person, and settled on a "colored" woman as the most convenient story. Regardless of their validity, such accusations provided a trail that NYPD officers could follow to track down individual women who met these descriptions.[118] These reports also created a mutually reinforcing body of records that articulated a public health rationale for NYPD practices that broadly targeted Black women.

Women tracked down from contact reports or arrested by the NYPD resisted the authority of the police, the courts, and the hospitals to which courts remanded them for treatment. One doctor remembered "chasing one [patient] over the roofs of Harlem with a gun" as she tried to escape his monitoring and treatment in the fall of 1943.[119] Other patients provided hospitals with fake names and addresses in an attempt to protect their privacy, since hospitals sometimes shared information with the courts or attempted to track women after their release.[120]

Despite the activities of the NYPD and the city's health commissioner, army and navy officials were not satisfied with Valentine's efforts. In October 1944, they formed the Joint Army-Navy Disciplinary Control Board to survey and combat conditions "relating to prostitution, venereal disease, liquor violations, disorder and any other undesirable conditions as they apply to service personnel."[121] The board's first formal session occurred on November 3, 1944. A shore patrol officer testified about a midtown bar in which "soldiers seemed to predominate." Colonel B. W. Beers of the General Staff Corps, Security and Intelligence Division, and president of the board recommended that this bar and others like it be declared "out of bounds." Another member of the board suggested that the "out of bounds" label be applied to venues deemed "raided premises" by the NYPD, a designation granted to establishments in which vice arrests had occurred. A representative from the city's Health Department and medical staff from the army, navy, and Coast Guard supported these suggestions, arguing that such establishments served as sites of meeting for enlisted men and "patriotutes."[122] The control board did not put this suggestion into practice, but its efforts resulted in an escalation of NYPD monitoring of establishments with reputations for hosting servicemen and unescorted women. NYPD officers received orders to "make it as disagreeable as possible" to operate venues catering to enlisted men and single women.[123]

Conclusion

Valentine and La Guardia's augmented campaigns against wartime prostitution led the city to create new facilities to house arrested women, which endured beyond the end of the war. In early 1943, Health Commissioner Stebbins began advocating for the city to open a new rapid treatment center to house the increasing numbers of women forced into treatment for syphilis and gonorrhea. He led a committee of doctors and city officials who supported this plan, and procured federal funds through the Lanham Act to facilitate its implementation.[124]

Committee members conceived of the new center as serving for the detention and treatment of "women of the prostitute class." Participants articulated their visions for a "rehabilitation process" in which patients could work in the hospital or receive training and employment in war-related production. The treatment center, which opened a clinic at Bellevue Hospital and a facility on Welfare Island in April 1944, served as a physical manifestation of the city's expanded attention to policing and incarcerating women deemed to be "of the prostitute class" during the war.[125] Dr. Joseph Moore, chairman of the subcommittee on venereal disease of the National Research Council, described the importance of the new Bellevue clinic in terms of the prevention of lost "man-days." Moore celebrated that the New York City clinic and others like it around the country would reduce the rates of venereal diseases, which he estimated cost the army and navy "8,000,000 lost man-days."[126]

Though the wave of federal concern over sexually suspicious women crested and then receded with the end of the war, it left a lasting imprint on carceral systems in the city. The Bellevue clinic operated throughout 1945 and after the end of the war. It lost federal funds, but the city took over its financial responsibilities. In the years after the war, the NYPD continued to arrest, on average, between 4,000 and 5,000 women a year for prostitution, and all women arrested on such charges continued to be required to undergo forced venereal disease testing. If a woman was not convicted of prostitution but tested positive for a venereal disease, the city's Health Department continued to take her into custody and remand her to Bellevue Hospital for forced treatment. Author Scott Stern notes that after the 1945 adoption of penicillin in treatment centers like Bellevue, the forcible imprisonment of women to receive treatment for venereal diseases decreased. The pattern of profiling sexually suspicious women whom officials constructed as vectors of disease and disorder, however, continued.[127] In the fall of 1948,

Dr. Rosenthal, director of the Health Department's Bureau of Social Hygiene, described the city's public health powers over these women as a "gigantic screening device."[128] As the trajectory of the Bellevue clinic illustrates, even after the exigencies of the war subsided, the city's attention to policing women for prostitution persisted.

The mobilization for World War II unleashed a nationalistic call for enhanced policing of suspected prostitutes around the country. The federal infrastructure of the Social Protection Division linked domestic policing to the war effort through the conferences and pamphlets on anti-prostitution policing that the division produced. The May Act and Eight-Point Agreement codified both the wartime relationship between the federal government and municipal police departments and the responsibility of the latter to effectively monitor civilian populations. The Lanham Act provided federal funds to incarcerate these heavily monitored populations.

In New York City, La Guardia and Valentine embraced this responsibility and used it as an opportunity to expand the campaigns against suspected prostitutes that they had pushed throughout the 1930s. Working-class women who spent time on the street, sexually adventurous women, Black women and Puerto Rican women, and women in interracial relationships had no right to live freely in the city, according to the municipal leaders and their administrations. A central purpose of the city's police department was, in Valentine and La Guardia's reformist vision, to discipline and contain this racialized female threat.

When the United States entered World War II, the city leaders found widespread support and demand for this vision. They seized the moment, cultivating a militarized conception of the city's police department and expanding the department's anti-prostitution patrols. For La Guardia and Valentine, protecting the nation's servicemen made sex and gender regulation in the city both more permissible and more important. General language that described controlling women ran through these wartime policies, but they were inflected with the particular race and class concerns held by the leaders of the increasingly interracial city. However, while "unwholesome" women posed the most acute threat to enlisted men, wartime Gotham was also home to a younger and perhaps even more insidious peril: the juvenile delinquent.

7/20/29 – 152 W143 Bessie Roundtree – Disch.

7/24/29 – 42 W138 Gladys Fran___ 100 da

5/24/29 – 2542 8av. 3fl. Louise Washington 100da
Myrtle Morton P.C.

8/17/29 ⎤ Margaret Mitchell Disch.
165 W45 ⎬ anna Johnson Disch.
1st fl. ⎦ Mallinson Johnson Disch

8/25/29 – 133 W128, 2nd fl.
Bernice Miller – 100 days
anna Prather 180 "

8/16/29 – 490 Lenox av, 5 fl.
alma Lamb – 10 days

9/5/29 – Dorothy Howard – Bedford – Remand
9/5/29 – Eva Thomas – 100 days – Remand
arrested at 2704 – 8th ave. Room 15

9/20/29 – Louise Yates – 100 days – Norris
arrested at 136. W. 133d st. Room 4.

10/6/29 – 165 W 12__ 2fl. Josephine Green Prob.
Josephine Thomas – Prob Smith

10/8/29 2157 7av 2 fl. Mabel Shepard Disch.
Viola Shepard Disch Norris
Helen Bradley " "

10/20/29 – 108 W 129 Della Portick? Disch. Silb.
Lillian McKinney 100 days "

10/29/29 – 42 W138. 3fl. Gladys Moore Disch
Marg. Vinson 2days Silb.
" Frances Thompson 100 days "

11/19/29 – 68 W.138 st. 3 fl. _line Fulton – 180 days
12/7/29 – 133 W.128 st. Dorothy George – Prob
12/7/29 – 1 fl. right Eleanor Lee – 100 days
more Pros.

FIGURE 1 "Harlem." Names of women arrested and sentenced in one area of Harlem, collected by private anti-vice organization the Committee of Fourteen, 1929. Police Cards, Committee of Fourteen Records, Manuscripts and Archives Division, New York Public Library, Astor, Lenox, and Tilden Foundations.

FIGURE 2 "Negroes share in law enforcement. Negro policemen, Harlem, New York City." Black policemen on patrol in Harlem, 1929. Schomburg Center for Research in Black Culture, Jean Blackwell Hutson Research and Reference Division, New York Public Library.

FIGURE 3 "Police." NYPD officers beating person on the street, 1930. Irma and Paul Milstein Division of United States History, Local History and Genealogy, New York Public Library.

FIGURE 4 "LaGuardia, Fiorello H.—leading band." Fiorello La Guardia conducting police and firemen's band. New York World's Fair 1939 and 1940 Incorporated Records, Manuscripts and Archives Division, New York Public Library, Astor, Lenox, and Tilden Foundations.

FIGURE 5 "New York City—Police Dept.—Fiorello La Guardia (*far left*) saluting policemen with Harvey Gibson (*far right*)." Police Commissioner Lewis Valentine also pictured (*center*). New York World's Fair 1939 and 1940 Incorporated Records, Manuscripts and Archives Division, New York Public Library, Astor, Lenox, and Tilden Foundations.

FIGURE 6 "New York World's Fair employees—police—policemen and policewoman in uniform." New York World's Fair 1939 and 1940 Incorporated Records, Manuscripts and Archives Division, New York Public Library, Astor, Lenox, and Tilden Foundations.

FIGURE 7 "New York World's Fair—employees—police—Henrietta Additon and policewomen." New York World's Fair 1939 and 1940 Incorporated Records, Manuscripts and Archives Division, New York Public Library, Astor, Lenox, and Tilden Foundations.

FIGURE 8 "Women's House of Detention." Print by artist Nan Lurie, Works Progress Administration, 1935–43, Schomburg Center for Research in Black Culture, Art and Artifacts Division, New York Public Library.

FEDERAL ART PROJECT
NYC WPA

FIGURE 9 "April." Print of Black police officer on horse by artist Fritz Eichenberg, Works Progress Administration, 1935–43, Schomburg Center for Research in Black Culture, Art and Artifacts Division, New York Public Library.

FIGURE 10 Ann Petry photograph by Carl Van Vechten, 1948 © Van Vechten Trust.
Carl Van Vechten Papers Relating to African American Arts and Letters, James
Weldon Johnson Collection in the Yale Collection of American Literature,
Beinecke Rare Book and Manuscript Library.

CHAPTER FOUR

Is This the Freedom We Are All Working So Hard For?

Gender, Race, and Wartime Juvenile Delinquency

The kids were not alright. Or at least that's what many adult New Yorkers contended. By Mayor Fiorello La Guardia's election and Police Commissioner Lewis Valentine's appointment in 1934, the idea of policing youth to detect and deter what the commissioner described as "crime-conscious[ness]" was well established, even if the definition of the behavior that fell into this category was not.[1] At the turn of the twentieth century, first in Chicago and then in other urban centers, reformers began arguing that the criminal justice system should distinguish between children and adults instead of housing all prisoners together regardless of age. Two interlocking and sometimes contradictory theories undergirded the call for a separate carceral track for children. The first was what historian Tera Eva Agyepong has referred to as "the rehabilitative ideal—the notion that children were inherently innocent and entitled to a justice system separate from adults."[2] The second was what we might call the preventive ideal—or the idea that misbehavior among youth, which might be *problematic* but not *criminal*, would lead to future criminality unless an authority figure intervened.

The first ideal justified the creation of youth courts, jails, and prisons; the second dramatically expanded the purview of police over youth.[3] If the purpose of juvenile justice was to separate young criminals from their older counterparts, then the definition of criminality would not change based on age. If, however, the goal was *preventing* youth from *becoming* criminals, then police officers or other surveillance agents were required to monitor all types of youthful behavior. As historian Carl Suddler notes, the introduction of preventive surveillance, or the monitoring of "potential delinquents," vastly increased the number of young people on the NYPD books in the 1930s.[4] In addition to monitoring the plastic category of "potential delinquents," the juvenile justice system was also charged with housing neglected children who had no safe adult to care for them. Agyepong shows that race, rather than situation or behavior, often dictated whether children were deemed "dependent" and in need of care or "delinquent" and in need of punishment.[5] The mutability of juvenile delinquency was reflected in the White House Conference on

Child Health and Protection in 1935, which defined delinquency circuitously as "any such juvenile misconduct as might be dealt with under the law."[6]

By the early 1930s, police officers and young people in cities across the country had a well-developed antagonistic relationship. Conflict was particularly sharp between officers and children of color as well as young members of the urban working class.[7] In New York City, throughout the first decades of the twentieth century, patrolmen had chased, harassed, and arrested youth who played or worked on the city's streets. These children saw officers as an annoyance—a "boogy-boo"—at best and a danger at worst.[8] "They hated to see us having fun," one author reflected about the police in an autobiographical novel about growing up poor on the Lower East Side.[9] Valentine remembered dolefully the "dimly lit streets of yesteryear when the boy lurked behind a lamp post, waiting for the policeman to move on so that he could break the nearest window and steal a piece of merchandise."[10]

For NYPD officials throughout the 1930s and 1940s, children's antagonistic attitudes toward police officers became, like their behavior, another target of surveillance and reform. Historian Tamara Gene Myers has argued that during these years, policing in North America underwent a "youth turn" in which police departments devoted increased attention to children and adolescents.[11] Policing youth was not only about preventing the types of smash-and-grab crimes that Valentine associated with "yesteryear." Monitoring young people also proved central to the NYPD project of crafting law-abiding adults who valued and submitted to police authority. By the 1940s, the commissioner celebrated, "in the crowded New York neighborhoods where 'Cheese it, the cop!' was once the juvenile slogan . . . the current young generation greet the policeman with a new friendliness."[12] The mobilization for war further heightened the commitment of the police and the mayor to controlling youth.

In New York City, officials put the project of controlling the attitudes and behavior of young people into practice through the Crime Prevention Bureau, first imagined under reform police commissioner Arthur Woods in the 1910s. The bureau was created as part of a move to make policing take on elements of community assistance or "social reform."[13] Police Commissioner Grover Whalen later revived it in 1930 with a particular focus on "prevent[ing] the spread of crime among adolescents," and Whalen's successor, Edward Mulrooney, made the bureau an official part of the NYPD in 1931 with a staff of 199.[14]

Commissioner Valentine, who contended in his autobiography, "Nothing has concerned me more than the neglected boy and girl," saw molding children into law-abiding adults as an important police priority.[15] After Valentine took over as leader of the department, he and La Guardia reorganized and expanded the NYPD's Crime Prevention Bureau. La Guardia was critical of the preexisting bureau, believing it to be ineffective and expensive.[16] He ordered Valentine's predecessor to "pep it up, put some vision into it and see that it obtained results."[17] Still unsatisfied with the bureau's "pep," La Guardia and Valentine renamed the office the Juvenile Aid Bureau (JAB); drove out its director, Henrietta Additon; and pushed the new department to interact with more youth.[18] Though La Guardia and Valentine's vision of crime prevention differed from Additon's, the duo were deeply committed to policing Gotham's youth and sought to do so through the JAB.[19]

The new JAB had an expansive mandate and reach. Valentine and La Guardia added six branches to the ten that operated under the former bureau so that each NYPD division command office had a corresponding JAB unit.[20] Every officer received "JAB2" cards on which they were required to record identifying information about children engaging in "delinquent conduct" that was not serious enough to merit arrest.[21] The JAB then followed up on these reports. Though parents, social workers, teachers, and other community members could report children, police officers initiated far more JAB cases than these alternative sources.[22] Valentine named twenty-seven-year-old Princeton graduate and society-page regular Byrnes MacDonald to replace Additon as head of the new JAB.[23] MacDonald was a strong supporter of La Guardia in his mayoral campaigns, and after his stint running the JAB he would go on to serve as first deputy commissioner of the Department of Welfare and later as personal secretary to the mayor.[24]

As head of the JAB, MacDonald advocated a wide-ranging youth surveillance program that relied on collaboration with the Bureau of Education in an early iteration of what today is often referred to as the "school-to-prison pipeline." In MacDonald's words, the purpose of the JAB was to guide children's leisure time "as constructively as possible, and to develop their sense of responsibility."[25] In the NYPD's annual report for 1934, Valentine further elaborated on the goals of the JAB as "(1) bringing about a change in the behavior of delinquent minors who come to the attention of the police, (2) finding and removing community conditions which make for delinquency, (3) building up constructive forces for the prevention of crime, and (4) developing a different attitude in general on the part of our youth toward the law and law enforcing agencies, and of the community toward the efficient treatment of incipient crime."[26]

To achieve these goals, MacDonald organized the new JAB to collect names of truant children from the Board of Education as well as lists from the principals of public and parochial schools of children who were "showing tendencies towards irresponsibility, such as lying, stealing, and cheating."[27] The JAB's surveillance efforts were so extensive that one journalist described it as "commendably assuming the shape of the many-legged octopus."[28] By 1937, even Additon, who had doubted La Guardia and Valentine's commitment to surveilling youth, was "amazed at the interest various police officials took in the discussions on child delinquency" at a crime prevention conference hosted by Governor Herbert Lehman.[29]

MacDonald's youth surveillance network was further enabled by the formalization of the Police Athletic League (PAL) and the creation of new clubhouses where young people could engage in NYPD-approved activities. The PAL developed in the early 1930s out of informal games overseen by patrolmen. The league became an organized recreational program intended to spread positive messages about policing to working-class youth, create opportunities for NYPD-approved recreation, and enable expanded police surveillance.[30] By spring 1935, the PAL was regularly holding organized sporting events around the city attended by thousands of children. Acting Captain (and later police commissioner) Arthur Wallander wrote of one such event that "efforts to teach the neighborhood boy to shoot squarely can be directed with excellent results by encouraging him to go in for athletic competition."[31] Though PAL facilities were open to girls, athletic activities aimed at boys were the heart of its program.

PAL programs extended the reach of the NYPD into the lives of children. PAL facilities were often named after police officers killed while on duty, popularizing a conception of policing as a dangerous job that required self-sacrifice for the good of the community.[32] Though NYPD officers did not generally supervise the children who frequented these facilities (Works Progress Administration employees or civilian NYPD members usually staffed the clubhouses), the department collected information about young people and patrolmen mingled with the community at PAL events. "Without the children knowing it," MacDonald shared in an article on the JAB in the NYPD's *Spring 3100* magazine, "there is a daily attendance and attitude record kept of each one of them by the worker of this Bureau assigned to the center."[33] This information could then be used by the NYPD to categorize or criminalize the city's youth.

Gender, Race, and Juvenile Delinquency in the 1930s

For NYPD leaders and officers, both in and outside the JAB, the process of criminalizing young people was structured by gender and race. Deputy Chief

Inspector and Dean of the Police Academy John J. O'Connell described this dynamic passively, observing that "boys who come before the juvenile courts usually present delinquency problems different from those of girls."[34] Despite O'Connell's choice of words, children did not "come before" the juvenile courts; they were brought there, often after being identified as problematic by a police officer.[35] The central gender difference in how officers made these identifications among girls and boys was that officers and city and court officials criminalized sexual experience (including abuse or assault) among girls.

The Wayward Minor Law, introduced in New York City in 1882, facilitated this criminalization. As historian Cheryl Hicks describes, the law was first introduced to apply to prostitutes with "a desire to reform," then broadened to include "incorrigible girls," and later expanded to apply to all youth between sixteen and twenty-one "in danger of becoming morally depraved."[36] The fact that one of the main legal devices used to criminalize young women initially applied to sex work illustrates that conceptions of female juvenile delinquency were rooted in sex. By the 1930s, both "wayward minor" and "juvenile delinquent" were gender-neutral categories that officials assigned in response to gender-specific behaviors. For example, during 1934, girls reported for offenses of "incorrigibility—wayward minors," "sex offenses," "running away," or being "unmarried mothers" formed 64 percent of all of the JAB's new female cases and 24 percent of new male cases.[37] By 1936, the city opened the Wayward Minors' Court within the magistrates' court, designed "specifically to handle the delinquent adolescent girl, between the ages of sixteen and twenty-one."[38] While officials criminalized girls for their sexuality, boys were labeled delinquent for offenses related to theft or violence, though the theft could be as minor as entering the subway without paying or hitching a ride on a trolley, particularly if the boy was Black or Puerto Rican. In 1934, 60 percent of all new male cases who received "social treatment" from the JAB were for offenses of theft or violence.[39]

The criminalization of young women's sexuality justified carceral state surveillance over women and girls in a wide variety of cases, including cases in which the arrestees were victims of sexual violence, as well as instances of young women seeking to exert autonomy. Officers arrested thirteen-year-old Elenore with the thirty-nine-year-old man who abducted her in May 1935. The child cried while a Brooklyn magistrate "asked her if she knew that she had done wrong" by allowing herself to be taken by her assailant. Elenore was labeled a wayward minor.[40] In the summer of 1934, eighteen-year-old Louise was arrested and found guilty of being a wayward minor for running away with a paramour who did not meet parental approval.[41] Nettie Harris, the first

African American woman in the NYPD and a member of the JAB in Harlem's Thirty-Second Precinct, identified nineteen-year-old new mother Katherine as in need of police assistance in early 1937. Harris found Katherine "depressed and despondent" and kept her under "constant supervision," while providing her with employment assistance.[42] Elenore's, Louise's, and Katherine's experiences with juvenile policing differed, but all centered on their sexuality.

Katherine's experience with Harris was unusual, since Black girls and young women rarely encountered Black policewomen (there were only two in the whole NYPD in 1929 and six by 1945).[43] Harris's "constant surveillance" of Katherine was partly informed by a desire to assist the young mother, which white NYPD leaders and members did not usually feel for Black girls and young women. Even well-intentioned surveillance, however, could impede the autonomy of young women like Katherine and entrap them within the reaches of the carceral state. Without the intervention of Harris, though, Katherine would have most likely received harsher treatment from both the NYPD and the courts; the city's policing and court system generally treated struggling, sexually active young women of color as criminals.

How gendered conceptions of criminal behavior intervened in the lives of children and young women was deeply racialized. For young white girls and boys, a protective impulse justified and undergirded the carceral state's interference in their lives. White police officers, NYPD leaders, magistrates, and city officials articulated a desire to protect white girls from predatory men and from their own autonomy and to keep white boys from getting involved with organized crime. These state interventions were often unwanted and detrimental to the well-being of the children involved. More dangerous still, however, was being criminalized without the ethos of protection, as many Black children discovered. City and NYPD officials regularly placed Black children outside any protective framework while criminalizing them at higher rates than their white peers. This dynamic meant that NYPD officers and court officials were far more likely to assign the gendered categories of delinquency to Black children than white. While white children were more likely to be seen as temporarily wayward dependents, Black children were treated as irretrievable delinquents.[44] A 1934 report on juvenile delinquency in Gotham initiated by Edward Boyle, presiding justice of the children's court, found that Black children were overrepresented in juvenile court in Brooklyn, Manhattan, and Queens at a rate of at least double that of their representation in the general population.[45] In the racially segregated landscape of New York's carceral youth institutions, magistrates then regularly committed Black boys and girls to facilities reserved for the most serious youth offenders.[46] Being labeled a juvenile delinquent, therefore, carried higher stakes for youth of color than for white young people in 1930s and 1940s New York City.[47]

Although officials depicted the city's youth as falling into one of two racial categories, Black or white, these categories did not encompass the racial diversity of young New Yorkers. Young Puerto Ricans were another growing demographic group in the city who were often criminalized along with Black New Yorkers, though not regularly mentioned by NYPD leaders. Lorrin Thomas has described Puerto Rican New Yorkers in the 1930s as "personae non gratae in the black-white political relations of Harlem and in the city at large."[48] Puerto Rican youth were discussed less frequently than Black children by NYPD and city officials, but in the early 1930s about 11,000 Puerto Rican children were enrolled in New York City schools. By the mid-1940s the number had increased to about 25,000.[49]

Many of these children lived in East Harlem, where they were under heavy surveillance from the NYPD. Activist groups like the East Harlem Committee for Racial Cooperation worked to defend Puerto Ricans against criminalization and other racist attacks in the late 1930s and 1940s.[50] Despite these efforts, Valentine encouraged NYPD officers to racially profile youth, declaring that most crimes committed in or near Harlem were perpetrated by "Negro boys," although "Puerto Rican, Mexican and other Spanish-speaking boys have also been involved." According to the commissioner, "up in Harlem . . . even my own men are not safe" from the threat of groups of boys from twelve to sixteen years old.[51]

The racist and racialized perceptions of youth articulated by Valentine were also shared by rank-and-file members of the department and reflected in its broader culture. Illustrations of the way NYPD members racialized crime and the work of the JAB can be seen in short stories published in *Spring 3100*. Every month, the magazine's editorial staff, headed by Valentine, selected a short story to appear in the issue from a collection of entries. The published stories, therefore, can be seen as an impressionistic reflection of the values embraced in the department. When *Spring 3100* covered female juvenile delinquency, its authors did so through girls like Ruth, who appeared in a 1939 prize-winning short story. Ruth had "blue eyes" and was the "well dressed [sic] and attractive" daughter of a "Connecticut merchant," but had been lured into the city by an older man and her own misguided sense of adventure. Luckily, she was rescued by an intrepid policewoman and returned home to her loving parents.[52] Though they were heavily policed and disproportionately represented in court, Black girls rarely appeared in the pages of the departmental magazine. Rather, the female juvenile delinquent was racialized as white. This depiction reflected the way that race-based notions of protection and femininity justified the policing of young women, even though in practice Black girls who were framed as outside these categories were regular police targets.

In patrolman Alex Greenbaum's story "Off Tackle," the author imagined a close relationship between white working-class boys and a patrolman, who together team up to thwart a duo of darker-skinned criminals, described as "a big, heavy-set gorilla" and a "small, swarthy runt."[53] In addition to these short stories, *Spring 3100* ran cartoons that depicted Black children as stupid or uneducated and images relying on racist pickaninny iconography.[54]

The dehumanized depictions of fictional Black youth cultivated in *Spring 3100* translated into police violence against real Black children, which became an explosive issue for Black New Yorkers. In 1935, fifteen-year-old William Chase was watching a fight between two other youths when he stumbled and fell to the ground, perhaps connected to his epilepsy. A police officer at the scene tripped over the youth while attempting to disperse the crowd. The *Amsterdam News* recounted that when the crowd laughed at the officer, he became angry and started beating Chase before taking him to the station house, where the youth was beaten further.[55] When Lino Rivera, a sixteen-year-old Afro–Puerto Rican boy, was arrested in March 1935 for shoplifting from a store on 125th Street and taken into the store's basement by a member of the NYPD's Crime Prevention Bureau, rumors spread through the neighborhood that Rivera was being assaulted by the police. Shoppers became incensed and demanded to see the boy, but the police who had arrived at the scene ignored their requests.[56] Community members and protesters gathered outside, some of whom began breaking windows at the store and others nearby. The uprising spread across several blocks and lasted throughout the night. Participants engaged in property damage and looting, not violence, but the police responded violently. By the end of the night, seventy-five people had been arrested, sixty-four injured, and five killed, including Lloyd Hobbs, a sixteen-year-old boy, who was shot to death by the police.[57] An officer shot Hobbs through the chest and hand, without ever directing the youth to stop or turn around, when he was on the way home from the movies with his brother. The boy died at Harlem Hospital a few days later.[58] Hobbs's murder demonstrated exactly the type of police disregard for Black lives that had instigated the uprising in the first place.

The day after the uprising, La Guardia formed an interracial commission to investigate its causes. Harlem residents and organizations and Black New

Yorkers around the city followed its work closely.[59] Many residents testified before the group about discrimination in housing and employment as well as their experiences with the NYPD. Participants reported being harassed, abused, and assaulted by the police. A central theme running throughout many participants' comments was "the insecurity of the individual in Harlem against police aggression."[60] As the experiences of Hobbs, Chase, and numerous other Black boys and girls demonstrated, this insecurity extended to children. The vulnerability of even the youngest Black New Yorkers to police brutality and criminalization motivated residents to take to the streets and to demand that city officials change NYPD practices.[61] Ultimately, the commission completed a report that was deeply critical of city officials and made numerous recommendations for reform in city policies.

La Guardia and Valentine chose to ignore the commission's suggestions and to bury the report, further incensing residents and neighborhood institutions. The report only became public when the *Amsterdam News* published it against the mayor's wishes.[62] In the aftermath of the uprising, Valentine received demands from the newly formed United Civil Rights Committee of Harlem that the post-uprising police occupation of the neighborhood be lifted and that officers accused of brutality be punished. Valentine declined to take action on either front and dismissed the report of the mayor's commission as "false and dishonest."[63] The chairman of the New York City Civil Liberties Committee remarked that for Valentine the "only solution for a problem created in part at least by the unusual concentration of police in Harlem is to send in more police."[64]

Instead of taking police out of Harlem or disciplining officers, law enforcement leaders maintained a heavy police presence in the neighborhood and expanded programs to foster positive perceptions of the NYPD among heavily policed youth. A year after the uprising, the *Amsterdam News* reflected that, since the conflict, there had been "fewer reported cases of police brutality [and] less indignation over the reputed violations of civil rights," but Harlem had been occupied by more uniformed police than "at any other period in its history."[65] In 1936, the JAB created "neighborhood councils," which were led by police precinct commanders and guided by local business owners.[66] These councils were aimed at "solidifying public opinion in support of the [Crime Prevention] bureau's efforts to stamp out the evil influences in the community," according to the *Amsterdam News*.[67] The neighborhood councils bore similarities to the PAL, and the NYPD relied on both to shape the behavior of young New Yorkers. A 1939 article in *Spring 3100* entitled "Police Athletic League of All Nations" celebrated the interracial PAL as place where youth were taught to "obey the rules," "control [their] temper—win or lose as a true sportsman," and "live a clean and honest life."[68] As the nation prepared for a possible entrance into the escalating global conflict, city leaders became increasingly committed to surveilling and controlling young New Yorkers.

Rising Concern about Juvenile Delinquency during War

Mayor La Guardia and Commissioner Valentine both fueled and responded to rising concern in public opinion about the activities of youth during the war. Many New Yorkers embraced a widespread notion that a national military mobilization would increase juvenile delinquency.[69] Journalists spread this idea, residents expressed it in letters to the mayor, and criminal justice figures at the municipal, state, and national levels sought to popularize it. Proponents argued that in a nation at war, working mothers left children unattended, young women pursued enlisted men with abandon, increasingly interracial cities became sites of racial conflict, and blacked-out streets lured youth to misbehavior.[70] These unsupervised children, Valentine and La Guardia argued, were not only an urban problem but a threat to national security.

Two motivating concerns drove Valentine and La Guardia's approach to policing youth during the war. Above all else, the pair believed that soldiers and sailors needed protection from young women who sought them out for sex and company. These wayward girls threatened the nation's military strength by weakening the moral fiber of enlisted men and exposing them to venereal diseases. Throughout the war, Valentine and La Guardia directed NYPD officers to scour the city, especially the Times Square area, for young women. When found, these young women were to be taken into custody and either sent home or placed in a reformatory. Protecting enlisted men from venereal diseases justified heightened policing of young women and restrictions on their social and sexual autonomy, both of which were further structured by racialized conceptions of sexual experience and criminality endemic to Valentine's police department.

Valentine and La Guardia's approach to juvenile delinquency was further motivated by their desire to prevent racial unrest in the wartime city. The thinking of the two leaders diverged slightly on this issue. Valentine viewed Black youth as instigators of racial disharmony. He was generally sympathetic to white parents who complained that Black children made their neighborhoods unsafe, and he allocated significant police resources to monitoring youth in Harlem.

La Guardia had more ambivalence about the racialized policing of youth. He believed that racism led some white parents to perceive delinquency in what was actually just normal childhood behavior. "Boys will be boys and girls will be girls, regardless of race, color and creed," he noted in response to one such complaint.[71] He was also aware that racist policing of youth could serve as a catalyst for protests or uprisings, as in the case of the arrest of Lino Rivera and the Harlem uprising of 1935.[72] Both the mayor and the commissioner wished to avoid a similar episode during the war. At the same time, the mayor felt that youth crime destabilized the city, something that he could not afford during a military mobilization, and he accepted the idea that crime was higher in Black and interracial neighborhoods for economic and cultural reasons. The increased attention to juvenile delinquency during the war created an opening that conservative white residents in interracial neighborhoods used to demand a heavier police presence. Black New Yorkers, civil rights organizations, and Communist Party activists created an alternative narrative, arguing that during the war racialized accusations of delinquency were not only racist but un-American. Ultimately, however, for La Guardia and Valentine the increasing urgency of maintaining order in the wartime city and protecting enlisted men from sexual threats (which they incorrectly assumed to be coming solely from women) justified expanding the NYPD's attention to young women and boys of color. As the nation waged war around the world, NYPD officers worked to combat youthful threats at home.

The war was an exciting time for the many teenage girls whom officials depicted as dangerous delinquents. Increased entry into the paid workforce provided new economic opportunities for some young women and a reduction of parental authority for others, as mothers left the home for the factory.[73] Young women were part of the almost 15 percent of civilians who moved away from their home counties or states during the war years. Along with these economic and social opportunities came new sexual possibilities for young Americans, who now engaged in premarital sex at higher rates than their prewar counterparts.[74] Many young women resisted attempts by the state or their families to surveil and control their social and sexual behavior, sometimes going to extreme lengths to preserve their freedoms.

Law enforcement and political leaders in Gotham and in Washington expressed dismay over the changes in young women's behavior. They believed these behavioral shifts posed a sexual threat to the military strength of the nation and put the morality and safety of teenage girls at risk. Police and public health officials distinguished this threat from that posed by professional sex workers or promiscuous adult women, imbuing the former with an element of paternalistic concern. The misbehavior of young women constituted part of a broader wartime increase in juvenile delinquency, officials argued, which for young women took the form of inappropriate sexual activity. Magistrate Henry Curran described these young women as "the runaway girls who hate their homes, the devil-may-care girls swept up in the fever of war, [and] the girls who stand at the crossroads between life and death—for prostitution is death, dragging and painful to most those who practice it."[75] The Eight-Point Agreement, the May Act, public health provision 17B, and the heightened attention to policing suspected prostitutes applied to girls labeled juvenile delinquents. These young women were also, however, subject to laws and NYPD practices devoted particularly to them, including the Wayward Minor Law and surveillance from the JAB.[76] During the war, officials constructed these young women as both dangerous and endangered and strengthened a web of policing systems to control them.[77]

In the prelude to U.S. entry into the war, officials worked to expand the city's juvenile justice infrastructure to meet an anticipated increase in delinquency. Justice Stephen Jackson of New York City's Domestic Relations Court presented a proposal to La Guardia in early 1940 promising to reduce juvenile delinquency by devoting more resources to monitoring youth and launching anti-delinquency publicity campaigns.[78] La Guardia pronounced Jackson's plans "not only impressive but workable" and placed the justice at the head of the newly formed Bureau for the Prevention of Juvenile Delinquency.[79] The possibility of a wartime surge in delinquency both created a wider opening for Jackson's suggestions and rendered them more necessary than ever in the eyes of many New Yorkers.

Officials who worked in the Wayward Minors' Court argued that the social disruptions likely to accompany mobilization would increase the numbers of delinquent girls. In December 1941, two days before the Japanese attack on Pearl Harbor, Dorris Clarke, a liaison officer at the Wayward Minors' Court and one of the city's experts on female juvenile delinquency, completed a multiyear report on the functioning of the court. Clarke was the first woman appointed chief probation officer for New York City's magistrates' courts and a Wellesley College graduate. She received her certification as a probation officer in 1935. While serving in this position, she attended night school on a scholarship at New York University's Law School. By the end of the war, she had been admitted to the bar and appointed to the top probation post of the magistrates' courts.[80] In her report, Clarke argued for an expansion of police powers, writing that "under the present emergency, and with the increasing number of young girls found on the streets, in bar rooms, and in places of disrepute, consideration should be given not only . . . to broadening the charges under which adolescent girls could be brought within the jurisdiction of the court, but as well, to assuring full powers of apprehension and detention of such adolescents found in questionable circumstances."[81] Clarke found the Wayward Minor Law of 1941 too limited in scope and contended that the mobilization for war required expanded police and court powers over young women.

In her report, the probation officer reflected on the gender and class dimensions of the enforcement of the Wayward Minor Law. Clarke argued that juvenile delinquency among girls presented "a distinctly different type of problem" from that of boys. Clarke contended that while adolescent boys "commit offenses against person and property," adolescent girls should be considered "actual or potential sex offenders."[82] She also highlighted the role of class in determining whose behavior merited the label "delinquent," arguing that though there was no difference between the actions of young working-class women and their wealthier counterparts, only the former appeared in juvenile courts. "The latter are simply shipped off to boarding school," Clarke observed, "or allowed to give vent to their adolescent effusions in expensive night clubs."[83]

She did not add editorial comments on the role of race in structuring girls' experiences of being labeled wayward minors, although she documented racism in sentencing and racial disparities in arrests. Clarke recorded, for example, that "PRACTICALLY THE ONLY FACILITIES AVAILABLE FOR NEGRO GIRLS ARE THE HOUSE OF DETENTION, A CITY PRISON, OR WESTFIELD STATE FARM, A STATE REFORMATORY."[84] The author's use of caps seems suggestive of frustration with the limited capacity for housing Black girls, but the fact that she includes no discussion about the role of racism in girls' experiences in court is notable given her comments about class. Black girls were significantly overrepresented among girls brought before the Wayward Minors' Court. In 1939, girls labeled "Negro" made up 27 percent of the total number of girls who came before the court and 38 percent of wayward minors in Manhattan, where more than half of the wayward minor cases originated.[85] Regardless of her limited critiques of the wayward minor practices, Clarke called for the expansion of that system to meet wartime conditions.

After the attack on Pearl Harbor and the U.S. entrance into the war, concern about the impact of war on youth was no longer hypothetical. In early 1942, the mayor reorganized the JAB, cutting some investigator positions in order to meet budget restrictions. Many New Yorkers responded to this reduction in personnel with outrage, arguing that during the war juvenile delinquency was certain to surge. A minority bloc in the city council passed a resolution calling for the investigators to be reinstated and for the JAB to add additional probation officers.[86] La Guardia received dozens of letters from a wide swath of New Yorkers, including the Civilian Defense Volunteer Office, the Midtown Business and Professional Women's Club, and even the Young Communist League of New York State, criticizing this move in a time of war.[87] The *New York Post* excoriated La Guardia for "shrugging off the problem" presented by "hundreds of young girls on the loose along dimmed out Broadway with the soldiers and sailors on leave." The only answer to this youthful female threat, according to the *Post*, was to increase the rolls of the NYPD "many times."[88] In 1943, following the criticism about the JAB cuts, the mayor increased the bureau's budget.[89] This episode demonstrates the popularity of connecting support for the war with support for policing youth and the opposition facing proposals that challenged either of these goals.

Politicians and law enforcement agents at the federal, state, and city levels were deeply concerned about the wartime threat of obstreperous girls. FBI director J. Edgar Hoover, an enthusiastic proponent of sexual policing, sought to capitalize on wartime anxiety.[90] In September 1942, he warned a gathering of the nation's law enforcement leaders that "juvenile delinquency is mounting rapidly" and that they should "expect another era of lawlessness such as swept the country after the last war."[91] A month after Hoover's remarks, Justice Stephen Jackson addressed a large meeting of representatives from city agencies in New York City about the "urgent war-crime problem" of juvenile delinquency among adolescent girls.[92] In January 1943, Governor Thomas Dewey alerted the legislature to the perils of juvenile delinquency, decrying its recent increase.[93] One month later the National Conference of Juvenile Agencies aptly declared that wartime anxiety about youth crime presented their profession with a "golden opportunity for total growth."[94]

Racialized Wartime Policing of Girls

In New York City, La Guardia and Valentine expanded city resources devoted to policing young women, paying particular attention to girls out with enlisted men or those in Manhattan's central Times Square neighborhood. The neighborhood housed the high-end Astor Hotel, theaters that had survived the Depression, dancehalls, bars, and cheap cafés. In the evenings servicemen loitered on the streets, forming what journalist Meyer Berger described as a "GI gauntlet" for the young women entering the Forty-Second Street subway.[95]

In the summer of 1942, Valentine assigned a special squad of twelve patrolmen and twelve policewomen from the JAB to monitor the entertainment district in civilian clothes. These plainclothes officers roamed midtown from 10:00 at night to 6:00 in the morning and focused particularly on dancehalls, bars, grills, taverns, theaters, and rail and bus terminals. Department leaders charged officers assigned to Times Square with searching for "victory girls," or, as a member of the department's Division of National Defense described them, "young girls . . . who enter New York City for the specific purpose of following the movements of service men."[96] Throughout 1942, this unit apprehended 431 young women. In 1943, the number increased to 587, and from January 1 to August 31, 1944, officers took 568 young women into custody.[97] Probation officer Dorris Clarke's concern that "twelve and fourteen-year-old girls were being arrested for prostitution, most of them in Times Square in the company of soldiers and sailors," was justified.[98]

The case of Betty, who was arrested in March 1943, though not for prostitution, provides a clear example of the dynamic that so concerned Clarke. On the evening of March 22, three officers in the JAB came upon Betty while patrolling Midtown Manhattan. Patrolmen Julius Weiss and Frank Esposito and Patrolwoman Evelyn Kaplon stopped the fourteen-year-old girl and a male sailor as the couple enjoyed an evening stroll. The officers later recounted that Betty's "youthful appearance and scanty attire" had aroused their suspicions.[99] The officers separated the pair and divided the work of interrogating them along gender lines. Although both Betty and the sailor relayed similar stories of viewing a movie and going for coffee, the officers determined Betty's gender, age, appearance, and responses to be suspicious. The patrolmen found themselves "impressed with [the sailor's] innocence and truthfulness," and released him without recording his name. Kaplon, however, labeled Betty "reluctant and evasive." The officers took Betty to the Eighteenth Precinct, where she was further interrogated. Officers then contacted her mother, who worked the night shift at the Bendix Aircraft plant in Brooklyn, and her father, who worked as a truck driver, and booked her as a juvenile delinquent.[100] Any gender solidarity that Kaplon may have felt toward Betty did not prevent her from mistrusting the young woman's statements and labeling her delinquent.

Betty's experience proved illustrative of common concerns raised by officials and residents about delinquency and ways that police officers monitored young women in light of these concerns. She sought out entertainment in Times Square and the company of soldiers and sailors. She rebelled against authorities at home and school, choosing to make her own schedule and stay in rooming houses around the city. When found in the company of a sailor, it was her behavior, not that of the sailor, that officers found problematic and in need of correction. A patrolwoman interrogated Betty during her arrest and after she was booked to extract information about the details and causes of her "misconduct." At Betty's hearing, the defendant pledged to be a "good girl" going forward; her working mother "admitted her neglect" and "accepted the entire blame" for Betty's misdeeds. Records do not include the whereabouts of Betty's father during the hearing.[101]

NYPD leaders considered combing the city for young women like Betty central to the "special wartime services" required of officers in the JAB. These services included "strict supervision of premises frequented by men of the Armed Forces and to which young girls are attracted" and "special attention to the growing problem of . . . unsupervised children" whose parents were engaged in war work.[102] JAB officers worked closely with schools, branches of the armed forces, and community members. Official policy directed the commanding officers of precincts to visit the principals of all high schools and colleges within their jurisdiction at least once a month to discuss collaboration with the police. Sergeants were required to visit schools once every month, and to check in with custodians.[103] Young women were also monitored through the precinct coordinating councils the JAB set up in November 1943 to fuel a "militant community movement to curb juvenile delinquency."[104] By 1943 the number of arrests for juvenile delinquency had increased 33 percent over those of 1941.[105]

Throughout the spring and summer of 1944, the NYPD worked to maintain a vigilant presence over young women in the city's central entertainment district. La Guardia expressed frustration after reading a salacious Sunday news exposé in which the author recounted seeing young women dancing with, and supposedly coming to blows over, enlisted men in uniform. "What I cannot understand," the irate mayor complained to Commissioner Valentine, "is that if this reporter saw these children, why do not the police see them, the Juvenile Aid Bureau, and the Patrolwomen?" The mayor directed Valentine to increase nightly patrols in dancehalls and declared that patrolmen should interrogate any girl in these establishments who appeared under age.[106]

Young women of color in New York City also set out in search of social and sexual freedoms and faced particular forms of violence and repression from the city's expanding policing network. Novelist and journalist Ann Petry represented these young women through the character of Annie May, who stays out late, shops, and wears "too much lipstick," in a 1946 short story entitled "In Darkness and Confusion."[107] These young women had to contend with higher arrest rates than their white counterparts. African American girls were disproportionately represented among children alleged to be delinquent in children's court. In the first two months of 1942, 1943, and 1944 the court recorded that African American girls constituted 44, 33, and 37 percent of the total numbers of girls brought before the court, respectively, though Black New Yorkers formed only about 6 percent of the city's total population. These records described arrestees as "white," "negro [sic]," or "other," so the information that can be extracted about the racial or ethnic identities of these children is limited.[108] Demographic information about young women arrested as wayward minors after 1939 is also limited since the NYPD did not analyze arrest statistics by race. Valentine spoke freely to the press, however, about the threats he saw embodied in Black and Puerto Rican boys and adult women in Harlem.[109] Given these remarks and the racialized record of arrests in children's court and in the Wayward Minors' Court in 1939, it is reasonable to surmise that young Black and Puerto Rican women were targeted as delinquents during the wartime intensification of juvenile policing.

In addition to higher rates of arrest and more punitive incarceration, young women of color also faced risks of police violence generally unknown to white teenage girls. In March 1943, the same month as Betty's arrest, an officer in the transit police assaulted Ethelen, a fifteen-year-old African American student, in a subway station at 211th Street. Ethelen had been passing through the turnstile when the officer ordered her to move faster and slapped her after deciding she was not complying. When the teenager responded by trying to kick the officer away, he dragged her by the hair into the men's toilet, shutting the door. The officer also struck at a group of students who had gathered and tried to intervene for Ethelen's protection. One white student in the crowd, Harriette, called the NYPD's Thirty-Fourth Precinct and reported that a girl was being beaten in the subway station. Shortly thereafter a group of policemen arrived and pulled Harriette into the bathroom with Ethelen before taking both girls to the precinct.[110]

Ethelen's schoolmates, family, and community were outraged at the attack, which they framed within the larger contexts of police relations with Black New Yorkers and the national war mobilization. They launched a campaign to remove the officer with the support of the *People's Voice* newspaper, the NAACP, the National Negro Congress, the Harlem People's Committee, and the New York Communist Party.[111] Journalists reporting on the incident for the *People's Voice* capitalized "MEN'S TOILET," emphasizing the ways that white police officers did not apply ideas about femininity to Black women and girls. This form of what scholar Moya Bailey has dubbed misogynoir rendered Ethelen and other Black girls like her vulnerable to physical and sexual violence from police officers, risks that were heightened when a child like Ethelen was isolated with a police officer.[112] In addition to cultivating police brutality and contributing to the criminalization of Black girls, misogynoir led officers to ignore crimes committed against Black girls. Writers made this connection by recounting a case when police declined to follow up on a report of a series of attempted assaults on a fifteen-year-old African American girl.[113]

During the war, Black Gothamites connected anti-Black violence in the United States to Nazi campaigns against Jews in Europe. One mother wrote to the *People's Voice* expressing her horror at the attack on Ethelen, which she imagined could easily have happened to her own daughter. The author described Harlem as "overrun with police" and wondered, "Can you tell me the difference between Gestapo attacks on Jewish people in Nazi occupied Europe and anti-Negroism in Harlem?"[114] Although the officer responsible for the attack on Ethelen served in the transit police, a unit technically independent from the NYPD, the mother writing to the *People's Voice* connected the teenager's experience to the police presence in Harlem. She argued that for young women like Ethelen, an increased police presence around the city, and particularly in predominantly Black neighborhoods, could increase the risk of such assaults. Despite a significant organizing campaign, the transit officer successfully argued that he had been acting in self-defense during his assault on the teenager. He returned to work following a three-week suspension.[115]

Most parents who criticized the NYPD did so after a violent assault on a child like what Ethelen experienced. Many families, community members, and even children themselves embraced the NYPD's policies of monitoring and arresting young people in the city. Civil rights organizations, African American community groups, the Communist Party, and some interracial liberal organizations criticized police brutality against children but accepted police surveillance projects like the JAB and the PAL. Some New Yorkers likely accepted the NYPD's policies toward youth as the only bulwark against real physical and sexual dangers that children, particularly girls, could encounter in the city. In Black and interracial communities that were underserved by city resources, residents and activists often requested additional JAB or PAL services as part of a larger set of demands for equitable municipal services. Many Gothamites also embraced the popular idea that young women posed a threat to the health of servicemen and, therefore, the national war effort. Additionally, city and NYPD leaders invoked the military mobilization to silence critics, arguing that Gothamites should contribute to the war effort by submitting to police authority.

A small number of parents, however, did take issue with the department's heavy wartime surveillance of youth. In the spring of 1944, Elmer Robertson, a father from Long Island, wrote to the mayor protesting the treatment his daughter had received from police officers at a skating rink. Robertson noted that officers "singled out" his fifteen-year-old daughter and her friends, removing them from the skating rink in front of other patrons. The officers held the young women in an enclosed office and refused the girls' requests to telephone their parents. In his letter, the father described his daughter's experience of being "deeply humiliated" and treated as if she had committed a serious offense. He connected his criticism of the police officers' behavior to the war effort, wondering, "Is this the freedom we are all working so hard for?"[116] In a response to Robertson's letter, La Guardia expressed sympathy for the girl's embarrassment. The mayor also, however, scolded Robertson for allowing his daughter to be out at night, informing the father that according to "most of the mothers who have written me . . . teen age girls should not be out late at night."[117] In the eyes of the mayor, the fault lay with the female skaters and their parents, not with the officers who detained and interrogated them.

Some young women resisted the state's authority on their own behalf. During a heat wave in August 1944, five white teenage girls launched an elaborate escape from the Society for the Prevention of Cruelty to Children's reformatory in downtown Brooklyn. Mary, Margaret, Estelle, Carmen, and Jean had been remanded to the institution after being tried for juvenile delinquency at the Manhattan Children's Court. While at the court, one of the young women received a manicure file as a gift. Days later, in the hot August night, the young women used the file to scrape through a brass padlock securing the window guard in their dormitory. Once they had broken the lock, the girls climbed out of the window and onto the roof of the building, carrying their bedsheets with them. They then knotted the sheets together and climbed down onto the roof of the building next door, fleeing down the stairs and onto the street. They succeeded in hailing a cab, despite lacking shoes and wearing white shelter uniforms.[118] After their escape, the young women parted ways. One traveled to Coney Island to meet her boyfriend. In spite of attempts on the part of their family members, police, and the courts to control them, many young women were, in the words of another nineteen-year-old under JAB surveillance, committed to "getting a good time while [they were] young."[119]

Racism, Politics, and Youth Policing in Bedford-Stuyvesant

Geography intersected with racism and partisan politics to structure the city's approach to delinquency and communities' responses. Valentine and La Guardia saw Times Square as ground zero for female misbehavior. They dispatched members of the Division of National Defense and members of the auxiliary City Patrol Corps to the entertainment center to prevent girls from meeting the soldiers and sailors who flocked to the district. The pair worried less about these trysts in other neighborhoods. In more residential parts of the city, like Harlem and the Brooklyn neighborhood of Bedford-Stuyvesant, debates about delinquency served other purposes. In Harlem, officials contended that delinquency was one of the many supposed problems that justified the NYPD's significant presence in the neighborhood. In Bedford-Stuyvesant, white conservative residents claimed that misbehaving Black youth threatened their security and property values. These accusations resulted in a monthslong controversy about racism, delinquency, policing, and citizenship in the fall of 1943 that dominated the city's papers, provoked controversy within the NYPD, weakened the mayor, and elicited protests from a wide swath of civil rights organizations. Though La Guardia and Valentine generally supported aggressive policing of youth, they did not always control the narrative around wartime juvenile delinquency.

A few months after Ethelen's attack in Manhattan, white residents in Bedford-Stuyvesant began complaining about delinquency in their Brooklyn neighborhood. Brooklyn's Midtown Civic League, a white supremacist group with a history of using terrorism to try to drive Black residents from the neighborhood, raised the issue throughout the summer of 1943.[120] League members claimed crime was causing white residents to vacate Bedford-Stuyvesant, resulting in the loss of millions of dollars in real estate and mortgage investments.[121] As historian Craig Wilder shows, it was actually federal financial and insurance policies that funneled money away from central Brooklyn, not the actions of Black residents.[122] The material conditions caused by these policies and the NYPD's criminalization of Black youth encouraged white residents to blame Black neighbors for reductions in their property values and to associate a growing Black population with increased crime. In late summer 1943, county judge Louis Goldstein, who one year later would give two Black male trolley operators multiyear sentences in Sing Sing for defending themselves against violent attacks from white passengers, appointed a grand jury to investigate crime in Bedford-Stuyvesant.[123] The jury was then charged with issuing a presentment, or a written statement, describing the result of their investigation.[124] In their report the grand jury framed crime, particularly juvenile delinquency and prostitution, as the neighborhood's primary problem, but the records of their work suggest that their biggest concern was living near Black New Yorkers.

Brooklynites who served on the grand jury and can be found in the historical records came from the borough's white professional class. Of the all-white grand jury's twenty-three members, eleven could be found in the 1940 census or in newspaper articles discussing the presentment.[125] More than half of these jury members owned their homes, and all but two were engaged in professional fields including insurance, banking, business, sales, and law.[126] The jurors heard testimony from over one hundred witnesses, only one of whom was African American, before releasing their report on crime in the neighborhood.[127] With the exception of an unlisted number of "representative citizens," the mayor, and the police commissioner, most witnesses were criminal justice professionals, business or homeowners, or clergymen. The grand jury's public statement reflected the racialized perceptions of criminality held by white members of this professional class, as well as their disapproval of Mayor La Guardia.

The grand jury contended that their criticisms of Bedford-Stuyvesant were not influenced by the race of residents, but racist assumptions and racially coded language pervaded the report. Authors declared that the neighborhood hosted an "extremely deplorable state of lawlessness" partly caused by "a great influx of people from out of the State," likely a reference to African Americans migrating from the South. They claimed that "groups of young boys armed with penknives . . . roam the streets at will" and that "prostitution is rife" in the neighborhood, which jury members described as "a cesspool of filth and venereal disease."[128] Monsignor John Belford of the R. C. Church of the Nativity at Classon Avenue and Madison Street, who did not serve on the jury but publicly supported its work, shared with the *Brooklyn Daily Eagle* that "anarchy does exist in the area where Negro youth dare to say to police 'if you lay a hand on me I'll complain to the Mayor.'"[129] Jurors complained that "colored boys" were receiving sentences that were "too lenient" in court.[130] The grand jury's defensive comment that "many eminent, responsible and trustworthy Colored citizens of this area" concurred with their assessment further suggested that the presentment's authors were, in fact, saying something about Black residents. La Guardia made the jury's concerns explicit when he stated, "This is the Negro question we are talking about. . . . When a neighborhood changes its complexion that way there is bound to be trouble."[131] Craig Wilder describes this comment as La Guardia "introducing *race*" into the debate, but the text of the jury's presentment suggests that racism was already a central facet in the investigation.[132]

In response to this "trouble," the grand jury called for harsher and more intensive policing and criticized the mayor. They recommended increasing the number of patrolmen in the neighborhood, adding more JAB officers, lengthening sentences for young offenders, investigating relief rolls in the neighborhood, expanding the Colored State Guard, a volunteer military unit under the control of the governor that was created in 1942, and even prohibiting public gatherings.[133] They also called for more violent policing, arguing that police in the neighborhood had "not adopted sufficiently the 'muss em up attitude' that this kind of lawlessness deserves and requires."[134] The jury's use of the phrase "muss em up" was a verbatim reference to a 1934 directive from Valentine to his officers to beat arrestees, illustrating that the commissioner's statements shaped how the public conceived of policing. Jurors levied some soft criticism against Valentine but saved their most vehement accusations for the mayor.[135] "The fault lies . . . with the Mayor of this city," the report declared, for "failing to invoked all the powers at his command to prevent the lawlessness we have referred to."[136]

City forces allied themselves with or against the grand jury along lines of politics and civil rights. Supporters of the mayor or of civil rights for Black New Yorkers criticized the grand jury's report, while opponents of civil rights or of the mayor came out in support of the presentment.[137] La Guardia and Valentine both argued the entire investigation was driven by political motives. This accusation was likely a subtle reference to tension between the mayor and Brooklyn's Democratic district attorney, William O'Dwyer, who had unsuccessfully challenged La Guardia in the 1941 mayoral election and who possessed a significant base of power in the borough's justice system. The conflict around the presentment was structured by both party politics and racial politics in the city.

Members of the Midtown Civic League sought to capitalize on the presentment to fan the flames of racial resentment. A week after the presentment appeared in the press, the league hosted white patrolman David Liebman, who broke department ranks to criticize the mayor and to discuss low morale in the NYPD, which he attributed to the influence of the "sunburnt element" on city government. Henry E. Ashcroft, an African American lawyer and probation officer at the Brooklyn Court of Special Sessions, was also in attendance at the meeting. Ashcroft attempted to counter Liebman's derogatory statements but was shouted down by the audience.[138] Yvonne Gregory of the *People's Voice* declared that, though attendees at the meeting purported to be engaging in rituals of "good citizenship," the discussion revealed "the distorted features of fascism."[139]

For NYPD higher-ups, Liebman's language proved a problematic and inflammatory articulation of the ideology that implicitly undergirded department policies: that African Americans did not belong in New York City and should not influence city government. Following the meeting, NYPD officials moved quickly to bring charges against Liebman, who was suspended for violating Section 161 of the Department Rules and Regulations, which forbid department members from making public speeches on police matters.[140] La Guardia and Valentine worried about the possibility of racial unrest during the war and sought to avoid blatant displays of racial prejudice. The NYPD charged Liebman with "causing a condition that might have led to a riotous condition," for his use of a racial slur.[141] City officials were especially sensitive to the possibility of unrest in the fall of 1943, since Harlem residents had broken out in protest the previous August after an NYPD officer assaulted two people. Not all department members, however, shared Valentine's outlook. A disgruntled delegate in the Patrolmen's Benevolent Association publicly criticized Valentine and his departmental allies for refusing to stand behind officers. "It is high time the membership wrest control from this craven group," the delegate declared, "who . . . volunteer as witnesses against one of their number."[142]

La Guardia's effort to dissipate interest in the jury's presentment proved unsuccessful, and under pressure from conservative white residents the mayor directed Valentine to initiate a new survey of crime in the neighborhood. On November 20, 1943, Valentine produced a report directly addressing the claims made in the grand jury's presentment. Valentine's report took issue with the overall assessment that the NYPD's inadequate policing of Bedford-Stuyvesant was leading to rampant youth crime. He argued, in contrast, that the numbers of patrol and detective forces assigned to the neighborhood had been increased during the war, when other precincts were losing officers to military release.[143] Valentine sought to deflect the grand jury's claims of a particular problem with delinquency in Bedford-Stuyvesant by citing a general increase in the misbehavior of youth during the war.[144] In his report, the commissioner attempted to frame the NYPD's presence in

Bedford-Stuyvesant in a way that would satisfy the white Brooklynites calling for more police without offending Black residents or civil rights activists.

Black residents of the neighborhood and their allies had already begun mobilizing against the attack on the neighborhood. Herbert T. Miller, executive secretary of the Carlton Avenue branch of the YMCA, spoke out against the presentment, arguing that Bedford-Stuyvesant was targeted because of racism rather than concern about crime. Miller hosted a gathering at the YMCA at which participants passed a resolution calling for an interracial committee to "repudiate statements of the grand jury presentation, which are false and misleading," a group to explore Black unemployment and racial discrimination at plants in Brooklyn, and publicity about the lack of playgrounds in the neighborhood.[145]

Activists referenced the war effort, arguing that the grand jury's accusations were driven by the same fascist impulses against which the nation was at war. Shortly after Miller's criticism, residents and supporters organized a public event opposing the presentment. White Communist city councilman Peter Cacchione described the grand jury's accusations as "an organized fascist attack" orchestrated by enemies of the government seeking to "help Hitler and prolong the war." The Brooklyn chapter of the NAACP also held a rally in opposition to the presentment. Edward Strong, executive secretary of the National Negro Congress, presided over the rally, which was attended by over 200 people, including members of the Congress of Industrial Organizations, American Federation of Labor, Teachers Union, American Labor Party, and Brooklyn Urban League.[146] City councilmembers Adam Clayton Powell Jr. and Cacchione joined other speakers addressing a crowd of over 1,000 people at a November 25 event at the Brooklyn Academy of Music. Critics described the presentment as an attempt to "set brother against brother," and Powell dubbed the leader of the Midtown Civic League "a native fascist."[147]

Despite this significant organizing campaign and La Guardia's conflict with the grand jury, Valentine assigned additional officers to Bedford-Stuyvesant in response to the presentment. After the NYPD investigation, the commissioner assigned 133 additional police officers to the neighborhood, including 32 detectives, and established a new unit of the JAB, which included 2 officers, 10 patrolmen, and 10 policewomen.[148] Valentine also reorganized NYPD operations in Bedford-Stuyvesant.[149]

The episode in Bedford-Stuyvesant was an example of anti-Black racism expressed through a conflict over how to identify and respond to wartime juvenile delinquency. White conservative Brooklyn residents mobilized charges of delinquency and criminality in an effort to expand the police presence in the neighborhood and make Black residents unwelcome. Valentine and La Guardia, aware of the racial dynamics at play, sought to present police activity in the neighborhood as adequate but not racially discriminatory. Black residents and civil rights activists attempted to reframe the presentment as a racist attack that proved dangerous and anti-American during the war. Though Valentine and La Guardia were not generally sympathetic to the supporters of the grand jury report, in the militarized context of the war the pair responded to the controversy with additional police forces.

Conclusion

By the last year of the war, legislators in Albany were taking note of the demand for more aggressive policing of young women in New York City. Senator Fred Young of Lewis County, a sparsely populated region north of Syracuse, and Assemblyman MacNeil Mitchell of Manhattan collaborated on bills to strengthen police power over young women. Young and Mitchell, inspired by reports from New York City court magistrates Henry Curran and Raphael Koenig, sought to expand the Wayward Minor Law. In February 1945, they sponsored companion bills adding a new category to the pre-existing law. Their bills broadened the category of wayward minor to include young people between the ages of sixteen and twenty-one who flouted parental or state authority.[150] Although the bill used gender-neutral language, Mitchell described its true targets in a letter to Governor Dewey requesting the governor's support. Mitchell explained that his goal in expanding the statute was "to permit the court to take jurisdiction in the ever-increasing number of cases of runaway girls."[151]

Koenig and Curran argued that female juvenile delinquency was on the rise, and that the NYPD needed freedom to exercise greater control over "these young girls."[152] Curran connected the need to expand police power over young women to the war effort, but also argued that the situation would continue after the end of the hostilities. He argued to Dewey that "these are not only war emergency bills, but also they go to the root of the whole future of this Wayward Minor Court for Girls."[153] Koenig elaborated on the rationale behind the bills in a report to the governor. Koenig first stated that the existing wayward minor statute generally required that a parent or guardian raise a complaint. He argued that this provision restricted the ability of police officers to use the law, which was particularly problematic in New York

City. Further, he explained, the new provisions "are primarily designed to enable a Police Officer or someone in a similar capacity to be the complainant." Koenig lamented that "New York City is a haven for runaway girls" and that "the police are seriously handicapped in dealing with that problem." Koenig and Curran argued that the new laws would set up the state to more aggressively police young women in the postwar period, when "the rate of delinquency will unquestionably rise."[154]

Koenig and Curran overstated the "handicap" that police officers faced under the pre-1945 Wayward Minor Law. Throughout the war, police officers initiated a significant majority of cases referred to the JAB. In 1942, officers referred 66 percent of the total cases, while parents and relatives referred 9 percent.[155] In both 1943 and 1944, police officers in the JAB or other departments referred 94 percent of the cases accepted by the bureau for ongoing attention. Parents and relatives, in contrast, referred 0.5 percent of cases in 1943, and 1 percent of cases in 1944.[156] Under the Wayward Minor Law, however, parents could revoke or refuse to lodge a complaint regarding their child, and therefore, if the offense had been disobedience, the court would lose the ability to prosecute. This was the situation that probation officer Dorris Clarke had fretted over in 1941.[157] The bills Young and Mitchell sponsored removed this restriction, thereby facilitating convictions.

Dewey signed the Young bill into law on April 16, 1945. He described the bill as "designed to meet the new conditions arising from the spread of delinquency among young people, particularly those who have left their homes." When signing it, Dewey declared that "with millions of fathers away and millions of mothers helping the war effort of the nation in industry, it is our task to take unusual measures for our boys and girls."[158] The Young bill used concern about wartime social disruptions to expand the carceral state's reach over New York's youth, even as the *New York Times* reported on Allied successes in "whittl[ing] down the area of Germany still in enemy hands."[159] In the months after the Allied forces declared victory in Europe and later in the Pacific and the nation embarked on a program of demobilization, there was no effort to roll back carceral state expansions that had been justified as a wartime necessity. In fact, political interest in juvenile delinquency and policing youth would increase significantly in the years after the war.[160] New York State's Wayward Minor Law would remain in use until 1972, when the Supreme Court affirmed a lower court's ruling declaring unconstitutional the portion of the law that permitted the imprisonment of persons between sixteen and twenty-one years of age deemed "morally depraved" or in danger of becoming so.[161]

Throughout the war, La Guardia, Valentine, and other city officials argued that exigencies of the mobilization required heightened surveillance of Gotham's youth. The duo, particularly Valentine, had pushed youth surveillance throughout the 1930s as a means of preventing young people from developing into criminals and forming them instead into adults who valued police authority. The requirements of the war, however, provided a useful opportunity to expand NYPD practices. The municipal leaders reframed the priorities of the NYPD around protecting soldiers and sailors traveling through the city and preserving wartime urban order. The officials enthusiastically pushed for intensified monitoring of young women and were responsive to white Brooklyn residents who claimed that delinquency from Black youth required a heavier police presence in their neighborhood. City leaders were so successful in making these claims that policy makers in Albany expanded the state's ability to surveil and incarcerate youth. While city leaders worried about the threat that juvenile delinquency posed to wartime Gotham and fretted about what misled youth might signal for the nation's future, they also turned their attention to policing gambling in the city, which they believed threatened to undermine male labor, the nation's most important wartime human resource.

CHAPTER FIVE

Gamblers Warned to Work or Fight
Policing Male Gamblers, Soldiers, and Sailors

Gendered and racialized anti-vice policing under Mayor Fiorello La Guardia and Police Commissioner Lewis Valentine did not exclusively target women. Men were also criminalized for behavior that city leaders believed violated masculine responsibilities of citizenship. Gambling proved the most infuriating example of this violation for the mayor and police commissioner. To La Guardia, gamblers were shirkers, deceivers, and predators who neglected their duty to participate in legitimate work and conned other men into doing the same. In Valentine's view, gamblers enabled and depended on corrupt police, the types of officers he despised and had worked to root out for his entire career. Though women gamblers faced arrest and punishment as well, they made up a small proportion of female arrestees and did not provoke the same ire from city officials as their male counterparts due to the gendered discourses around gambling and labor. From the start of their tenure, La Guardia and Valentine launched an aggressive onslaught against gamblers in the city. Black New Yorkers, whose neighborhoods—particularly Harlem—were both criminalized and constructed as sites of illicit amusement, bore the brunt of much of this onslaught.

In 1939 and 1940, when the country began preparing for war, these campaigns picked up speed and urgency. During the war, discussions about gamblers in New York reflected larger national debates about citizenship, male labor, and the boundaries of the coercive powers of the wartime state. In the prewar years, a male gambler might be seen as neglecting his duties to provide economically for his family or to participate in the legal economy. Once the nation began mobilizing a military campaign, however, male labor was framed as essential to the mobilization. Any illegitimate use of this labor, as in the case of gambling, was a violation of the patriotic responsibilities of masculine wartime citizenship. Male gamblers, therefore, became saboteurs, stealing their own labor from the war effort and undermining the efforts of their fellow citizens, in uniform and out of it. Many New Yorkers, in fact, wrote to La Guardia to complain of their own wartime sacrifices in contrast to the profligacy that they perceived to be on display by known gamblers in their neighborhoods. La Guardia recommended examining the draft status of civilian men arrested for gambling, and some floated the idea of drafting arrestees.

La Guardia and Valentine's approach to gambling among enlisted men diverged dramatically from the tough stance they adopted toward civilians. Men in the armed forces were already using their labor appropriately. They therefore were to be *protected* from both arrest and the moral and financial perils of gambling. The Manhattan district attorney clearly articulated this mind-set to NYPD members in 1943: "If a soldier gets into trouble and must appear in our courts as witness, complainant or defendant, valuable days of training and of service are forever lost with possibly fatal consequences to someone fighting in our cause."[1] Though officials described this policy as applying to enlisted men generally, in practice only white men in the armed services enjoyed the full benefits of police protection. Black members of the military passing through Gotham's boroughs and even those stationed in the city, as in the case of the soldiers at the Fox Hills army facility in Staten Island, were not exempted from intense police surveillance, arrest, and violence. Throughout the 1930s, La Guardia and Valentine developed a gendered and racialized approach to anti-gambling policing that intensified and took on new significance during the war years.

Prewar Gambling, Corruption, and Organized Crime

Betting on games of chance including dice, cards, billiards, and lotteries has a long history in Gotham's public cultures. Lotteries were common in the American colonies in the eighteenth century and increased in scope and popularity throughout the nineteenth century.[2] Gambling of many varieties was popular during these years in public houses as well as in the emerging socially stratified restaurants that catered to working- or upper-class men and prostitutes. These restaurants, taverns, and saloons were embedded in the city's political life, since many tavern owners also served as political bosses or aldermen. They therefore had close connections with the police.[3] Because of these connections, in the nineteenth and early twentieth centuries saloons were centers of illicit entertainment, and many allowed gambling on policy, cards, and billiards.[4]

All aspects of life in New York were racially stratified during these years, and gambling was no exception. Black betters were often excluded from official lotteries, but formed their own gambling pools in which they bet on lottery numbers for lower prices and lower winnings. This practice became known as insuring the lottery and later developed into policy gambling.[5]

Though betting and games of chance were embedded in Gotham's white male social world, racist cultural productions depicted Black men as eschewing legal work in favor of gambling, theft, and living off proceeds of prostitution. Songs portraying these and other racist messages proliferated at the turn of the twentieth century in response to the migration of Black Americans to New York City from the South. Employers used these cultural stereotypes to justify discrimination against Black men. The numbers of Black men employed as hostlers, porters, and waiters dropped significantly in the first decades of the twentieth century.[6] As historian Douglas Flowe has argued, in pre-Prohibition New York City, Black-owned saloons provided spaces for Black men, who were demonized and excluded in many other areas of city life, to pursue economic advancement, leisure, and community.[7] Gambling could overlap with any one or all of these three areas of life.

While white elites' racism and sexism led them to view Black Gothamites as likely gamblers, gambling did play particular economic and cultural roles in Black New York. This was especially true of policy gambling, a type of lottery in which players chose a three-digit number that was then compared with a winning number selected from bank clearing totals and later the New York Stock Exchange.[8] The game became increasingly popular in New York City throughout the 1920s and 1930s and played important roles in Harlem.[9] For Black New Yorkers, policy provided much-needed avenues for extra income through winnings or the jobs associated with the game. The policy economy included jobs for number runners or bet collectors, operators who ran pads where bets were collected, psychics who predicted winning numbers for pay, and, for a select few, owners who ran their own policy bank.[10] These opportunities proved significant since Black New Yorkers faced severe employment discrimination. Indeed, historians have argued that policy gambling should be considered within the context of "Black business history" because of the "essentially economic nature of the whole enterprise."[11] Furthermore, the policy system was inscribed into the flow of social, political, and cultural life in Harlem. Historian LaShawn Harris has shown that policy banker Madame Stephanie St. Clair publicly decried racism at the hands of the NYPD, worked to educate Harlemites about how to protect themselves from police harassment, and funneled her profits back into institutions to assist Black immigrants.[12] Policy betting was woven into the neighborhood's social and cultural fabric as well, and "dream books" advising readers how to place bets based on their dreams were best sellers.[13]

Though policy gambling provided financial opportunities for Harlem residents, NYPD members exploited its illegality to extort bribes. Policy arrests featured prominently in Samuel Seabury's 1930 investigations into corruption in the city's municipal functioning. Investigators found a "pernicious system" of corruption that was "especially prevalent" in the "thousands" of policy arrests that the police department performed every year and particularly concentrated in the Fifth District Court, known as the Harlem Court. Lawyers found that though policy gambling was illegal according to Sections 974, 975, and 976 of the penal law, NYPD officers allowed certain bankers to operate in return for payoffs. Reportedly, employees of these bankers even received buttons that provided them immunity from arrest.[14] Seabury's investigators documented tens of thousands of dollars of unexplained income for many NYPD members, much of which likely stemmed from policy extortion.[15] St. Clair testified that she had paid $6,000 to "a lieutenant and plainclothes officers."[16] Influential African American journalist Ted Poston wrote regularly about gambling and police corruption in mid-twentieth-century Gotham throughout his career.[17] Poston described a system of payoffs that flowed throughout the ranks of the NYPD from the "cop on the beat" to "sergeants, lieutenants, captains and, in many cases, to some of their superiors."[18]

NYPD officers regularly used claims of searching for policy slips, which were ubiquitous, as justification for harassing Black New Yorkers and worked with white gangsters who were seeking to expand into Harlem.[19] St. Clair launched a campaign against this police harassment. One of her approaches was to share her experiences with police harassment in the *New York Amsterdam News*. She called for city officials to halt these "brutal mistreatments" of Harlemites in a public letter to Mayor Jimmy Walker. In an indication of the transactional way city politics functioned under Tammany, St. Clair ended her letter by explaining what Harlem could do for Mayor Walker: "Your Honor, I am going to organize my people in Harlem to work and support you in the coming election. We want and need you to be re-elected Mayor of New York City, and I am going to do all I can to help you."[20] Though St. Clair was a prominent and unusual figure in Harlem, the experience of being arrested or harassed under the guise of policy policing became increasingly common in the neighborhood throughout the 1920s. As Harris has noted, the number of arrests for policy violations reported by the NYPD increased from 7 in 1920 to 13,692 in 1935.[21]

In the early 1930s, the landscape of policy gambling changed in ways that further disadvantaged Black bankers and policy workers. As alcohol prohibition came to an end, major players in the illegal liquor business sought to diversify their holdings by moving into policy gambling.[22] Crime leaders including Frank Costello, Phil Kastel, and Arthur Flegenheimer, known as Dutch Schultz, made millions from controlling slot machines and policy gambling.[23]

Schultz was one in a line of gangsters who benefited from their connections to Tammany Hall. In particular, Schultz worked with Jimmy Hines, a Tammany boss described by the *Amsterdam News* as the "political overlord" of the city's Eleventh Assembly District.[24] Harris notes that Hines was on Schultz's payroll and that the municipal leader pressured police, prosecutors, and judges to target employees of Schultz's Black competitors.[25] When federal agents raided a drug operation run by the gangster Arnold Rothstein, they found Hines's telephone number. A police informant testified in the Seabury investigations that Hines directed vice squad members to drop certain cases.[26] The *Amsterdam News* noted in 1938 that the collaboration between Hines and Schultz had "been common gossip in Harlem for a long time."[27] In 1931, when then–assistant U.S. attorney Thomas E. Dewey had prosecuted numbers boss Henry Miro, Dewey offered Miro a deal if he would testify against Hines. Miro, however, refused, reportedly claiming that if he did so, his "life wouldn't be worth a nickel."[28] Dewey went on to win the Manhattan district attorney race and was appointed special prosecutor overseeing a grand jury investigation targeted at Schultz and Hines. In 1938, Dewey charged Hines with helping Schultz drive out Harlem's policy competition. Hines was convicted and sentenced to four to eight years in prison.[29] Hines's connection to Schultz's network was emblematic of the ways that Tammany, the NYPD, and powerful gangsters collaborated throughout the 1920s. La Guardia took advantage of the public revelations of these connections in 1930 to push his alternative vision of city life, one free from corruption, gangsters, and gambling.

Immediately upon taking office, La Guardia sought to remedy the corruption revealed in the Seabury investigation. Campaigns against gambling lay at the center of this effort. For the new mayor, gambling and police corruption existed in a symbiotic relationship, each protecting and enriching the other. Corruption within the police department and gambling in the city would be banished together, to be replaced with a new era of municipal law and order. "A police department utterly free of political domination will war upon gangs of criminals that have had official protection," the *New York Times* reported the mayor telling a group of 200 ranking officers at police headquarters in January 1934.[30]

As part of this effort, under the new mayor the NYPD expanded its antigambling efforts. Throughout 1934, the police department embarked on a "determined and relentless attack on commercialized prostitution and gambling," which resulted in a 63 percent increase in arrests for policy gambling over 1933. Arrests for "gambling, miscellaneous" increased by 46 percent and arrests for "disorderly conduct (cards)" rose by 70 percent in 1934. Not all gambling-related arrests increased: arrests for "disorderly conduct (craps)" decreased slightly, as did those for maintaining gambling establishments. Arrests related to slot machines decreased significantly, likely due to La Guardia's campaign to remove and destroy the gambling machines throughout the city. Overall, however, there was a noticeable increase in the NYPD's anti-gambling activity between 1933 and 1934. In the department's magazine, *Spring 3100*, the NYPD celebrated that "marked inroads have been made on the deep-rooted organization of the policy racket, with particular success in relation to the bankers and control rooms, which constitute the backbone of the racket."[31] Throughout the 1930s, La Guardia and Valentine launched high-profile crackdowns against gamblers. By 1938, La Guardia declared that the city was "getting modernistic" in its destruction of slot machines by crushing them with a concrete cutter.[32]

When La Guardia promoted Valentine to police commissioner in fall 1934, he gained a committed ally in his campaigns against gambling. In a January 1935 radio address, the mayor announced that "a determined attack on commercialized vice and gambling shows results. The slot machine evil has been eradicated. Inroads have been made on the so-called policy racket. . . . Commissioner Lewis J. Valentine is on the job."[33] Both La Guardia and Valentine framed Tammany as in bed with gambling interests in the city. Valentine had built his career, in part, on opposition to Tammany's control of the police department and viewed gambling as inextricably tied to police corruption. The commissioner reflected in his autobiography on how, in his early career, New York City had "played host—thanks to rotten police and politicians—to 1,000 policy slip establishments."[34] Valentine also recollected his experience serving in the police department's confidential squad, which was devoted to "the uprooting of thieving policemen."[35] Despite Valentine and La Guardia's commitments to eradicating police graft, corruption remained endemic to the regulation of gambling throughout the 1930s. Valentine reflected in his autobiography that "even while I was Commissioner, gambling was still the main source of police graft."[36]

Prohibitions on gambling provided opportunities for police harassment as well as graft. In the spring of 1935, Harlem residents took to the streets in rebellion against racism in many facets of city life, especially their experiences with the police. Following the uprising, La Guardia organized a commission that held public meetings on life in Harlem and later produced a report on its findings. In these meetings, many Harlem residents shared their experiences with police harassment. The reports' authors noted, "One of the excuses which the police offer for illegal searchers of persons and their property is the quest for policy slips." The authors found that possession of policy slips accounted for 32 percent of the arrests in Harlem in the first six months of 1935. More than twenty-six attendees at the meetings shared that they had been illegally searched for policy slips, only one of whom admitted to possessing the slips at all.[37] The search for policy slips was clearly a popular justification for police intrusion into the lives of Harlem residents.

Throughout the 1930s, La Guardia, NYPD leaders, and state officials combatted gambling. When the war broke out, city officials' battle against gamblers both took on increased relevance and gained new tactics. As the mayor declared in the fall of 1940, he had had "the heat turned on gambling and vice for some time, [and] this was no time to let down."[38]

Gambling as Inappropriate Wartime Use of Resources

As the nation prepared for the possibility of war, gender became increasingly central in relations between Americans and the state. Policing was no exception. The landscape, goals, and strategies for policing men during the war differed from those used to monitor women and children. Women and children in New York City presented sexual and social threats to military preparedness, according to Valentine and La Guardia. Male labor, in contrast, was understood to be essential to the nation's war effort, and men were expected to contribute through serving in the military or working in defense production. Valentine and La Guardia directed members of the NYPD to protect the men who were performing these duties from temptations to engage in gambling or vice and to refrain from arresting or detaining those who proved unable to resist these enticements.

Officers in the military police and the shore patrol bore responsibility for policing soldiers and sailors, but NYPD members also interacted with enlisted men. "If that shore patrol gets in your way," La Guardia informed sailors arriving in New York City, "just call a city cop. He'll help you."[39] Like all of the NYPD's policies, this leniency was refracted through the racial politics of the city and the department. Department members did not treat African American service members stationed in the city with the same tolerance as their white counterparts, and Valentine was sympathetic when white New Yorkers claimed that Black soldiers were a source of crime and disorder. The stated policy of the department toward men seen as performing their wartime duty, though, was one of leniency.

Toward civilian men who withheld or misused their labor, Valentine and La Guardia adopted another approach altogether. Men who shirked their wartime responsibilities constituted a treasonous threat to the nation's ability to wage war. For the moralistic duo, no group embodied this threat more fully than male gamblers. La Guardia and Valentine had worked to penalize New Yorkers who worked or played in the extralegal gambling economy since they took up their respective positions. "It has been my policy to keep racketeers, crooks, gangsters, and other species of punks out of this city," declared La Guardia in a public letter to Chief Magistrate Henry Curran in January 1940. The mayor was writing to "make it clear" to the magistrate that in cases of vagrancy, evidence that an arrestee possessed financial resources should not be sufficient to merit an acquittal of the charge. Arrestees with evidence of revenue sources, La Guardia argued, may have earned such revenue from gambling or theft. "It goes without saying that no innocent person should be convicted," the mayor proclaimed, "on the other hand, the community must be protected."[40]

La Guardia and Valentine saw gamblers as disrupting the proper functioning of the city. The mayor viewed gamblers as predators from whom working-class New Yorkers required protection; to Valentine bookies and policy bankers were punks in league with corrupt members of the police department. Reformers, in government and outside it, argued that leisure should be orderly and in keeping with middle-class values of productivity and Christianity.[41] Gamblers challenged this framework by winning money without performing visible labor and by, in some instances, avoiding regular work. In the context of the mobilization of men into the armed forces and the national emergency of the war, male gamblers became not only lazy or predatory but a treasonous threat to national strength.

During the war, two dynamics related to the policing and monitoring of gambling became increasingly pronounced. First, opponents of gambling in city government, the courts, and the police department argued that during wartime, gamblers proved not merely irresponsible or immoral but unpatriotic. Male gamblers, particularly, received criticism from city officials, NYPD members, and their own neighbors for neglecting their wartime duty. Their presence in public, or in some instances their visible displays of wealth, became a reminder of the sacrifices engaged in by other New Yorkers, who argued that male gamblers should be drafted or working in defense industries.[42] Second, La Guardia's emphasis on protecting the "community" from gamblers during the war took on new weight as the "community" expanded to include white soldiers and sailors. These enlisted men had to be protected from both the lure of gambling and the enforcement of anti-gambling laws. An episode in Staten Island in the spring of 1945, in which white residents, NYPD officers, and much of the city's press described a supposed "crime wave" perpetrated by African American servicemen stationed on the island, suggests the racist parameters of these narratives of police protection.[43] During the war, city officials, NYPD leaders, and New Yorkers developed new ways of talking about and policing men for gambling violations. These wartime critiques of gambling and gamblers constituted part of a larger debate about the power of the wartime state and the blurry boundaries between military and civilian responsibilities.

From the passage of the Selective Service Act in September 1940 to demobilization in 1945, federal policy makers, municipal officials, and citizens debated the appropriate limitations of state power. Many agreed that mobilizing for war required expanded state interventions into the lives of citizens; the Selective Service Act provided one clear example of this expansion. Officials, along with many Americans, however, wondered how much civilian liberties could or should be curtailed during the war and whether the military draft was an appropriate stick to use in the service of these restrictions. Could civilian men and women be required to work in essential industries? How would the state treat civilians who refused to comply, broke the law, or went on strike? Could the military draft be used as punishment for these noncompliant citizens? Officials did not apply the same level of concern to the attacks on the civil liberties of Japanese Americans, the continued limitations of rights for African Americans, or the mass arrests of women for suspected prostitution. Officials did, however, worry about how much the federal government could dictate work responsibilities for white American men and what role the draft could play in these interventions.[44]

While officials in Washington argued about the appropriate scope of state control over the economy, Manhattan district attorney Frank Hogan was mobilizing an unlikely ally to monitor the city's docks. In March 1942, officials from naval intelligence met with Hogan to express concerns about the security of the docks.[45] Following this meeting, Hogan reached out to members of organized crime groups including Socks Lanza, Albert Anastasia, Meyer Lansky, and Frank Costello for assistance. The group struck a deal provided that Lucky Luciano was released from prison, where he was serving a thirty-to-fifty-year sentence won by Thomas Dewey when he had served as special prosecutor. They collaborated with police, monitored docks, and passed information to navy spies. In return, when the war ended in 1946, Governor Dewey commuted Luciano's sentence.[46] In his 1947 autobiography, Valentine devoted multiple pages to a heroic recounting of Dewey's take-down of Luciano during his time as district attorney, remarking only in passing that in 1946, while serving as governor, Dewey pardoned Luciano for having "made some contribution to the nation's war effort while he was in prison."[47] Valentine clearly preferred to dwell on the conflict rather than the collaboration. The collaboration between Hogan and Luciano, and the latter's subsequent postwar pardon, however, reveals a counterintuitive way in which the war changed the political calculations involved in policing and punishment in the city. Though the official line of the NYPD and the city remained opposition to gamblers and organized crime, the priority of maintaining control and surveillance on the city's docks, where, in the first four months of 1942, more than 114,000 railroad cars with war supplies were unloaded for transfer to ships, superseded this policy in practice.[48]

In April 1942, a month after Hogan's meeting with naval intelligence of-ficers, President Franklin Delano Roosevelt created the War Manpower Com-mission (WMC) in response to ongoing debates about production and civil liberties. Paul V. McNutt, head of the Federal Security Administration, over-saw the new agency and occupied a central position in these debates.[49] McNutt, an ambitious Democrat from Indiana, had his work cut out for him. He oversaw a nine-person committee whose initial purview consisted pri-marily of producing recommendations. The work of the commission was opposed both by critics who viewed its recommendations as an infringement on the rights of organized labor and by those who argued that the war de-manded a harsher federal policy.[50] The creation of the WMC reflected de-bates about how to control the nonenlisted population. In New York City, La Guardia and Valentine argued that men who abused their wartime liber-ties by gambling deserved to be drafted into the military or essential war pro-duction. Officers in the NYPD played multiple roles in this landscape; they enforced state policies, while also being subject to wartime provisions like the mayor's revision of retirement requirements.

La Guardia regularly reminded NYPD officers of his administration's pol-icy toward gamblers. Addressing the NYPD's "second war class" in Septem-ber 1942, the mayor spent a significant portion of his speech discussing this particular threat to order in the city. La Guardia reminded the new officers that "there is no place in the department for a rummy or a gambler." When the new patrolmen encountered a gambler, in fact, the mayor, raising his voice, cried that officers should *"sock him in the jaw, I'll stand back of you."*

The mayor believed that professional gamblers preyed on other men and lured them into illegal activity. He compared such gamblers to "petty thieves stealing food from children," and accused them of "enticing [other] men to spend their money on bets." Finally, he passed judgment, declaring of gamblers, "they're no good for the community."[51]

Other city officials put the mayor's words into action. Paul Moss, La Guardia's commissioner of the Department of Licenses, supported the mayor's crusade by demanding the removal of all sheets that provided tips on horse races or information on policy games from the city's newsstands. He informed the press that he had made his decision "because of this growing evil" of gambling and tipster sheets.[52] The NYPD launched a series of raids that same month.[53] A week later, at a meeting of police officials to discuss the upcoming election, Valentine emphasized the continued importance of wiping out gambling establishments as a means of protecting sailors and soldiers from gamblers and prostitutes.[54] Throughout the fall of 1942, while the British Royal Air Force targeted Germany's manufacturing centers and New York enacted its first daytime air raid drill, La Guardia and Valentine kept the attention of residents and police department members on gamblers.[55]

Some civilians agreed with the mayor's staunch attacks on male gamblers. Frustrated and angry New Yorkers wrote to La Guardia criticizing gamblers for rejecting their wartime responsibilities. Although many women gambled throughout the city, wartime criticism of gamblers focused primarily on men. One New Yorker, writing to La Guardia in the spring of 1942, griped that when walking through his neighborhood, he had to "wade through bookmakers, touts, and horseplayers who crowd doorways, infest the telephone booths and congregate on the corners and midblock." The writer requested that police enforce laws against public loitering and "clear out these gentry who should be drafted and made to do an honest day's work for home and country instead of pursuing their illegal trickeries."[56] Another writer complained to the mayor in September 1942, "As I go around the Borough of Brooklyn, groups of men, eight, ten, or twelve of them of all ages, play on street corners for hours at a time." The writer wondered, "Who is supporting them? Are they on home relief? . . . Why does the Police Department allow card playing on Street Corners . . . ? Why are these young men not in the draft, and other able men not working?"[57] On September 20, 1942, La Guardia reflected on similar themes in his Sunday WNYC broadcast. The mayor commented on the insidious danger that gambling presented to the wartime nation. "What are we fighting for?" the mayor asked his audience, before responding, "To perpetuate our institutions and American life.

What is the basis of everything that we hold dear, what is the foundation of American life? It is the American Family. Surely we will not permit disreputable, dishonest, lawbreaking thieves and racketeers to destroy the American family. I refer to the tin-horn book maker, the number racketeer, the professional gambler."[58] To the mayor and many other New Yorkers, male gamblers undermined the current military strength of the nation and the future security of American ideals. For persistent foes of gambling, like La Guardia, the ever-present threats posed by "numbers" games escalated during the war. Men were being mobilized to fight for the vision of "American life" that, according to La Guardia, gambling devalued. New Yorkers who may have considered gamblers a mere inconvenience outside wartime now called for the state to bring repressive force against men evading an "honest day's work for home and country."[59]

A minority claimed, however, that it was La Guardia's vigorous attacks on gambling that truly threatened the American family. In September 1942, former president of the Board of Education James Marshall spoke out against a public statement by La Guardia that young boys should write to the mayor if their fathers were losing money by gambling. The mayor had suggested that "little boys who see the family happiness destroyed because some thieving tinhorn is robbing his daddy of money on horse races or gambling, also please let me know." Marshall worried that such a dynamic might create "bad family relationships" and commented that the mayor surely did not mean to suggest "that American children adopt the practice current in Soviet Russia and Nazi Germany of reporting their parents to the authorities."[60]

Marshall was outnumbered, and the dominant anti-gambling attitudes played out clearly in the case of Henry G. Hoffman. On November 18, 1942, William Sullivan was arrested in Hoffman's apartment by Patrolman Thomas Higgins. Sullivan was charged with bookmaking and accepting bets on racehorses. Higgins confiscated policy slips and a telephone from the apartment. Evidence suggested that the phone belonged to Hoffman, who was then also arrested and charged with bookmaking in December 1942. The thirty-two-year-old married father pleaded guilty and received a fine of $100 and sentence of thirty days. Hoffman described himself as a professional painter who also accepted bets on horse races. The commanding officer of the investigating squad disagreed, stating in his reports of Hoffman, "His hands seem to indicate that he never did any painting in his life. In my opinion he is a bookmaker and nothing else."[61] In this description, the officer used Hoffman's engagement in the illicit economy to undermine the arrestee's claim to a lawful profession.

Hoffman's neighbors denounced him for what they perceived to be his lack of participation in the war effort. The NYPD investigated the painter and bookmaker after receiving an anonymous tip wondering "why Hoffman is not called for service in the Army or made to work in defense."[62] Another complaint went to Hoffman's local draft board in Ridgewood, Queens: "How come bookmakers are not drafted or are they some special class that are essential for the war effort? Why is it Mr. Hoffman doesn't have to get into an essential defense industry or go into the Army like lots of ordinary people." The author criticized Hoffman's seeming ability to receive extra gas rations when "I work in an airplane plant and have to take public busses."[63] In these statements, neighbors expressed their frustrations with their own wartime sacrifices through criticism of Hoffman's perceived liberties, which they called on the state to curtail.

Though Hoffman's neighbors felt their wartime sacrifices deeply, some government officials worried that American men were not doing enough to contribute to the war effort. In January 1943 in the face of such anxiety, the WMC's Paul McNutt suggested a "work or fight" order. Anna Rosenberg, regional director of the WMC in New York, perhaps best articulated the ideology behind the order when she noted that "every able-bodied man" is on "loan from the military to civilian life."[64] McNutt argued that draft boards should focus less on whether a man had dependents and more on his occupation when determining whether to grant deferments. He contended that deferred men working nonessential jobs should be drafted or moved into essential industries.[65] This proposal was highly controversial and opposition to it led to the passage of a 1943 law reaffirming the significance of fatherhood as the paramount factor in assigning deferments. The debates continued throughout the war, however. In December 1944, the Selective Service System issued a work-or-fight order that applied to men labeled IV-F, or unfit for the military. Only about 12,000 men were drafted under this program, but the threat of the draft was used to break strikes in aviation, mining, railroads, and public transportation.[66] Although federal officials differed over the degrees of coercion they wanted to embrace, the entire conversation illustrates the ways that the requirements of war provided opportunities to redefine the responsibilities of citizenship.

In this landscape, complaints about idleness took on increased significance. For African Americans, such accusations existed within a larger context of racism and debates about crime and migration that had been ongoing since Reconstruction.[67] In New York, southern migrants were a particular focus of such racialized critiques. Kings County judge Franklin Taylor articulated tropes common to these accusations in September 1943 when he spoke out against home relief. Since the initiation of the home relief policy, the judge claimed, "the social flotsam has trekked into New York City. . . . Once here and on relief these people further deteriorate. . . . The men stay home during the day so as to remain on relief. Being idle, they spend the time drinking cheap liquor and gambling." Though Taylor did not explicitly name African Americans as the target of his ire, Dan Burley, writing in the *Amsterdam News*, argued that Black New Yorkers understood the judge's remarks as directed at them. Burley criticized Taylor for his remarks and noted that Black New Yorkers would move off home relief when "the doors to jobs have been opened to all, regardless of race or color."[68]

Black journalists in New York differed in their assessment and analysis of the war's impact on gambling patterns in the city. One reporter in the *Amsterdam News* described an increase in gambling and partying during the war, declaring that "Harlem is wild" with New Yorkers reaping the benefit of wartime jobs and wages. The limited wartime consumption options enabled people to engage in "wanton waste of money in gambling." The author contrasted those "wasting" money on gambling with the "solid folk" at the post office bond window investing their money in savings and "also, no doubt for Uncle Sam."[69] The journalist connected thrift and patriotism, focusing on gambling as an issue of consumption rather than production. Though the author criticized gambling as a waste of resources, he, unlike La Guardia and Valentine, acknowledged that many gamblers also held productive jobs.

Carolyn Dixon voiced an alternative opinion in the newspaper two months later. Dixon wrote that "with a decent job at respectable wages [former gamblers] reason, there's nothing to be gained in trying to 'out-figure' the number bankers." She concluded, "It doesn't pay, even the bankers are saying, to attempt to beat Mayor LaGuardia and Uncle Sam."[70] For Dixon, gambling was a profession rather than a pastime, and one that did not pay in the punitive wartime context.

In his column in the *New York Amsterdam News*, the academic and activist W. E. B. Du Bois argued against gambling during and after the war. Du Bois proposed a "future program" for the paper's African American readers: "Let us ignore luxury, waste, gambling, and keeping up with the Joneses. . . . Let us learn the new economics which refuses to build wealth on theft from the poor and aims to re-distribute wealth so as to make a steady demand for consumable goods, whose consumption helps and does not hurt men. Let us aim at production for use and not for profit, and eschew chance as a legitimate means of livelihood."[71] Du Bois's perspective on gambling was similar in many ways to La Guardia's. Du Bois, however, situated gambling within the larger frameworks of the war's impact on African Americans and his Marxist conceptions of production and consumption.[72] The writer's concluding line, "With such a program they can't keep us down and they know it," indicates the higher stakes that existed for African American men labeled unproductive or wasteful.

Gamblers were guilty of wasting more than just their own labor, according to city officials. In May 1943, the mayor directed NYPD officers to patrol neighborhoods surrounding race tracks and record the license plates of cars parked in the vicinity. Officers were then required to report these numbers to the Office of Price Administration to investigate inappropriate use of gasoline rations. "The OPA considers horse races the least essential of all forms of recreation," La Guardia declared in a May 1943 broadcast.[73] La Guardia connected the races with absenteeism and argued that the federal government should prohibit horse racing for the duration of the war. Some of the most influential players in the federal bureaucracy agreed. Southern New Dealer and "Assistant President" James F. Byrnes had served on both the Senate and Supreme Court before moving to lead the Office of War Mobilization.[74] In December 1944, Byrnes declared that beginning on January 3, 1945, all animal racing was to be suspended to conserve labor and materials.[75] In response to the announcement, La Guardia gleefully proclaimed, "I'm for Jimmy [Byrnes] for President."[76] The mayor advised Valentine to shift officers to preventing the always prohibited off-the-track betting and to targeting number runners.

Though the most vehement wartime concern about number runners and betters focused on men, some women arrested for gambling were criticized for neglecting their wartime duties and violating the expectations of their gender. On December 6, 1942, a group of women came before a magistrate in Brooklyn's weekend court for charges related to gambling. A patrolman charged Belle Braham with keeping sets of policy numbers in a bible on the table in her bedroom. Mary Rabinowitz had been arrested at her candy store on Fulton Street for accepting horse racing bets, which she told the court she did to make good on a debt. "It looks as though they're taking over for the duration," a court attendant remarked of the Brooklyn women.[77] In March 1943, a Bronx magistrate lectured twelve women for "passing their time gambling instead of doing war work."[78] When Florence Anderson came to court in Flatbush on charges of bookmaking in October 1943, she received a scolding. "If your mother had been told when you were a little girl that in 1943 her daughter and other women would be bookmakers," the magistrate admonished, "she would have thought it a fantastic story by [science fiction writer] H.G. Wells."[79] The cases of these women, though deeply upsetting to the magistrate, provoked less attention than those of their male counterparts during the war because of the gendered expectations of wartime citizenship. Women were not subject to the draft, and though they volunteered with the military and many more worked in war-related manufacturing, female wartime citizenship was not imbued with the same expectations of physical contribution to the armed forces or wartime production.

As the war progressed, La Guardia encouraged Valentine and the city's Selective Service director to treat all men arrested for gambling like arrestee Henry Hoffman. "Look here, Lew," La Guardia declared, addressing Valentine, "every arrest that you make for gambling, check the military information, the draft board cards, and report them immediately to Colonel [Arthur] McDermott [New York City's Selective Service director]. Detain the gamblers and physically deliver them to the colonel or to the draft boards."[80] In January 1945, La Guardia announced on his weekly broadcast that anyone arrested in a gambling raid would have his draft status "carefully scrutinized," and anyone classified with a deferment would have his case revisited by his local draft board. To the mayor, refusing to work at a "war job" constituted a crime "as low and despicable as treason." The mayor had been inspired to remark on the need to draft gamblers by the case of Max Katz, who had received a class 2-A deferment and was arrested in September 1944 for running a numbers bank.[81] The national director of the Selective Service declined to comment on the legality of La Guardia's proposal, remarking to the *New York Times* only that he had not considered such a policy.[82] The mayor's approach illustrated the ways that the wartime mobilization crystallized gendered requirements for citizenship and militarized the home front with the support of the NYPD. For civilian men, the always inappropriate practice of gambling became treasonous during the war because of their responsibilities to participate in staffing, arming, and feeding the nation's war effort.

For men in the armed forces, however, the practices and arguments around gambling differed significantly. La Guardia and Valentine considered these men to be performing their wartime duty. Gambling or getting arrested for gambling could interrupt that duty. To the mayor and police commissioner, therefore, gambling among civilians was an indication of their rejection of wartime responsibilities; enlisted men who were already performing this responsibility, in contrast, needed to be protected from the distractions and dangers of gambling.

Give Some Protection to Those Sailors and Soldiers: Protecting White Enlisted Men from Gamblers and Gambling Arrests

While city officials and residents viewed civilian gamblers as irresponsible traitors, these same Gothamites argued that enlisted men needed to be protected from both predatory gamblers and the possibility of being arrested for gambling themselves. Reformers had made similar arguments about the need to protect vulnerable men from conniving con men and their own poor judgment in the 1930s, but during the war this demand took on a patriotic tint. Department leaders directed NYPD members to prevent gambling throughout the city as a means of protecting the time and income of enlisted men. At a department communion breakfast in April 1943, Valentine reminded the 2,100-person audience that department members must "see to the welfare of the thousands of members of the armed services to be found in our midst. New York City is the largest staging area—point of embarkation if you'd prefer calling it that—in the United States, and we have got to protect those thousands of our boys on their way through—and during their stay—in our city."[83]

At a communion address one month later, Manhattan district attorney Frank Hogan was even starker in his discussion of wartime police responsibility. Hogan alerted attendees, "Your work was never more important than it is now." He reminded officers that enlisted men came into New York City from Schuyler, Totten, and Hamilton Forts, as well as from Manhattan Beach, Harts Island, Governors Island, Mitchel Field, and Floyd Bennet Field. Men also came off the naval and merchant ships docked in the city and traveled from camps as far as one hundred miles away to spend their furlough in the city, Hogan noted. "It is safe to say," the district attorney declared, "that there are more service men in this city than you would find in any military camp in the country." Of these men, Hogan warned NYPD officers, "All of them are in your care."[84]

Civilian New Yorkers joined in the cause by alerting the mayor to conditions they considered dangerous to servicemen. A concerned resident described one of the "noisiest places" on the Upper East Side where an "informant" had found "drunken soldiers and prostitutes right on the street."[85] Another New Yorker wrote to the mayor in January 1945 describing a "gang of thugs" playing a "shell game and a three card monte game" on the Interborough Rapid Transit platform at Penn Station. According to the author, the game was "promoted for the boys of the Armed Forces coming from the Penn R.R. Station." The writer demanded that the mayor "give some protection to those sailors and soldiers arriving at that point."[86] Following the complaint, the NYPD's Third Division in Manhattan kept the station under close surveillance but witnessed no further gambling. Despite this absence of visible lawbreaking, "all concerned have been . . . instructed to give location complained of special and continued attention."[87]

The introduction of a national curfew provoked a revealing response from city officials regarding the rights of Gotham's entertainment industry and the enlisted men who patronized its venues. In February 1945, James Byrnes issued a nationwide curfew of midnight for all places of entertainment in an effort to conserve coal and reduce labor needed for nighttime travel.[88] La Guardia, always believing in New York City's exceptional nature, requested an extra hour curfew exemption for Gotham's nightlife. Byrnes diplomatically denied the mayor's request.[89]

Members of the NYPD received clear instructions on how to enforce—or not enforce—such a curfew. Chief Inspector John J. O'Connell telephoned all borough commanders with the directive "not to arrest or molest soldiers, sailors, marines, or other members of the armed forces found by police in unlicensed premises, or premises where curfew violations were being committed." The order emphasized that no charges in connection with the violations were to be brought against servicemen, though civilian customers of such places were to be taken into custody. Police were directed to inform enlisted men of the "curfew-violating status" of the establishments and to suggest that the soldiers immediately vacate the premises.[90] Unlike that of the civilian gamblers or women found in such establishments, enlisted men's time and mobility were considered essential to the war effort and therefore were not to be infringed on through arrest or incarceration.

Though the exemption from arrest for curfew violation protected enlisted men from incarceration, gambling could also pose other dangers. An anguished letter sent to the mayor at the end of the war articulated other ways that gambling could undermine the security of men in the military. The letter writer, who signed his name "veteran World War II," declared, "Thank goodness I returned safely but to what a strained family relationship and not one dollar saved, but plenty of debts." He recounted how he and his mother had extracted a promise from his father to cease gambling and save money from his wartime defense job. Despite this foresight, "gambling is the very cause of our predicament." The writer stated he had "thought wartime put a stop to this," but he had discovered his father's regular spots to be "as brazen as ever, if not more so." He attributed the spots to "a gangster clique" operating with the support of "pigs that are in back of them and protect them."[91]

In his letter, "veteran World War II" articulated the ways that some New Yorkers felt exploited and victimized by the city's gamblers. This was one of the central concerns that motivated the mayor's anti-gambling crusades. He shared the letter with listeners of his weekly broadcast on August 26, 1945. He then wondered, "Look here, Mr. Inspector. . . . Why should this boy come home to find even his allotment stolen from his father by bums and thieves?" The mayor ordered, "You fellows on post there, what have you got a night stick for? I want those bums cleaned out of that neighborhood. I don't want to get letters like this from veterans."[92] To La Guardia, the letter writer's status as a veteran made his exploitation by gamblers all the more despicable. Having fulfilled his civic responsibility abroad, he returned to, in the mayor's framework, find his family's security undermined by a threat at home.

Although the mayor, the police commissioner, and many in the public viewed gamblers as antipatriotic at best and traitorous at worst, some New Yorkers disagreed. Gotham's gamblers framed restrictions on civil liberties as the true violation of the spirit of the American war effort. The members of the Sporting Women's Moral Club, for example, who identified themselves as "a group of twenty women, some of [whom] are mothers of veterans, some are wives of businessmen," proclaimed their commitment to the races. They criticized the mayor for denouncing horse race players and, seeking to turn La Guardia's own moralizing against his administration, threatened to publicize the names of "many of the officials that you appointed [who] are carrying on in an adulterous state."[93] Mrs. Bush wrote to La Guardia to "register her protest" against the arrest of two men in Madison Square Garden for "harmless" betting. She argued police protection was lacking "in my own neighborhood. Meanwhile police are employed in such foolishness."[94] These critics, though creative, represented a small minority. They were far outnumbered by those who wrote in support of the mayor's anti-gambling campaigns like "veteran World War II."

The assumption that predatory gamblers lured innocent enlisted men into vice was punctured in August 1945 by the case of George Sturm and Josephine Allen. Patrolman Henry Schnitzer arrested Sturm, a navy yeoman assigned to the Naval Induction Center in Grand Central Palace, for taking bets on horse races. Schnitzer claimed to have heard that "a pretty waitress" at a bar and grill on Third Avenue was accepting bets and turning them over to a uniformed sailor, who, in turn, relayed them via a nearby telephone. Following their arrest, Sturm and Allen, the waitress, each sought to point the finger at the other. Sturm denied accepting any money from Allen. Allen cleverly invoked gender and class stereotypes, stating, "I guess I'm a dumb waitress and not a clever bookmaker." Allen also implied that she had felt compelled to assist an enlisted man, stating that she had accepted bets but "only to help out the sailor, without getting any money for it." A gobsmacked Magistrate Joseph Glebocki of the gamblers court declared, "This is the first time I ever heard of a United States sailor being charged with bookmaking." The *New York Times* recorded the "amazement" of everyone in the courtroom over the circumstances of a member of the navy caught in such a predicament.[95] Although Sturm's actions disrupted the perception that men in uniform were solely the victims of gamblers, the widespread surprise at his case reveals the rarity of this type of arrest during the war. NYPD officers were directed to protect — not arrest — white servicemen. Their Black counterparts, however, faced a very different type of policing.

"Rumor, Vicious Innuendo, and False Reports": Policing Black Servicemen on Staten Island

While wartime policing was organized around protecting white enlisted men from the risks associated with gambling, Black soldiers and sailors enjoyed no such protection from even the most unfounded accusations of gambling and other crimes. In the spring of 1945, charges of gambling, disorderly behavior, and attacks against white women levied against Black soldiers stationed in northeastern Staten Island were met with the "largest concentration of police in the history of Staten Island," in the words of the *New York Herald-Tribune*.[96] The police formed part of a "small army," according to the island's daily paper, the *Staten Island Advance*, comprising "police, detectives and MPs [military police] imported from Manhattan — more than 200 in all — [who] patrolled a three-mile square area."[97] While the NYPD and military police patrolled the streets outside, enlisted men inside the camp were denied weekend passes and had their persons searched for knives up to three times a night.[98] Soldiers stationed at Fox Hills told an investigator for the NAACP that they felt like "prisoners of war."[99]

The events that culminated in this frenzy of surveillance and racist hysteria began in February 1945. A small group of white business owners and residents, led by Staten Island district attorney Farrell M. Kane, began complaining about a "wave" of crimes that they attributed to the Black soldiers stationed at Fox Hills. Most of these complaints stemmed from vague references to rumors of crimes rather than actual incidents. The small number of Stapleton residents who did report specific crimes later either retracted their statements or were contradicted by evidence provided by other witnesses. Regardless of their spuriousness, these accusations launched a monthslong debate about racism, crime, and policing on Staten Island during the war. The response from city officials and the NYPD to these debates revealed the white-only parameters of the department's policies of protection and leniency toward servicemen.[100]

The criminalization of the soldiers on Staten Island was one example among many of the racism that Black men experienced in the armed forces. Three million Black men registered for service in the armed forces, where they worked under segregated and discriminatory conditions.[101] As historian Kimberley L. Phillips has noted, with the passage of the Selective Service Act in 1940, each branch of the military adopted a "Negro Policy" that restricted the numbers of Black enlistees and circumscribed their responsibilities.[102] The hypocrisy of experiencing racial discrimination while being called on to fulfill duties of wartime citizenship in a war "for democracy" ignited many acts of protest within the military and among civilians.[103] Furthermore, Black soldiers served as meaningful civic symbols and leaders both during and after the war.[104]

Black residents of New York City encountered discrimination and hypocrisy in the armed forces in numerous ways. More than a million city residents across races served in the military throughout the war, which would have included roughly 600,000 Black Gothamites, if Black enlistment was proportional to the city's population.[105] The journalist Nat Brandt estimated that the Black population of Harlem decreased by about 25,000 people after 1940, many of whom, he proposes, left for military service or defense jobs.[106] Despite this participation, many Black New Yorkers questioned the wartime priorities of the U.S. government and doubted that the wartime commitment to democracy would extend to their own lives. A spring 1942 survey from the U.S. Office of Facts and Figures interviewed about 1,000 Black New Yorkers and 500 white Gothamites regarding their perspectives on the war. Between 34 and 45 percent of the Black respondents stated that the nation's foremost concern should be establishing democracy at home instead of defeating enemies abroad.[107] Additionally, 18 percent of Black respondents surveyed by Black interviewers believed that their lives would be improved if Japan won, illustrating relatively widespread Afro-Asian solidarity and distrust in postwar racial advances under American rule.[108]

Those who stayed behind in New York worried about their enlisted family members, who were often sent south for training. For Black civilian

Americans, the mistreatment of family members, friends, and comrades in the military was a source of indignation and concern, as the pages of the *Amsterdam News*, the *New York Age*, the *People's Voice*, and many other Black newspapers attest. Black Gothamites also witnessed racist treatment of soldiers stationed in or passing through the city limits. Black New Yorkers who enlisted in the Coast Guard in 1942 were housed in segregated sleeping quarters and mess halls at Brooklyn's Manhattan Beach training facility.[109] In 1943, Harlem residents rose up in protest after a white police officer shot a Black soldier during an altercation with a Black woman at the Braddock Hotel. Though La Guardia sought to reduce racial tensions in the city following the uprising, Black soldiers continued to experience racist treatment and attacks. Almost two years after the Harlem uprising, the mistreatment of Black soldiers in Staten Island led to a citywide controversy.

Black soldiers first arrived at the Fox Hills Army Housing Facility in the predominantly white neighborhood of Stapleton, Staten Island, in the spring of 1944. They quickly encountered discrimination and hostility inside and outside the walls of the facility. The soldiers numbered between 2,000 and 3,000, and they hailed mostly from the South. At Fox Hills, they worked as stevedores and porters, loading ships at the nearby Staten Island Terminal, before shipping out around the world.[110] They labored alongside higher-paid civilian members of the American Federation of Labor and Italian prisoners of war working in Italian service units. In interviews with the *New York Amsterdam News*, soldiers stationed at Fox Hills expressed frustration with "being used as laborers when they are capable of doing other things" and with racial segregation at the encampment.[111] At the end of their day, a military police officer accompanied the soldiers on a march back to the Fox Hills facility. The Italian prisoners of war, in contrast, received rides to and from their detail.[112] During the course of the soldiers' marches, which reminded some men of chain gangs of imprisoned Black workers in the South, white civilians from the surrounding neighborhoods gathered nearby to jeer at the passing soldiers.[113] As Martha Biondi has noted, though "racial harassment of Black soldiers is mostly associated with military bases in the South, it happened wherever the segregated military happened to be, including Fox Hills."[114] Despite being stationed in New York City, far from the battlefronts in Germany and Japan or the terrorism of the American South, the soldiers were still in dangerous territory.

Fox Hills had been open for less than a year when Staten Island district attorney Farrell M. Kane began launching public accusations against the servicemen stationed at the facility. Kane, who was a politically ambitious

Democrat, regaled the press and military authorities with a description of petty crimes purportedly committed by the enlisted men. Kane stated that, though additional police and detectives had already been assigned to the East Shore area, robberies and misbehavior like gambling from the soldiers were on the rise.[115] In response to Kane's complaints, the NYPD assigned additional patrolmen and detectives to monitor the areas around the army facility.[116] Though city officials, NYPD officers, and many residents viewed white enlisted men as people in need of protection, the Richmond County district attorney, Valentine, NYPD members, and some white Staten Island residents viewed Black servicemen as a danger from which they required protection.

Kane's claims surged through the city's presses. The *New York Times*, the *Brooklyn Daily Eagle*, the *Daily News*, and the *Herald-Tribune* all covered the "crime wave" regularly and salaciously.[117] The *Amsterdam News* and the *People's Voice* conducted their own investigations and determined the concern about crime around Fox Hills to be untrue and racially motivated. The more conservative Black paper the *New York Age* also wrote frequently about the accusations, but with a different analytical bent.[118] On Staten Island throughout March and April 1945, residents could read write-ups of Kane's campaign in almost every issue of the *Staten Island Advance*, the borough's most widely circulated paper.[119]

The citywide press coverage included inflammatory and inaccurate stories like one that ran in the *New York Times* under the headline "Staten Island Widow of Hero Is Attacked." The story described the accusation from a white woman that a Black soldier had raped her. The journalist labeled the woman the "widow of a soldier killed in Europe," though she was later found to be the wife of a deceased civilian. Additionally, her accused rapist was never found and many inconsistencies emerged within the woman's account.[120] The theme of imperiled white femininity ran through many of the stories white residents and journalists shared about the soldiers. By emphasizing the woman's relationship to an enlisted man, the author situated the story within a larger narrative that Kane and his supporters were constructing in which patriotic white citizens in Staten Island were sacrificing for the war and having their security undermined by criminal Black soldiers. The persistent press coverage of the accusations of crime around Fox Hills kept the issue on the minds of city officials, activists, and Staten Island residents.

Business and homeowners' associations worked with Kane to spread a narrative that framed their animosity toward the soldiers through both a race-neutral rhetoric of criminality and a timely threat of racial conflict. The Stapleton Businessmen's Association shared its concern about crime with the press and floated suggestions that businesses close early for the protection of owners and patrons.[121] The association held and publicized meetings with the commander of Fox Hills to discuss how they could "further guard" against the criminal activity of soldiers.[122] On March 13, 250 residents and business owners signed a petition asking for additional police protection to "end hoodlumism" among troops stationed at Fox Hills. Authors informed authorities that "the situation seems to be getting out of hand . . . [and] unless such action is taken at once, serious race disorders may result."[123] Rather than explicitly stating their opposition to living near Black soldiers, signatories relied on racially coded language of criminality and invoked "hoodlumism" and "race disorders." The threat of such "disorders" loomed large in the minds of Mayor La Guardia and Commissioner Valentine after the unrest in Detroit and the uprising in Harlem in 1943. Avoiding any similar conflicts, more so than ensuring civil rights, was a wartime priority for the municipal leaders.

Journalists writing for the city's Black newspapers combatted this narrative and argued that the accusations against Black soldiers were an expression of racism that predated the soldiers' arrival. Journalists called into question the details of the assaults and elevated inconsistencies that had been reported by the police or the military. The *People's Voice*'s Llewellyn Ransom, who often covered policing, commented that it was the opinion of "some" that "Negro troops were never wanted in this area by prejudiced elements in the population."[124] In the *Amsterdam News*, Carl Dunbar Lawrence declared, "There is no crime wave on Staten Island . . . but there is rumor, vicious innuendo, and false reports that Negro soldiers are morally unfit for service." Lawrence went on to point out holes in other reports of supposed crimes committed by the soldiers. Some of the discrepancies that Lawrence highlighted were later affirmed in police investigations.[125] During a later grand jury investigation into the accusations, Lawrence argued that the rumors about enlisted men on Staten Island were "actually a conspiracy to make it appear that our boys in uniform are primarily concerned about white women, cheap liquor, and gambling."[126] Despite the inconsistencies in many of the accounts, the calls for a heavier police presence from Kane's supporters persisted.

In response to these calls, La Guardia, Valentine, and the army responded with a public show of force and a covert effort to dissipate concern from the city's Black communities about violations of the rights of the soldiers. The mayor announced that he was working with the army to "prevent conflicts of violence between civilians and servicemen" and that he supported sending extra police officers to "guard the section."[127] Army officials and Valentine both dramatically increased their surveillance of the soldiers stationed at Fox Hills. Soldiers were searched before leaving the grounds and heavily policed once they exited the facility. The army added over 120 officers from both the Second Service Command and the Staten Island Terminal to monitor the area.[128] More than 200 officers in the NYPD and the military police patrolled the neighborhood surrounding the camp.[129] In addition to this band of patrolmen, the NYPD also called in supervising officers from Manhattan and Queens.[130]

At the same time, La Guardia's administration embarked on a less public effort to investigate and de-escalate the situation in Staten Island. In the wake of the Harlem uprising of 1943, La Guardia had formed the interracial Committee on Unity, whose central mandate was to preserve order in the city. The committee supported gradual policies to improve life for minority New Yorkers, with the goal of deterring mass protests or uprisings.[131] Staten Island borough president Joseph Palma, a racial liberal with similar politics to La Guardia's, had formed a comparable committee for the borough, known as the Council for Democracy. In the wake of the rape accusation, the Staten Island council reached out to the Committee on Unity to request assistance, which the committee quickly provided.[132] Members of the committee found that two soldiers, Privates Curtis Williams and Haywood Arrington, who had been arrested as part of the "crime wave," were being imprisoned without representation. The committee further made note of "widespread apprehension in the Negro communities of the city that the legal rights of these men would not be adequately protected." Lawyers affiliated with the committee volunteered to represent the men in an effort to "safeguard this situation," and the group began its own quiet investigation.[133]

The widespread coverage of the campaign against the Fox Hills soldiers had also provoked the attention of Roy Wilkins, national acting secretary of the NAACP. Wilkins, who worked out of the organization's Manhattan office, determined to find out "just what the situation is" around Fox Hills, overruling the relatively minimal actions that were being taken by Staten Island's NAACP branch and its leader, Clarence De Hart.[134] Wilkins hired white investigator A. B. Owens to interview Staten Islanders.[135] The acting secretary also wrote to La Guardia about the treatment of the soldiers in Stapleton. "Negro citizens protest this smear campaign against a whole race and call upon you to require the police of the city to have no part in it," Wilkins proclaimed to the mayor.[136]

Ultimately, the army, the mayor's committee, and the NAACP all launched covert investigations into the accusations of the crime wave. All three investigators found evidence of racism among white residents but believed that the "crime wave" rumors had spread from borough politicians, particularly Kane and Staten Island councilman Frederick Schick, down rather than from residents up. The army's investigator stated that "these rumors are being spread by people whose interests would be furthered by the removal of these soldiers from this community."[137] Owens concluded that "from this office [of Kane] has come all the loud noise that has resulted in much rumor and gossip prevalent on Staten Island."[138] The executive director of the Committee on Unity made a similar comment in a thinly veiled criticism of Kane in a 1946 issue of the *Journal of Educational Sociology*.[139]

While the army, the mayor's committee, and the NAACP worked on the undercover investigations, Kane and his allies sought to keep their version of events in the public eye. Kane launched a grand jury investigation into the crime rumors, which began on March 20, 1945.[140] Kane's supporters constructed an argument that emphasized the wartime sacrifice of white Staten Islanders and framed their criticism of Black soldiers as an expression of white citizenship rights. On March 21, Schick—of whom the *New Yorker* wrote in fall 1944, "In his four terms in the council [he] has not opened his mouth except to yawn or incert [sic] a cigar"—raised the issue before the council.[141] The councilman asked that "adequate steps" be taken by police and the military to protect the lives and property of Staten Islanders. Schick's resolution described Staten Island as "a community of law-abiding citizens, consisting of families whose sons are fighting in foreign lands for the preservation of peace throughout the world."[142] In this rhetoric, the councilman implicitly claimed that it was Staten Island's white residents who were performing the duties of citizenship, rather than the enlisted soldiers stationed at Fox Hills. City councilman Ben Davis, the representative from Harlem and a leading member of the Communist Party, objected to Schick's resolution, which was then tabled.[143]

The ultimate results of the complaints and the presentment were heightened surveillance from both the city and the army, increased criminalization of the soldiers, and political advancement for the politicians at the center of the episode. Army officials transferred over 1,000 soldiers off the island and received funds from the War Department to build a new guardhouse, a service club inside the facilities, and a fence to enclose the perimeter of the camp, all of which would further separate soldiers from the Staten Island community.[144] More than 200 additional NYPD officers patrolled the area.[145]

For Kane and Schick, the "crime wave" proved politically profitable. Kane continued to serve as district attorney until August 1947, when he went on to win election as a city court justice on a joint Democratic and Liberal party ticket.[146] Schick won his reelection in 1945 and used his position to introduce bills to allow police officers to gain raises more quickly and to oppose tax increases.[147] For Haywood Arrington and Curtis Williams, however, who had been arrested during the crime wave accusations, there were costs. Both pleaded not guilty to charges related to their involvement in a fight and had the support of other service members stationed at Fox Hills at their trials.[148] Regardless of this testimony, Judge Thomas J. Walsh of Richmond County Court at St. George sentenced Arrington and Williams to two and a half to five years and twelve and a half to twenty-five years, respectively, at Sing Sing Prison.[149]

Conclusion

Throughout the 1930s and 1940s, La Guardia's administration and the NYPD declared themselves at war with Gotham's gamblers. This battle was partly symbolic; La Guardia and Valentine positioned gamblers as representative of Tammany corruption and the violence of organized crime during the Prohibition years. Furthermore, La Guardia throwing slot machines into the Long Island Sound or shouting about driving gamblers from the city limits made for good press. But these campaigns were about more than publicity. The administrators believed in their own symbolism and thought that aggressive enforcement of anti-gambling laws was central to the creation of a meritocratic, equitable, and preeminent city.

They also put significant resources behind this effort; in 1940, the roughly 18,000 members of the NYPD made 34,006 gambling-related arrests.[150] Though these arrests did not always result in long imprisonments, they did disrupt people's lives and serve as justification for police surveillance that further restricted the ways that New Yorkers moved through their neighborhoods and their lives. For Black New Yorkers, who were constructed as likely gamblers and whose neighborhoods received disproportionate attention in these gambling crackdowns, the costs were particularly high.

The war rendered this policing more important than ever in La Guardia's and Valentine's minds and provided new ways of justifying increased surveillance. Debates about the appropriate scope of the wartime state structured this policing, as did gendered conceptions of masculine citizenship. For Valentine, La Guardia, and many New Yorkers, gambling among civilian men during the war symbolized their rejection of the wartime duties of male citizenship. The NYPD's treatment of gamblers was influenced by this ideology and diverged depending on men's relationship to the wartime state.

The episode on Staten Island revealed the unspoken racial limitations of the calls to protect enlisted men. La Guardia, Valentine, city magistrates, and other NYPD officials invoked the need to safeguard servicemen from being preyed on as a justification for cracking down on gamblers. Police department leaders directed NYPD officers to avoid arresting soldiers and sailors caught gambling or breaking curfew, to further shield them from the consequences of these violations. The success of white Staten Island residents in levying accusations of criminality against Black soldiers indicates that these narratives of protection did not extend to Black servicemen. African American soldiers not only merited less protection than their white counterparts but, according to white Staten Islanders and city officials, presented a danger from which white New Yorkers deserved protection. White Staten Islanders' complaints about criminality also increased the racial segregation of leisure in their community by justifying the creation of more onsite recreational facilities inside the Fox Hills facility. Anxiety among residents and city officials about interracial leisure was not limited to Staten Island. Throughout the war, calls to protect white servicemen from contracting venereal diseases and from being exposed to immoral entertainment legitimized more aggressive policing of entertainment, with a particular focus on working-class and interracial spaces.

CHAPTER SIX

They Do Not Go There to Say a Padre Nostre
Policing Nightlife in Wartime Harlem

Throughout the 1930s and 1940s, Gotham's dancehalls, cabarets, buffet flats, taverns, and theaters became sites where NYPD officers, performers, leisure workers, patrons, and city officials clashed over conceptions of criminality and the rights of urban citizenship. Mayor Fiorello La Guardia and Police Commissioner Lewis Valentine's campaigns against the sex workers, juvenile delinquents, and gamblers whom the duo viewed as disrupting the morality and social order of the city penetrated into spaces and neighborhoods that city leaders associated with these groups. Officials worried that in these venues barriers of race, class, and sexuality could be violated or reimagined, with perilous and unpredictable consequences.[1] La Guardia, Valentine, and Commissioner of Licenses Paul Moss, another key player in these efforts, sought to imprint their vision of urban order on the city's leisure landscape by enforcing the city's prohibitions on "disorderly spaces."

La Guardia, Valentine, and Moss's approach differed from that of their Tammany Hall predecessors. Under the Tammany system, a venue's status was often determined by the owner's connections to the Democratic club or ability to pay the required bribes.[2] La Guardia, Valentine, and Moss, in contrast, sought to rid the city completely of establishments they dubbed sites of "depravity." They contended that such venues "endanger[ed] public morality" and proved "a disgrace to the people of the City of New York."[3] Venues could be labeled disorderly if their owners or managers allowed criminalized groups, including sex workers, gamblers, youth, gay and gender-nonconforming New Yorkers, and interracial parties, to patronize or work at the venue. Because of the gender, race, and class associations that undergirded these criminal categories, venues that catered to Black audiences, working-class patrons, or single women also became subject to aggressive policing. City leaders' efforts to segregate, homogenize, and desexualize the city's nightlife, however, met resistance from criminalized populations, venue owners, and the courts in the prewar years.[4] The mobilization for war changed the political context for these leisure policing campaigns and weakened opposition.

After the nation's entrance into World War II, city leaders intensified their nightlife surveillance and met with greater success in their efforts to combat venues that they now argued posed a threat to the sexual and moral health of enlisted men visiting the city. The national Social Protection Division, U.S. Army, and municipal Health Department all contributed resources to bolster these campaigns. These collaborations, combined with the wartime necessity of protecting enlisted men, strengthened the ideological incentives and institutional forces mobilized against spaces of social and sexual experimentation and interracial mixing. To La Guardia and his allies, such spaces were always a threat to the city; during the war, they became a threat to the nation itself.

This chapter explores efforts by the mayor, Valentine, Moss, the city's health commissioner, and military officials to surveil, restrict, and criminalize nightlife in Harlem, the neighborhood on which officials most intensely focused these campaigns, as well as how residents and activists combatted these intrusions. The war became a justification for increasing the NYPD's presence in the neighborhood and closing down its most well-known dancehall, the Savoy Ballroom. In contrast to other cities, where local police and the Social Protection Division demonstrated a degree of disinterest in the sexual practices of Black women during the war, in New York City Black women and the spaces where they supposedly met white servicemen were an intense focus of La Guardia and Valentine's police campaigns.[5] Despite mass activism and resistance against racist policing led by Black women themselves, La Guardia and Valentine succeeded in expanding surveillance and policing in Harlem during the war under the rationale that, as the mayor proclaimed in a 1944 letter to the commandant of New York's Naval District, when soldiers and sailors set out for Harlem's dancehalls, burlesque theaters, saloons, and taverns, "they d[id] not go there to say a Padre Nostre."[6]

The NYPD's Leisure Surveillance Infrastructure

Throughout his tenure as police commissioner, Valentine sought to bolster the department's penetration into the world of New York's nightlife. This advance reflected one of Valentine's core policing philosophies: that "the best efforts of the police should be directed against morals offenses."[7] So-called morals offenses were legal violations and crimes that disrupted racist, classist, gendered, and heterosexist hierarchies. Valentine, rightly, believed that some establishments in the city's leisure landscape provided opportunities to violate these divisions by allowing people to socialize freely. After assuming office, he launched mass raids on nightclubs throughout the city to restrict these freedoms, rounding up suspected gamblers and sex workers, and fought for expanded police power to arrest people with criminal records in nightclubs or dancehalls.[8]

In early 1938, unsatisfied with the department's progress in combatting vice, Valentine reorganized the NYPD's vice department. He moved twenty-five ranking lieutenants into leadership positions in plainclothes anti-vice units and assigned fifty "top-ranking patrolmen" to special training on morals law enforcement, with the possibility of vice assignments depending on their progress. Additionally, department members assigned to morals law enforcement would no longer have the option of refusing their assignment, which had been prior department policy. "Now the commissioner is giving his best men the task of cleaning up the city with orders to deliver, or face demotion," the *New York Times* proclaimed of the change.[9] NYPD tactics for cleaning up late-1930s Gotham built on practices previously embraced by investigators of private anti-vice associations, such as the Committee of Fourteen, which included undercover surveillance. In the economic Depression of the early 1930s, the Committee of Fourteen folded, no longer able to garner sufficient funds. The NYPD stepped into the breach, shouldering an expanded role in nightlife policing. Through mass campaigns and reorganizations, Valentine sought to both expand and depoliticize anti-vice policing, key priorities in the post-Seabury policing landscape.

La Guardia, Valentine, and Moss crafted their approach to policing 1930s nightlife in a landscape that was being reshaped by the legalization of alcohol. The 1933 passage of the Twenty-First Amendment repealing alcohol prohibition moved venues that served alcohol out of the underground economy and into the regulation of the state. As historian Anna Lvovsky notes, the amendment "did not just bring legal alcohol back into American bars. It also brought the police."[10] In New York City, these police included uniformed patrolmen, plainclothes detectives, members of NYPD vice squads, and investigators with the newly formed New York State Liquor Authority (SLA). The SLA possessed the power to grant, refuse, or revoke liquor licenses. SLA agents worked with members of the NYPD to surveil suspect establishments. Bar owners and managers themselves were also newly incentivized to prohibit "disorderliness" to keep their liquor licenses.[11]

If bar staff failed to uphold these responsibilities, the NYPD had a wide range of prohibitions governing leisure venues, the violation of which could lead to temporary or permanent revocation of licenses or criminal charges for owners or employees. For example, the NYPD Manual of Procedure in 1940 stated that women entertainers and employees of cabarets were not permitted to "mingle or sit with patrons or guests," prohibited employment of "homosexualists or persons pretending to be such," and stated that employees were required to "promptly report" any "unlawful or disorderly act[s]" committed in the venue to the nearest precinct. Dancehalls were directed to ban "disorderly, obscene, or immoral conduct or dancing" and to bar "persons with criminal records, gangsters, racketeers, prostitutes, pimps, procurers, degenerates, homo-sexualists or persons pretending to be such."[12] Furthermore, any establishment in which a morals law violation occurred could be labeled a "raided premise," which would result in the stationing of a uniformed member of the force on the premises. These vague and wide-ranging prohibitions gave NYPD higher-ups, plainclothesmen, and uniformed officers broad latitude to surveil and police the city's nightlife.

Policing Leisure in 1930s Harlem

Valentine directed his officers to use their latitude aggressively in Harlem, the city's largest and most influential Black neighborhood. The NYPD's nightlife policing served as one excuse for the department's heavy occupation of the uptown Manhattan community. This dynamic was the result of the racist policies of the NYPD, which constructed Black women and men as vice law violators and criminalized interracial socializing, but it was also influenced by the racialized histories of licit and illicit entertainment and employment in Gotham.

New York City across boroughs, and Harlem in particular, was transformed by the Great Migration in the early twentieth century. From the violent termination of Reconstruction through World Wars I and II, Black Americans fled the U.S. South to urban centers in the North and West in a process that Isabel Wilkerson describes as transitioning from "a little-noticed march of the impatient" to a "flood of the discontented" to eventually become "a virtual rite of passage for young southerners."[13] Afro-Caribbean immigrants also moved to New York City in large numbers during this period, and Gotham's Black population increased by 66 percent between 1910 and 1920 and by another 115 percent between 1920 and 1930.[14]

Though Black migrants came to the city seeking improved economic, social, and political opportunities, many struggled to find housing or work. Housing discrimination meant that Harlem was one of the few neighborhoods in which Black residents could secure lodging.[15] Lutie Johnson, the protagonist of writer Ann Petry's groundbreaking 1946 novel *The Street*, reflects on the effects of housing discrimination in cities like New York, noting, "They set up a line and say black folks on this side and white folks on this side, so that the black folks were crammed on top of each other."[16] This discrimination overcrowded the housing stock in Harlem and robbed Black New Yorkers of many choices in where to make their homes.

The neighborhood, however, was also a destination and reprieve for many Black people. In *The Street*, Johnson reflects that upon exiting the subway in Harlem, Black New Yorkers were "freed from the contempt in the eyes of the downtown world" and able to laugh and take up space.[17] The city within a city became a center for Black cultural and political creativity, including a vibrant and diverse nightlife. Venues like the Savoy Ballroom, as well as more underground spaces and networks for leisure, were important sources of employment and income for Black New Yorkers, who were excluded from so many of the city's labor sectors.[18] The Great Depression further circumscribed Black New Yorkers' already limited employment options.[19] In addition to discrimination in housing and employment, Black New Yorkers had to contend with white Gothamites' perceptions of Harlem as a place for their own leisure and sexual experimentation.[20] In this context, some Black activists called for a heavier police presence in the neighborhood as a means of reducing vice and crime.[21] These dynamics, both neglect and racist criminalization, structured the policing of Harlem. Ultimately, however, Commissioner Valentine and other NYPD leaders saw the neighborhood as a space for crime because Black people lived there.

Valentine framed Harlem and Black New Yorkers as particular sources of disorder, vice, and crime.[22] In the press, the commissioner described the uptown neighborhood as so dangerous that "even my own men are not safe" on its streets.[23] Valentine believed the city's growing Black and Puerto Rican population had "turned the whites right out" of Harlem, Bedford-Stuyvesant in Brooklyn, and Jamaica, Queens, and contended that these nonwhite residents were particular "problems" for the NYPD.[24] La Guardia was far less openly hostile toward Black residents than his police commissioner. He was, however, reluctant to take targeted steps to improve life for Black New Yorkers and declined to pressure Valentine to change racist NYPD practices. The cumulative effect of these forms of racism in the city's policing practices was that Black New Yorkers were regularly criminalized and attacked by police officers and rarely received any assistance from the police when they themselves were the victims of crimes. The overall impact of the NYPD on Black communities, therefore, was a violent one, which came in the forms of criminalization, physical attacks, and ignored requests for assistance or protection.[25]

Black New Yorkers protested their unequal experiences of crime and policing in a mass uprising in March 1935 and the investigation that followed.

In the wake of the uprising, which was spurred by a belief that police had killed an Afro–Puerto Rican teenager, Harlem residents publicly critiqued the NYPD's racist and violent policing practices. At hearings held by a mayoral commission investigating the uprising's causes, 160 residents detailed police violence, harassment, illegal searches of persons and homes, and arrests for walking in interracial couples.[26] In the commission's subsequent report, its authors cited Harlem residents' outrage over racist policing as a cause of the uprising. They also noted that police violence during the event worsened these feelings. During the uprising, police officers beat and arrested many Harlemites and shot and killed Lloyd Hobbs, a sixteen-year-old boy who was running away from police on the street. Commissioners noted that "lack of confidence in the police and even hostility towards these representatives of the law . . . has been built up over many years of experience with the police in this section."[27]

The commission proposed a slate of changes that could have radically undermined racist policing in Harlem. It recommended that police officers close down dancehalls or other venues that refused entry to Black patrons in violation of New York State's civil rights law. It suggested that police be directed not to bother interracial couples and that officers who violated this direction be dismissed from the police force. The commission proposed the establishment of an independent committee to which residents could bring complaints about police mistreatment, which would decades later be known as a civilian complaint review board, and that officers who violate the law be subjected to punishment by the district attorney "just as vigorously as where any other person is charged with a crime."[28] The idea that an independent body and the courts might hold police officers accountable to the citizens they policed would prove so threatening to police authority that when a version of the review board was created, it would be targeted by coalitions of racists, conservatives, and pro-police activists repeatedly from the 1950s through the 2020s.[29] In the 1930s, a review board could have protected citizens who made complaints against police from retribution and potentially reduced police violence and harassment against Black New Yorkers. Instead, the 1935 recommendations went unheeded, police assaults continued, and the political space for critiques of them narrowed. Police occupation of Harlem under the guise of surveilling "disorderly premises" intensified during the war and catalyzed another mass uprising less than ten years later.[30] The robust 1935 challenges to police authority would not be reiterated in the wake of the Harlem uprising of 1943. In the law-and-order context of the war years, such extensive criticism of the police would be framed as an unpatriotic attempt to undermine the war effort.[31]

Even in the prewar years of the 1930s, La Guardia and Valentine responded dismissively to the commission's report. Despite the broad public participation that went into its production, the mayor never released the document, and it was only through publication in the *Amsterdam News* in July 1936 that the report received a public audience. According to the commission, Valentine "maintained that there was no reason for disciplinary action against the police . . . and even justified the action of the police [in some cases]."[32] The commissioner declined to change the racist policies within the police department, which structured policing practices in Harlem. For example, rank-and-file members of the department and residents in Harlem and Bedford-Stuyvesant observed that white officers found guilty of being drunk on the job were sometimes assigned to precincts in these neighborhoods, though Valentine denied this practice.[33] Even in the face of such clear and widespread demands for change, the NYPD continued to criminalize Harlem, discriminate against Black department members, and shirk responsibility for responding to crime in the neighborhood.

The NYPD's refusal to take crime control seriously in Harlem was a source of distress and frustration for many residents. Criticism of police inaction took many forms and stemmed from varied political perspectives. Journalists and activists publicized cases in which Black New Yorkers were victims of violent attacks that provoked little to no police response.[34] Harlem residents contended that the NYPD permitted illegal businesses to operate uptown, allowing white owners of illicit establishments to extract profit from the neighborhood while forcing law-abiding Black residents to live in a dangerous and immoral environment. These complaints often came from property owners, but they were also voiced by working-class Black residents and expressive of intraclass conflict over questions of morality and informal labor.[35]

Though NYPD officers undoubtedly ignored requests for police responses to many kinds of crime in Harlem, they were quite active in arresting residents for vice law violations. Records suggest that by the mid-1930s, the police department was enforcing low-level anti-vice prohibitions in the neighborhood aggressively. Mayor La Guardia's Commission on the Harlem Riot reported that in the first six months of 1936, policy gambling and disorderly conduct arrests combined accounted for 61 percent of the total arrests of men made by Harlem's police precincts. During the same period, immoral conduct and vagrancy charges accounted for 80 percent of all arrests of women in these precincts. These records show that in the mid-1930s, not only was the NYPD enforcing low-level anti-vice policing in Harlem, but this enforcement was the vast majority of all arrests made by these precincts.[36]

Disorderly conduct, prostitution, gambling, and vagrancy arrests were both enabled by and a justification for police surveillance of leisure venues. During these prewar years, the NYPD monitored the Savoy and other Harlem hotspots, following up on Health Department reports that men had contracted venereal diseases from women they met on the premises of these establishments. Despite reports throughout the winter of 1938 and spring of 1939 that over a dozen patients at Health Department clinics throughout the New York area "had received their infection from girls whom they met at the Savoy Ballroom," the NYPD did not close the venue during this period.[37]

"An Insult to Negro Womanhood": Out-of-Bounds Policing and the Criminalization of Harlem Nightlife during the War

The Japanese attack on Pearl Harbor and the U.S. entrance into the war in late 1941 injected new wartime imperatives into the NYPD's responsibilities. Valentine regularly reminded department members that one of their primary wartime priorities was to protect enlisted men passing through the city. The experience of Private Robert Bandy, a Black soldier who was shot by an NYPD officer while in uniform in August 1943, and the treatment of Black soldiers stationed at Fox Hills in Staten Island, who were so criminalized and surveilled that they felt like "prisoners of war," make clear the racist limits of this protection.[38]

Valentine's attitude toward Harlem and nonwhite New Yorkers was refracted through the gender politics of wartime policing. Monitoring sexual and social interactions between men and women became an essential wartime responsibility of municipal police departments, according to this line of thinking. Building on anti–venereal disease policies enacted during World War I, federal enforcement agencies including the FBI and the newly formed Social Protection Division, as well as the military, provided municipal police departments like the NYPD with additional resources for the surveillance of women, particularly in interracial and nonelite leisure spaces with reputations for hosting enlisted men.[39]

While Valentine had continually framed Harlem as a source of crime and violence, he now constructed the neighborhood and Black women in and outside Harlem as a sexual threat to service members and men in wartime production. In remarks about a Black community in South Jamaica, Queens, the commissioner commented that police had "locked up so many women from there that we couldn't arraign them in the women's court." Valentine noted with approval that all the women arrested were forcibly tested for venereal disease, regardless of whether they were convicted of prostitution or any other offense. "We have been making progress," he remarked, ". . . and we hope [to] eliminate the number of infections not only in the armed forces but . . . in the men on the production line."[40]

Harlem was not the only neighborhood in the city that proved dangerous to enlisted men, according to Valentine, La Guardia, and Moss. The administrators also worried that Times Square provided a central point for vice and temptation with its theaters, burlesque shows, saloons, and taxi dancehalls, and that Central Park could host outdoor assignations.[41] Indeed, the United Service Organization's own Midtown Stage Door Canteen was a source of concern to some for its rejection of racial segregation.[42] Valentine assigned extra patrolmen and members of the auxiliary police agency, the City Patrol Corps, to monitor these neighborhoods. Over the course of the war, roughly 16,000 men and slightly under 2,000 women signed up for the patrol corps. The majority of these participants were working-class white men, some of whom joined for the opportunity to get into police work, while others did so under coercive threat of having their draft status reexamined.[43] NYPD officers shuttered dancehalls and burlesque theaters that had been accused of hosting immoral entertainment for soldiers and sailors, sometimes with assistance from patrol corps members.[44] The city leaders had attempted to close burlesque theaters in the late 1930s but were rebuffed by the state's appellate and supreme courts.[45]

The war mobilization presented a new context for this drive. Moss began refusing to renew licenses for well-known burlesque theaters in Midtown in early 1942 in a campaign the *Brooklyn Daily Eagle* labeled part of La Guardia's "drive to purify the city of burlesque for the protection of our boys in uniform."[46] Though La Guardia, Moss, and Valentine met opposition from theater owners, employees, and free-speech advocates, they succeeded in closing burlesque theaters in Midtown during the war. In April 1942, Judge Aaron Levy of the Supreme Court of the State of New York reversed the court's earlier ruling and sided with city officials, pronouncing the burlesque performances "predominantly offensive to public morals and decency."[47]

The same sentiments that justified closing burlesque theaters in Midtown undergirded an expanded police presence in venues and neighborhoods considered a threat to "public morals and decency" throughout the city. In the summer of 1942, in this context of heightened wartime surveillance, a fresh controversy arose over the practices of the NYPD in Harlem. The *New York Daily News* reported that, in conjunction with "the greatest vice campaign in the city's history" from Commissioner Valentine, the army and navy had declared Harlem "out of bounds for white service men."[48] The extant archives do not include a record of such an order, which would have barred white soldiers and sailors from the neighborhood and created official justification for NYPD officers, military police, and shore patrol to remove white men who violated the order. The archives do, however, include many communications between Valentine, La Guardia, and Major General T. A. Terry of the Second Service Command branch of the Army Service Forces at Governors Island in which the officials discuss their shared interest in protecting servicemen from prostitutes and venereal diseases. At semiregular conferences on anti-prostitution campaigns, these officials and their subordinates, along with representatives from the Health Department and the SLA, strategized about surveillance techniques to be used against what Valentine described as "the lower type of hotels, the 'taxi' dance halls, and the 'street-walkers.'"[49]

The surveillance network whose workers attended these meetings was both reactive, responding to accusations from men testing positive for sexually transmitted infections, and proactive, sending surveillance workers out to look for suspicious women. Both forms of surveillance were particularly intense in Midtown Manhattan and Harlem. Additionally, while the "out of bounds" report proved unsubstantiated in New York, the *Chicago Defender* reported on a similar order barring white sailors from parts of Chicago's South Side.[50] La Guardia would later suggest to a commandant of one of the city's naval districts that spaces declared "raided premises" by the NYPD be designated "out of bounds" for enlisted men.[51] The response of Harlem residents to the "out of bounds" rumor reflected this larger context.

Valentine, the health commissioner, and Terry all refuted the accusation after Harlem residents challenged the officials to explain the rumor.[52] The authors of the original *Daily News* article published another piece just one day later in which they stated that, according to Valentine, "there are no areas or locations within the city which service men are barred from entering." The authors commented obliquely on the source of the refuted designation, stating that "stories had been published, based on information from other police sources, that military and shore patrols had been assigned to keep white soldiers and sailors out of Harlem." The authors reflected that, "seemingly, the report among the police arose from the fact that roving patrols of M.P.'s and S.P.'s frequently had been seen there."[53] This statement suggests the practice of removing white enlisted men from Harlem was common enough among members of the military police and shore patrol that NYPD officers assumed it was official policy. If officially acknowledged, an "out of bounds" order would have made explicit the police department and military's practices of labeling Black women as prostitutes and venereal disease carriers, promoting segregated entertainment, and prioritizing the health and security of white soldiers over their Black counterparts. Such clearly articulated racist policing violated Valentine's approach of achieving these results through informal policies and practices.

Harlem activists and reporters took grave issue with the "out of bounds" rumor. The *People's Voice*, founded in 1942 by city councilmember and activist Adam Clayton Powell Jr., led the charge.[54] The *People's Voice* featured left-wing writers and activists and pulled some journalists from the more conservative *Amsterdam News*, including the *News'* first woman reporter, Marvel Cooke.[55] The *Voice* became one of the most vociferous critics of racist crime coverage and connected this criticism to police brutality against Black New Yorkers. The paper also became a platform and organizing tool used by Powell and other activists to speak out against police brutality and the criminalization of Harlem.[56] The *Voice* was widely read among Black New Yorkers; when over 1,000 Black Gothamites were asked about their reading habits as part of a survey by the Office of Facts and Figures in 1942, about 35 percent named the *Voice* as a paper they "usually read." Only the *Amsterdam News* was named more frequently. The authors of the same survey described Powell as the "one most important man in Harlem today" and said he occupied a "unique" position in the life of Harlem.[57] His efforts to generate activism around the "out of bounds" rumor rippled through the neighborhood and the city.

The *People's Voice* attacked the rumor on multiple fronts. When the rumor surfaced, *Voice* reporter Joe Bostic investigated the accusations and received assurance of their falsity from both Valentine and Health Commissioner Ernest Stebbins. Bostic emphasized that Times Square was a larger center of entertainment and vice and argued that "infinitesimal numbers" of white soldiers and sailors visited Harlem.[58] Protesters from the *People's Voice*, the Negro Labor Victory Committee, and the National Conference of Negro Youth picketed the *Daily News* with signs stating, "The Daily News Smears Harlem Again."[59]

A column penned by novelist and *People's Voice* staff writer Ann Petry explored the way Harlem women responded to the "out of bounds" rumor.

Many women felt personally insulted by the story. Isabelle Spiller was "boiling mad" when she heard the rumor. "I felt that the barring of white soldiers from this area because of prostitution was an insult to Negro womanhood," Spiller commented. Gladys Mason wondered, "If white soldiers are to be barred, what about Negro soldiers already stationed in this area?" Anna L. Moore shared that it was her "personal opinion that if the story is true it's a reflection on every decent woman in Harlem." These women and others interviewed, whom Petry described as "wax[ing] indignant," understood the rumor to be reinforcing the racist perception that Black women were prostitutes from whom white men needed police protection.[60] Photos of the *Daily News* pickets show women on the front line and making up a considerable portion of the protesters.[61] Protesters targeted the *Daily News* because of its regular practice of racist and sensualized crime coverage, an approach that was shared across many white New York dailies.[62] Accusations like the "out of bounds" order justified a large police presence in Harlem and increased the vulnerability of Harlem's Black women residents.[63]

Moore and Petry had recently formed a group that organized around issues like the "out of bounds" rumor that proved relevant to women of Harlem. The two women were, respectively, president and founding member of the organization Negro Women, Incorporated. The group held its first meeting in May 1942 in the *People's Voice* offices. Petry and Moore encouraged Harlem women to attend if they believed in "fighting for the rights of Negro women" or were "interested in yourself as a woman, in Harlem as a place in which to live during the war and after the war is over."[64] Negro Women Inc. was influenced by the housewives leagues and "don't buy where you can't work" campaigns that many Black women founded in the 1930s.[65] Petry had been involved with the Harlem Housewives League, and Moore had been the president of the Dunbar Housewives League.[66] Petry's interest in working-class Black women's experiences also informed her writing, including her novel *The Street*, which was published in 1946 and sold over 1 million copies. Reflecting on her writing later in life, Petry wrote, "Having been born black and female, I regard myself as a survivor. And so I write about survivors."[67]

Negro Women Inc. engaged in activism, political education, and community building.[68] Its members regularly wrote letters to municipal and federal policy makers, including La Guardia and Paul McNutt of the War Manpower Commission, as well as to city papers, demanding equitable treatment and sharing Black women's wartime experiences.[69] In 1944, Negro Women Inc. led voter registration drives and get-out-the-vote efforts and pushed for the inclusion of courses on Black literature at Hunter College's secondary school.[70] The group held meetings attended by as many as 300 people.[71] In Negro Women Inc.'s monthly newsletters, its leadership shared educational recommendations to help members form perspectives on "Allied war aims, proposed peace terms, the problems of returning veterans and even our own problems and achievements as Negroes," along with new member updates and recipes for ration-friendly dishes like "butterless cake."[72] Reflecting on their work in 1944, the group's leadership commended the "vocal expressions of approval and disapproval we have made on National and local issues" and shared hopes that their efforts would play "an increasingly vital part, not only in our lives as members of this organization, but in the world community in which we live."[73] In 1942, Negro Women Inc. led a boycott of the *Daily News* following the "out of bounds" article, demonstrating the affront that activist Harlem women took to the story.[74]

Shuttering the Savoy

The closure of the Savoy in the spring of 1943 occurred in this ongoing context of criminalization, policing, and protest. To many Harlem residents, it presented another example of city officials' commitment to racially segregating leisure, surveilling Harlem, and constructing Black women as carriers of venereal diseases. Activists protested the shuttering of the Savoy and connected it to larger themes of democracy and racial justice.

The ballroom, located at 141st Street and Lenox Avenue, was one of the city's hottest nighttime attractions. It was Harlem's largest dancehall and had been a neighborhood fixture since its opening in 1926. New Yorkers referred to the Savoy as "the Track" and the "home of Happy Feet."[75] Harlemites of all classes visited the dancehall, as did celebrities, bons vivants, and tourists of all races. The Savoy drew visitors impressed by its size and ambiance, as well as by its dance culture and musical acts. One dancer remembered feeling as if he had stepped into a different world upon first entering the Savoy. "I had been to other ballrooms, but this was different—much bigger, more glamour, real class," he recalled.[76]

The dancehall not only housed the hottest dance floor but also served as a key institution in Harlem's social and institutional life. As one of the few large ballrooms in the area, it regularly hosted fundraisers for Black organizations, no unimportant feat for a community denied equitable funding from the government and white-run institutions. It also held important social events. Bessie Buchanan, the wife of the manager, served as the chairwoman of a committee to bring theatrical entertainment to servicemen at the Harlem Defense Recreation Center. The Savoy provided 175 free-entry passes to the center each week during the war.[77] The Savoy's relationship with the center illustrates the centrality of the dancehall to Harlem's community and shows that the ballroom provided a welcoming space for Black service members in a city that was often anything but.

Within the city's segregated nightlife, the Savoy stood out as a site of interracial dancing and socializing.[78] At the ballroom, young zoot-suiters gathered, men and women mixed across lines of race and class, and guests and performers engaged in cultural and sexual creativity. Charles Buchanan, the African American co-owner and manager of the Savoy, who ran the venue along with his white partner Moe Gale, reflected in an interview that about half the club patrons were white and the other half Black, though the Savoy's clientele included Latinx patrons and musicians as well.[79] Petry described a visit to an Urban League event at the dancehall in a letter just a few months before its closure: "The regular Savoy jitterbug crowd was there . . . and I've never seen anything like them . . . little black gals in short dresses way above their knees with reddish colored stockings on, sailors with slick straightened hair, all sizes and shapes of females with too much rouge on their faces . . . jaded white women . . . and white men with pouches under their eyes reaching down to their insteps."[80]

The dancehall embodied the type of heterogeneous entertainment that city and police officials constructed as a threat to servicemen and to the gendered, racial, and class hierarchies embedded in the idea of wartime order in the city. The Savoy's closure in the spring of 1943, though temporary, signified the power of this hierarchy for many New Yorkers and worsened the already fraught relations between Black New Yorkers, the NYPD, and city hall. Buchanan recalled police opposition to the club's interracial patronage. "The cops used to hate it," he remembered. "They closed us down . . . in 1943."[81]

The Savoy appeared frequently in the correspondence between the army's Second Service Command, the Health Department, and the police department about venereal disease infections and prostitution. For example, from January through May 1942, dancehalls appeared as the "sites of meeting or contact" twelve times in such reports, eleven of which specifically named the Savoy.[82] "I would say that no day passes that the Savoy Ball Room is not listed in our records," Dr. Herman Goodman of the Health Department's Social Hygiene Bureau later testified at a hearing regarding the Savoy's license.[83] These records suggest that the Savoy was popular among soldiers and sailors, and that some may have contracted venereal diseases from (or transmitted them to) women they met on the premises.

The information collected on venereal disease transmissions, however, was self-reported and sparse, and some men likely misrepresented or misdiagnosed the circumstances of their infections. Black women were depicted as particularly likely to carry venereal diseases in educational materials about venereal diseases disseminated by the military and the leading public health experts, as discussed in chapter 3. The Savoy's co-owner, Buchanan, further argued that when enlisted men wanted to falsify their reports, they named the Savoy because it was "known to thousands of military men."[84] The records of the Health Department contain a long line of complaints against the ballroom. These records, regardless of their accuracy or spuriousness, justified police surveillance of the venue and the surrounding streets and made women vulnerable to arrest. One such woman, Eunice, a petite entertainer with a "fancy, high hair-do" who was employed at the Savoy, was arrested for prostitution in early 1943 while leaving the ballroom at the end of her 12:00–3:00 A.M. shift.[85]

The catalyst for the dancehall's closure was an incident that occurred on March 1, 1943. Following reports from the Health Department and the NYPD's wartime Division of National Defense about prostitution at the Savoy, the NYPD had stationed two undercover agents on the premises every night. In a later hearing, Patrolman Anthony Paduano testified that he had entered the Savoy the evening of March 1. The officer claimed that during his time at the ballroom, he had been approached by a men's room attendant who inquired if he wanted "any girls." When Paduano answered that he did, the attendant led him to another man, who then introduced the officer to four Black women. After paying the procurer, the officer left with two of the women, whom he then placed under arrest, before returning to arrest both the attendant and the intermediary.[86] After this incident, the operators of the Savoy received a notification from fourth deputy police commissioner Cornelius O'Leary to appear at a hearing on March 10, 1943, to show cause as to why the Savoy's license should not be revoked.[87] Two patrolmen, a lieutenant, a medical instructor from the Second Service Command, the assistant director of the Health Department's Social Hygiene Bureau, a venereal disease control officer with the navy's Pier 92 receiving station, and Buchanan participated in the March 10 hearing.

In Buchanan's testimony, the owner sought to defend the Savoy against NYPD allegations and revealed his beliefs about what prompted the venue's closure in the process. Buchanan stated that the operators of the Savoy did their best to deter prostitution and misbehavior, noting they had recently hired seven additional "housemen" to monitor the venue. He argued that management had successfully discouraged "white sight seers" from visiting the dancehall. "Once on a time our place used to be 30 percent white, it now has been cut down to 2 percent or 3 percent," Buchanan noted, adding, "The soldier element has been practically wiped out."[88] The fact that the manager emphasized the Savoy's declining popularity with white patrons and soldiers in his efforts to preserve its license suggests that he suspected the NYPD's true concern lay with the presence of white soldiers at the dancehall. Buchanan's testimony and the work of the venue's lawyers could not save the Savoy. The NYPD revoked the Savoy's license and closed the ballroom in late April.

Valentine considered the closure a success in the NYPD's ongoing battle against prostitution, but Harlem's residents and newspapers fought against the closure, which would last for six long months. Many critics argued that the Savoy was closed because of its tolerance of interracial dancing, rather than its role in spreading venereal diseases.[89] The *People's Voice* ran the most consistently critical and outspoken articles covering the police department's campaign of surveillance against the Savoy and subsequent closure. In a blistering piece, journalist Joe Bostic described numerous attempts by unnamed officials and police department members to deter interracial socializing at the dancehall. These officials had, according to the author, encouraged Savoy management not to advertise in white papers, because this might "draw white patrons to Harlem." Bostic also recounted that "various officials" had repeatedly inquired about whether white and Black patrons danced together at the club and suggested that management refuse entrance to white visitors.[90] The *New York Age* published a similar analysis, and the *Amsterdam News* named Deputy Police Commissioner O'Leary as the officer who suggested that whites should be denied admittance to the dancehall.[91]

Civil rights leaders in and outside New York spoke out against the closure. Philip Randolph, head of the Brotherhood of Sleeping Car Porters and organizer of the March on Washington movement, criticized the closure as an insult to African American New Yorkers.[92] Walter White, leader of the NAACP, requested that La Guardia intervene, but received a telegram from the mayor that the situation was out of his hands.[93] "While Negroes are losing their lives abroad," Adam Clayton Powell Jr. proclaimed, placing the closure in the context of the war, "Hitler has scored a Jim-crow victory in New York."[94] Powell had been growing increasingly critical of La Guardia's policies toward African American New Yorkers since early 1942, and the mayor's stance on the Savoy sharpened the conflict.[95]

The *People's Voice* contended that the targeting of the Savoy was racially motivated and part of a pattern of racist policing in Harlem. The *Voice* documented sex work and theft at the city's "better known" taxi dancehalls. These venues, according to the journalist, received support from the "same exponents of jimcro" who drove the Savoy closure.[96] Powell described the attacks on the Savoy as part of a larger dynamic of excessive wartime policing in Harlem; "during the time that Valentine and LaGuardia were crying about having an understaffed police force as many as a score of police officers were nightly assigned to the Savoy."[97] Though the total number of officers in the NYPD decreased during the war because policemen were not exempted from the draft, Valentine *increased* the number of officers assigned to monitoring venues like the Savoy. The poet and lyricist Andy Razaf penned a reflection on the Savoy's "guilt" for the *Voice*. In a poem highlighting the hypocrisy of demanding Black New Yorkers support a war in the name of democracy while their own municipal government implemented policies of segregation, Razaf declared the Savoy

> Guilty of national unity,
> Of practising real Democracy,
> By allowing the races, openly
> To dance and mingle in harmony.
> Guilty of its location — by now you can guess where the place is:
> Guilty of being in HARLEM
> And that's where the core of the case is![98]

Petry published an open letter to Mayor La Guardia in the *Voice* on May 22, 1943, in which she challenged the police department's depiction of the Savoy and the mayor's position of nonintervention. Petry explained that the Savoy was far more than a dancehall. It was, in her words, "a community affair," where essential fundraising and community building happened. More pointedly, the journalist cited racism as the source of La Guardia's inaction: "Mr. Mayor, you're doing something about NY's food situation, you've shifted people around on the Board of Education, you've stirred up in the Department of Welfare. It couldn't be because Negroes used the Savoy that you haven't done anything about it . . . ?"[99]

A photo accompanying Petry's letter hinted at the particular implications of the closure for Black women. The photo depicted Black women members of the American Women's Voluntary Service at a charity event hosted by the organization at the Savoy. In the image, four women in sharp uniforms and dresses chat together. Though Petry does not explicitly articulate it, the photo presents a visual refutation of the NYPD's narrative of Black women as sexual criminals who undermined the war effort. Petry notes that the photo was pulled "at random," suggesting that the newspaper's files were filled with many such images of this commonplace occurrence.[100] Vivian Wenham, recording secretary for Negro Women Inc., applauded Petry's missive in her own letter to the editor. Wenham proclaimed that "all of us . . . have been to the Savoy" and encouraged Black women to join her in opposing the closure. She declared, "Are we all diseased as they would have the world believe? 15,000,000 times no." She exhorted, "Negro women, all over America, to your pens!" to write to La Guardia protesting this closure.[101]

Buchanan and his partner Moe Gale fought the closure in court but lost on April 20, when the Appellate Division of the New York State Supreme Court upheld the revocation.[102] Justice Irwin Untermyer of the court shared his own assessment that the case was decided on "incomplete evidence."[103] Scholars have speculated about possible motivations behind the Savoy's closure, but what is clear is that the wartime aim of protecting enlisted men from venereal diseases and the collaborations between the NYPD, the Health Department, and the army's Second Service Command made the closure possible.[104] It would be six months before the venue would regain its license and reopen in October 1943. The extant records provide little evidence as to how the Savoy's reopening unfolded. When it reopened, however, the dancehall had been closed for a significantly longer time than the sixty to ninety days assigned to other venues closed by Deputy Commissioner O'Leary in the fall of 1943.[105] In the months in which the Savoy remained shuttered, tensions over policing in Harlem would escalate further.

The Braddock Hotel Incident and Growing Black Resistance

In the wake of the controversy over the Savoy, Harlem residents' frustrations with La Guardia and Valentine intensified. In response, the administrators worked to paint their policing efforts and broader municipal policies as racially inclusive. La Guardia met with prominent Black New Yorkers to discuss race relations in the city, and Valentine publicly shared plans to hire more Black officers. These efforts became increasingly important following the violence and property damage in Detroit in late June 1943. La Guardia and Valentine wanted to avoid any type of uprising, mass protest, or interracial violence in New York. Their gestures toward racial inclusivity, however, coexisted with a continued reliance on policing based on race, and the duo did not alter their wartime policies of racist and gendered surveillance of leisure spaces.

In June 1943, La Guardia sought information on what had caused the conflicts in Detroit. He received differing reports from Walter White and two NYPD officers, Edward Butler and Emanuel Kline, the latter the seventh African American to have joined the department, whom he sent to Detroit to investigate. White's report, "What Caused the Detroit Riots," emphasized the Detroit Police Department's inappropriate actions, while Kline and Butler accepted more of the analysis of Detroit police commissioner John Witherspoon that Black Detroiters were responsible for the episode. La Guardia and Valentine met with a group of African American leaders including Samuel Battle, the first Black officer in the NYPD, who had recently been appointed the city's first Black parole commissioner, and White to discuss how to avoid or respond to such a conflict in New York. The group agreed that in such an event, police violence should be avoided, bars should be closed, and police should protect Black passengers on public transit.[106]

In July, Valentine stated publicly in an interview with representatives from the New York Urban League and NAACP that he supported using African American policemen to quell racial conflict. The commissioner went on to express his willingness to work with groups that might assist him in recruiting Black officers, implicitly bolstering his own claims that the NYPD's disproportionately low rate of Black membership was due to lack of interest or qualifications on the part of Black New Yorkers and not the department's racist hiring practices. The *People's Voice* encouraged African American men interested in becoming members of the NYPD to register at the Urban League office on West 136th Street and suggested the initiation of a coaching course.[107] Twenty-two men answered the *Voice's* call and signed up just one week after the article appeared.[108] Before any of these men could begin training, however, a conflict between a police officer stationed at the Braddock Hotel and a guest on the evening of August 1 set off protests and property destruction throughout Harlem.

On the evening of August 1, James Collins, a white thirty-three-year-old patrolman from Queens, was on duty monitoring the Braddock Hotel. The hotel had been labeled a "raided premise" following reports that twenty soldiers had contracted venereal diseases there, and it had been under police surveillance for over a year in August 1943.[109] The Braddock Hotel was a well-known establishment located on West 126th Street, though it did not have the panache of the Savoy. Malcolm X remembered the bar at the Braddock as a "Negro celebrity hang-out" and became a regular there himself.[110] Margie Polite, also thirty-three, entered the Braddock Hotel at about 7:30 P.M. Polite may have been a married laundress who had moved to New York from South Carolina.[111] She had reserved a room but, finding the room unacceptable, complained at the front desk and sought a refund.[112] This request resulted in an argument with the front desk manager, at which point Patrolman Collins intervened aggressively to arrest Polite for disorderly conduct. Collins likely found Polite, a Black woman checking into a hotel alone, suspicious and may have labeled her a possible prostitute. During the altercation, a nearby Black serviceman, Private Robert Bandy, and his mother, Florine Roberts, intervened on Polite's behalf. Collins shot Bandy in the shoulder and then placed him, his mother, and Polite under arrest.[113]

Bystanders witnessed the attack and spread rumors that Bandy had been killed. Given the consistent police brutality in New York, the recent violence against Black Detroiters, and the ongoing reports of attacks against Black servicemen around the country, many believed the rumors. As James Baldwin reflected later, "This was certainly not the first time such an incident had occurred."[114] Harlem residents took to the streets in protest, breaking windows and taking items from stores, with particular concentration on the commercial stretch on 125th Street. Ann Petry wrote to her mother of the aftermath, "I don't think there's a whole piece of plate glass left from 110th Street to 150th Street from Fifth Avenue across to Eighth Avenue."[115] The uprising lasted for about twelve hours. La Guardia ordered all available officers into the neighborhood and telephoned military officials at Governors Island to send military police to remove soldiers and sailors from Harlem. Walter White suggested that La Guardia call back and request Black military police officers be sent in order to minimize racial conflict between military police and enlisted men. White also organized a group of prominent Black New Yorkers including Samuel Battle. The group rode through the streets announcing through a loudspeaker, "The rumor is false that a Negro soldier was killed at the Braddock Hotel tonight. . . . Don't form mobs or break the law."[116] The NYPD cordoned off the neighborhood and helmeted officers were stationed on the roofs of buildings and throughout the area, but the New York state guardsmen were not deployed. Six people were killed, all of them Black, and police arrested over 500 Black New Yorkers.

Harlem residents who reflected on the causes of the uprising named criminalization and wartime injustices as underlying frustrations that fueled the protests.[117] Baldwin remembered seeing policemen "everywhere" in the month before the uprising and described the neighborhood as "infected by waiting" for news from loved ones in the military or for racial conflict.[118] Petry centered the wartime injustices experienced by Black New Yorkers as a cause of the uprising in her short story "In Darkness and Confusion," originally published in 1946.[119]

"In Darkness and Confusion" follows Harlem resident William Jones through his day on August 1, 1943. Jones's day begins poorly. His coffee "didn't taste right"; he worries about the health of his wife, who is forced to climb many stairs to access their apartment; and his boss at the drug store berates him, calling him "boy." The overarching concern of his day, however, is the well-being of his son, Sam. Sam had been drafted into the army and is currently serving in "a camp in Georgia." William and his wife, Pink, have not heard from their son recently, causing both parents to worry. William carries this worry with him to the barbershop, where he encounters another soldier who had been stationed with Sam. From this soldier, William learns that Sam has been court-martialed and sentenced to twenty years at "hard labor" after a conflict with a white military policeman. The soldier recounts that after Sam refused to go to the back of a bus, the military policeman shot him, after which Sam took the gun and shot the white officer in the shoulder. William is horrified and overwhelmed by this information. He tries to process his son's traumas by walking around the neighborhood. He finds himself at a bar where a conflict between a white policeman and a "frowzy-looking girl" is unfolding. The conflict mimics that between Polite and Collins, and a soldier intervenes. The fictionalized Collins shoots the soldier in the back. Spectators believe the unmoving soldier to be dead, and crowds gather on the street. William bumps into Pink on the street and tells her about their son. In Petry's telling it is Pink, overwhelmed with anger, rage, and sadness, who throws a bottle through the window of a furniture store, crashing it with a "sound like a gunshot." The uprising swells around them, with Pink at its center. For Pink, however, whose health has already been taxed by poverty, racism, and sexism, the loss of her son and the trauma of the evening prove deadly. She collapses on the street with William next to her screaming "the sons of bitches" out to the night.[120]

Petry's interpretation was informed by her own life and the experiences of those around her. On July 31, 1943, the *Amsterdam News* ran a front-page story detailing the execution of Sergeant Edmund Reed in Georgia. Reed had shot a white police officer with the officer's own gun, which Reed's lawyer argued had been an act of self-defense since the officer had been beating Reed with a blackjack.[121] Petry's husband, George, was inducted into the army in early July 1943, and she worried about his treatment and well-being in the white supremacist institution. "I guess everything will be all right," she reflected in a letter to her mother and sister shortly after his induction, "—as long as he doesn't bop one of those cracker officers in the mouth."[122] As scholar Farah Jasmine Griffin notes, during his time in the army, George witnessed German prisoners of war receiving superior treatment to African American servicemen and was himself asked to leave a Roman Catholic church in segregated Washington, D.C.[123] Petry's exploration of why Harlemites took to the streets presents the author's view, informed by her own experiences, of how the war permeated life for many Harlem residents and intersected with other daily experiences of injustice in New York City.

Many scholars have explored the details of how the unrest in Harlem unfolded. Historians and sociologists have considered the underlying causes and responses from city officials, examined the participants and targets, compared the episode to other urban uprisings, and evaluated the impact of the uprising on African American rights in New York City.[124] Placing the uprising in Harlem within the landscape of wartime policing demonstrates that it was partly a response to the heightened gendered and racialized wartime policing in Harlem. The hotel had been labeled a "raided premise," and officers monitoring the Braddock sometimes barred interracial couples from entering, even entering rooms to eject white patrons.[125] In the cases of the Braddock and the Savoy Ballroom, one of the functions NYPD officers served was enforcing segregation. The NYPD's policies framed women as the "source" of venereal diseases and sought to identify locations where enlisted men met such "sources." Patrolmen, precinct captains, division commanders, and Commissioner Valentine relied on race and class distinctions when determining which locations to monitor or shutter. The campaign to keep enlisted men out of disorderly premises by closing them or stationing officers to monitor their patrons, combined with the NYPD's larger patterns of harsh and targeted policing of Black New Yorkers, created the conditions for Collins's conflict with Polite. The city's practices of discrimination and racism and the nation's mistreatment of African American servicemen drafted into a war fought in the name of democracy motivated the neighborhood's response.

Conclusion

The Savoy reopened in October 1943. Harlem residents celebrated the venue's return, but management accompanied the reopening with the adoption of new internal policies that mimicked those of the NYPD.[126] Buchanan signaled that the venue would collaborate more closely with the police moving forward. He alerted patrons and city officials that in the future "our policy will be toward building morale for the war effort."[127] The dancehall continued to appear frequently in venereal disease contact reports, though Buchanan disputed their validity. The NYPD dispensed undercover officers to the ballroom every night and military police and shore patrol officers patrolled the venue "constantly," according to a January 1945 interview between Buchanan and representatives of the Social Protection Division. Buchanan, however, sought to go even further and in early 1945 began "experimenting" with barring all unescorted military men from the premises.[128] After the Savoy reopened, therefore, Buchanan brought the city's regulatory practices into the dancehall himself and the reopened Savoy proved less challenging to Valentine and La Guardia's vision of wartime urban order.

In the months after the Harlem uprising and the reopening of the Savoy, the city's campaigns against venues that impeded morale by allowing dangerous socializing continued. La Guardia advocated cooperation between NYPD and military police in monitoring and deterring enlisted men from frequenting morally questionable dancehalls, theaters, and taverns. In a letter sent to both Major General Thomas Terry of the Second Corps Area and Rear Admiral Edward Marquart, commandant of Third Naval District, the mayor suggested that military police officers join NYPD members stationed at raided premises. In January 1944, La Guardia went further and advocated keeping soldiers out of such locations altogether, noting with frustration that "they do not go there to say a Padre Nostre."[129] This suggestion was not implemented through the military police, but the NYPD undertook the task. Later that same year, Valentine remarked that seventeen uniformed patrolmen monitored raided premises around the city on each of the day's three tours. Their instructions were to "compel all members of the armed forces to show identification cards and leave passes and all civilians to show their draft registration and classification cards. Harass and annoy."[130]

Throughout the war, efforts to monitor "unescorted women" and enlisted men resulted in an expanded policing network that structured the city's nightlife and included military police officers, members of the Social Protection Division, employees of the Health Department, and officers in the NYPD. Protecting soldiers and sailors visiting the city, particularly white soldiers and sailors, from immoral entertainment and women provided Valentine and La Guardia with the opportunity to temporarily shut down the Savoy. The city's focus on the Savoy highlighted the racialized and gendered ways that the NYPD mapped wartime policing onto the city's leisure establishments. These highly publicized campaigns were part of the larger crackdown on venues around the city with reputations for catering to immoral women or interracial socializing. Though city officials had opposed venues that they believed "impaired the morals" of civilian New Yorkers throughout the 1930s, the war provided new opportunities to expand their campaigns against these venues.

Through a focused examination of the policing of leisure spaces in Harlem, the NYPD's expanded campaign of targeted wartime surveillance becomes clear. During the war, city administrators' project of ordering, patrolling, and segregating the city's leisure spaces, a long-standing preoccupation of municipal governance, gained increased resources from federal and military sources and found a new justification as an essential component of military preparedness. City and NYPD officials sought to craft a gendered urban order informed by race and class hierarchies in the name of protecting white American servicemen, while also mobilizing the nation for a war launched in the name of global democracy. Many Black New Yorkers understood the racialized policing of leisure and vice to be interwoven with social and political inequalities. Activists protested the ways that Valentine, La Guardia, army officials, and the city's white press presented Harlem as a center of crime and vice, contending that such policing was undemocratic and anti-American. In the context of the larger military mobilization, however, city administrators argued that the restriction of New Yorkers' civil rights constituted a relatively insignificant casualty. The war intervened in an ongoing conflict over freedom and order in the city, strengthening the resources and rhetoric devoted to imposing and maintaining order.

Conclusion

In December 1944, a musical depiction of visiting sailors taking in the city's nightlife opened at the Adelphi Theater. The show, *On the Town*, was written by young, Jewish, left-leaning Broadway up-and-comers and became an immediate success.[1] A reviewer in the *New York Times* raved, "Everything about it is right."[2] It later became a hit movie in 1949 directed by Gene Kelley and starring Kelley and Frank Sinatra. The comedy follows three white sailors on a twenty-four-hour leave in the city. While on the subway, they examine a poster announcing Ivy Smith, the winner of the "Miss Turnstiles" beauty contest. When one of the sailors becomes besotted with the image, the group undertakes a citywide search to find the winner. They set off from the Brooklyn Navy Yard and take in high points of the city, including the Museum of Natural History, the Empire State Building, and Coney Island. Each of the other two sailors meets a young woman who joins in the search. They eventually find Miss Turnstiles and the three couples enjoy a night on the town, moving from dancehall to dancehall. Miss Turnstiles, however, sneaks out early to secretly travel to her job as a suggestive "cooch" dancer at Coney Island. The group tracks her down again, and she and her sailor engage in a tearful reunion in which she expresses shame at her profession. At the end of the twenty-four hours, the men return to their ship and the women kiss them goodbye. In the comedy, the city is an inviting landscape of entertainment and fun.

Offstage, the reality proved more complicated. Ivy Smith was exactly the type of young woman Lewis Valentine directed members of the Division of National Defense, volunteers in the City Patrol Corps, and NYPD officers to monitor and arrest.[3] Paul Moss, Fiorello La Guardia's commissioner of licenses, would surely not have approved of Ivy's place of employment. Ivy might have, in fact, lost her income and ended up on the picket line with the burlesque workers carrying a sign proclaiming she had "done no wrong," if Moss heard of sailors frequenting the club.[4] Had Gabey, the sailor who pursued Ivy, tested positive for a venereal disease, he might have remembered his tryst with Ivy and reported her as a "contact." Ivy then would likely have been arrested, forced to undergo a medical examination, and remanded to the Bellevue clinic for treatment. A working-class "cooch" dancer on a fling with a sailor in real-life wartime Gotham was a threat to national security, not the "all-American" darling Ivy Smith appeared as in the show.

On the Town's cast included African American performers playing sailors and a policeman who danced alongside white counterparts in a Times Square ballet.[5] In actuality, both the navy and the NYPD resisted accepting African Americans into their ranks. Those who did make it into these institutions faced further discrimination in their assignments, status, and treatment.[6] In New York City, Black members of the military, unlike those depicted in the show, might be criminalized, arrested, or harassed by police officers. In or out of uniform, Black servicemen also risked being assaulted by police officers, as Robert Bandy was in 1943. Young African American men and women, furthermore, did not enjoy the freedom to go out dancing or socializing, whether in Times Square, Harlem, or Bedford-Stuyvesant, without the threat of arrest for juvenile delinquency looming over their evenings. Unlike the racially inclusive pleasurescape depicted in *On the Town*, wartime New York City was heavily policed in discriminatory ways by a majority-white police department.

During the war, Valentine and La Guardia saw their policing strategies as both seizing an opportunity and rising to meet an emergency. They had pushed anti-vice or morals laws policing throughout their ten years in office, with mixed results and varying levels of support. As the nation mobilized to meet the wartime emergency, however, opposition to the enforcement of these laws decreased. With national security at stake, discriminatory policing, the violation of social and sexual autonomy, and restrictions on civil rights became easier to justify. The costs of failing to prohibit prostitution, juvenile delinquency, gambling, and disorderly leisure, the mayor and the commissioner believed, were immensely higher in wartime than in peace. As their colleague Magistrate Stephen Jackson declared, "All of the tanks, guns, planes, ammunition and firearms . . . are, in the last analysis, entirely and exclusively dependent on the men that operate them. Their effectiveness depends on . . . their moral fiber."[7] Valentine and La Guardia's anti-vice campaigns were reimagined as a home-front war to defend the moral fiber of enlisted white men against urban perils lurking throughout the city.

The justification of protecting enlisted men receded with demobilization, but many of the strategies Valentine and La Guardia embraced to surveil sexually profiled women would persist throughout the postwar period. Local-federal policing partnerships of the type that had flourished during the war expanded, and women's position in paid law enforcement continued, though it was often undermined by sexism within the police department.[8] In 1945

Valentine and other NYPD officials assisted the Social Protection Division in producing a pamphlet entitled "Techniques of Law Enforcement in the Use of Policewomen with Special Reference to Social Protection," which the division then sent to local politicians and police chiefs across the country. Contributors to the manual argued that the experience of the war illustrated the importance of the work of policewomen since they possessed particular skills necessary to monitor women and children. The authors recommended that departments appoint women who had served in war services including Women Accepted for Volunteer Emergency Service, the Women's Army Corps, and the Red Cross.[9] Additionally, the wartime repression campaigns launched against women's social and sexual freedoms did not cease postwar. Instead, they became increasingly racialized as white women's sexuality was decriminalized and police departments across the country increased their targeting of Black women for morals policing.[10] Though not exclusively directed at Black women, anti-prostitution policing in New York was already heavily racialized. As the Black women activists who challenged the racist and sexist policing regime during the war contended, the military and city's anti-prostitution policies were "an insult to Negro womanhood."[11] In this problematic advancement, Valentine's NYPD was ahead of its time.

The increased attention to juvenile delinquency from city officials, NYPD leaders, and residents that emerged during the war showed no sign of abating as the war came to an end. Leading criminal justice figures in New York City and at the federal level argued that law enforcement needed to prepare for a postwar crime wave. At his retirement speech, Commissioner Valentine alerted department members that they "are going into the postwar period with crime already on the increase," and J. Edgar Hoover predicted a postwar rise in juvenile crime.[12] In March 1946, the *New York Times* ran an article entitled "Rise of Juvenile Crime," which stated of 1945, "Our great year of victory abroad . . . was a year of defeat on one of the most vital sectors of the home front."[13] In 1946 experts gathered at the National Conference on the Prevention and Control of Juvenile Delinquency, and congressional hearings on juvenile delinquency in the mid-1950s kept national attention on the issue.[14] During the war, officials had tied youth crime to the social disruptions accompanying mobilization, but after demobilization, campaigns against delinquency, gang activity, and drug use flourished.[15]

Despite efforts to critique police brutality and racialized policing practices as anti-American during the war, African Americans continued to be disproportionately policed even during the victory day celebrations. Carl Dunbar Lawrence, writing in the *Amsterdam News*, commented on the "quiet" atmosphere in Harlem on V-E Day. With the exception of women whose husbands were overseas, Lawrence found that most Harlemites met the news with "a soberness that had been born out of the tragedy of the last depression and the jim crow experiences of this war." Lawrence suspected that La Guardia and Valentine had expected a different reaction, "judging from the number of cops assigned to the main uptown thoroughfares."[16] Dan Gardner noticed that V-J celebrations in New York City were "one of the few national celebrations in which the white man neglected or forgot to keep Negroes separate, Jim Crowed or segregated." Gardner's article gave vent to the complicated legacy of the war for many African Americans. The journalist felt that the "spontaneous gaiety" expressed by African Americans was "beyond comprehension" given that "the American Negro had less to be happy about than any other minority groups" and the only concrete civil rights gains made during the war were, in his estimation, the Supreme Court's ruling against white primaries and the passage of the Fair Employment Practice Act in New York State.[17] In New York City, campaigns against police brutality and racialized policing also made little progress during the war. Intense political pressure to demonstrate patriotism toward a nation at war constricted the space for the type of systemic criticism of the police department that many had voiced after the 1935 Harlem uprising. In 1943, La Guardia declined to launch an investigation into the uprising's causes and Black political leaders did not push for one. The Office of War Information collected informal responses from residents about what spurred the event, but much of the press coverage of the uprising's aftermath presented positive depictions of the NYPD's response.[18] The American system of racial hierarchy made it through the war mostly intact.

More so than lasting changes to the structure of urban policing, the wartime dynamics of the NYPD revealed the way that anti-vice policing in the city gained urgency and support from the national wartime emergency. Expansions of police power and restrictions on the civil liberties of New Yorkers of color and working-class women became necessary sacrifices to preserve the security of the nation and the health of its male troops. Police and military power reinforced each other. Brigadier General Ralph K. Robertson, who commanded District One of the army's Second Service Command from Governors Island, argued in 1944 that discharged military policemen, many of whom had been recruited from the ranks of law enforcement, would become "excellent additions to local police."[19] Police officers who served in the military could keep up with the department through its magazine, *Spring 3100*, and many did. Lieutenant Murray Trilling wrote to the magazine from "somewhere in New Guinea" about an increase in his responsibilities. He remarked that he now oversaw "shore patrol—sentries, guards, fire department, and base brig—" and noted that "being a N.Y. cop was responsible for the change." Trilling also commented that he found the magazine to be "a great morale builder."[20] Another writer, Edward T. Lynch, thanked the editors for sending him *Spring 3100* every month and bringing him "a touch of the sidewalks of New York." Lynch shared his copy with other servicemen, and remarked that "the Department can look forward to a few recruits from this neck of the woods when the boys down here come home."[21] Lynch's recruits may well have succeeded in joining the department, since La Guardia fast-tracked veterans into the NYPD without requiring the regular civil service examinations during demobilization.[22] The cover of *Spring 3100*'s January 1946 issue depicted this process with an image of a young white man handing off his military uniform to Uncle Sam and replacing it with NYPD blues.[23]

Valentine brought his particular strain of morality policing abroad after his retirement from the NYPD in 1945. The former commissioner was tapped by the War Department to oversee the reorganization of the civilian police department in occupied Japan.[24] Strengthening the department's anti-vice efforts, by creating "a detailed plan of attack exactly like the plainclothes system used in New York City," was high on his list of recommendations.[25]

The end of the war also spelled the end of Valentine and La Guardia's dual reign over the city. La Guardia reflected on his collaboration with the retiring commissioner. He criticized the "smelly big shot, thieving tinhorns," and remarked of his and Valentine's collaboration, "We have never let up on them . . . we went after the bums."[26] When La Guardia retired from office on December 31, 1945, John Rogers of the *New York Herald-Tribune* proclaimed that the mayor "was noted for going to fires and denouncing gamblers."[27] La Guardia and Valentine's program of harsh and nonpartisan policing in New York City was central to the influential mayor's vision of urban governance and to his legacy. La Guardia and Valentine had pushed expanded police campaigns against vice and disorder throughout the 1930s. During the war, this dynamic team of moralistic municipal leaders viewed these campaigns as more important than ever. With support from federal officials and some civilians, they directed an expansive onslaught against prostitution, delinquency, gambling, and disorderly entertainment. Valentine's post-NYPD career suggested that the arguments he and La Guardia had made about the centrality of policing New York City to the larger national military project had been heard.

La Guardia and Valentine's moralistic onslaught reverberated through the wartime life of the city. These campaigns curtailed the civil, social, and sexual liberties of New Yorkers, particularly Black and Puerto Rican women, men, and children; working-class women of all races; and young people. During the mass mobilization of the war, the preservation of internal social hierarchies gained new momentum and urgency. The conjoined processes of policing the city and mobilizing the nation for war became visible in the NYPD's "war within a war" against juvenile delinquency, prostitution, gambling, and urban disorder.[28]

In mid-twenty-first-century urban life in the United States, the approach to policing embraced by Valentine and La Guardia is so widespread among Democratic municipal administrators as to appear almost hegemonic. In major cities across the country, including New York City, Los Angeles, Chicago, San Francisco, Houston, Dallas, and Philadelphia, Democratic mayors responded to recent increases in crime ranging from slight to significant by calling for bigger budgets for police departments and more officers on the streets. While these politicians sometimes reference exploding inequality and the societal breakdown and mass death experienced during the COVID-19 pandemic when discussing crime, their proposals center on policing as the primary solution. Despite mass protests on a historic scale against police brutality and for racial justice in cities across the country throughout the summer of 2020 in the wake of the police murder of George Floyd, municipal leaders have, almost without exception, raised the budgets of police departments, while also making statements about their commitments to racial equality. Contemporary Democratic mayors tend to frame policing as a means of protecting the rights of "innocent" urbanites even as they propose policies that violate the rights of many city dwellers, usually working-class Black and Brown residents.

This dominant Democratic framework emerged in 1930s and 1940s New York City. At the heart of the liberal law-and-order framework lies a belief that professional police officers, uninfluenced by partisan politics, can enforce discriminatory conceptions of order in an equitable fashion. Law-and-order liberalism relies on a fiction that unbiased discretionary police power can craft an orderly and equitable city in a deeply unequal society. The history of La Guardia and Valentine's administration demonstrates that this vision has been flawed from its inception.

Notes

Abbreviations in Notes

APP   Ann Petry Papers, Manuscripts, Archives, and Rare Books Division, Schomburg Center for Research in Black Culture, New York Public Library

ASF   Army Service Forces, Records of the Deputy Chief of Staff for Service Commands, Entry 13, Record Group 160.2, National Archives

FLGC   Mayor Fiorello H. La Guardia Records, New York City Municipal Archives

HCR   Health Commissioner's Records, John L. Rice and Ernest Stebbins Subgroups, New York City Municipal Archives

JJCA   John Jay College Archives, Manuscripts and Special Collections, Lloyd Sealy Library, John Jay College

NAACP   Records of the National Association for the Advancement of Colored People, Manuscript Division, Library of Congress

NACP   Records of the Social Protection Division, Records of the Office of Community War Services, Record Group 215.2.5, National Archives

NDP   Nathan D. Perlman Collection, American Jewish Historical Society Collection, Center for Jewish History

OHA   Oral History Archives, Rare Book and Manuscript Library, Columbia University

SWHA   American Social Health Association Collection, Social Welfare History Archives, Migration and Social Services in the Archives and Special Collections Department, University of Minnesota Libraries

WCMA   Women's Court Record Book, Manhattan 9th District, Criminal Court, New York City Municipal Archives

WPA   Women's Prison Association of New York Records, Manuscripts and Archives Division, Astor, Lenox, and Tilden Foundations, New York Public Library

Introduction

1. Valentine, *Night Stick*, 232.

2. C. V. Terry, "Life-History of an Honest Cop," *New York Times*, September 21, 1947, BR4.

3. For more on the interconnections between Tammany's political power and control of the police department, see Golway, *Machine Made*, 50–55; Wallace, *Greater Gotham*, 106–7; and Czitrom, *New York Exposed*, 70.

4. "Moss Talks on Theatre," *New York Times*, June 18, 1937, 25; "Burlesque Shows of City Are Shut as Public Menace," *New York Times*, May 2, 1937, 1.

5. Naomi Murakawa shows that in the 1940s politicians at the federal level adopted an approach similar to La Guardia's. Federal officials argued that modernizing the state's carceral systems and removing individual racial bias from its ranks would advance the cause of civil rights. Murakawa, *First Civil Right*, 10, 29. I am also relying on Karen Miller's definition of racial liberalism; *Managing Inequality*, 4.

6. Address from Mayor La Guardia, *Spring 3100*, December 1935, 3.

7. "Valentine Willing to Add More Negroes to Police Force," *People's Voice*, July 17, 1943, 3.

8. Mason Williams, *City of Ambition*, 138–42.

9. Williams, 136.

10. U.S. Census Bureau, *1940 Census*, vol. 2, *Characteristics of the Population*, pt. 5, *New York* (Washington, D.C.: Government Printing Office, 1943), 137, 156, https://www2.census.gov/library/publications/decennial/1940/population-volume-2/33973538v2p5ch2.pdf; U.S. Census Bureau, *1950 Census*, vol. 2, *Characteristics of the Population*, pt. 32, *New York* (Washington, D.C.: Government Printing Office, 1953), chap. B, "General Characteristics," 94, https://www2.census.gov/library/publications/decennial/1950/population-volume-2/22980932v2p32ch3.pdf.

11. Nancy Foner notes that in 1930, about a fifth of the Black population of New York was of Caribbean origin. Foner, "Introduction," 4.

12. Sanchez-Korrol, *From Colonia to Community*, 30–34; Thomas, *Puerto Rican Citizen*, 133.

13. Glasser, *My Music*, 73. For more on the ways that city officials responded to Puerto Rican migration and the activism that migrants engaged in during the 1930s and 1940s, see Thomas, *Puerto Rican Citizen*, 133–53.

14. "Precinct Shifts to Its New Home," *New York Times*, November 24, 1940, 42.

15. The city would also eventually play an important role in military production by 1943, receiving 12 percent of all navy contracts. This was not the case, however, in the early war years, as Cheryl Lynn Greenberg discusses in *"Or Does It Explode?,"* 199.

16. Anne Gray Fischer describes how police departments used this discretion to enforce segregation in *Streets Belong to Us*, 27.

17. Police Department City of New York, Rules and Regulations, 1940, 394, Manuals of Procedure, JJCA.

18. Biondi, *To Stand and Fight*, 60–78; Clarence Taylor, *Fight the Power*, 9–33; King, "Murder in Central Park."

19. Office of Facts and Figures, *Negro Looks*, table 40.

20. Elmer H. Robertson to La Guardia, March 2, 1944, Folder 25, Roll 110, Subject Files: Juvenile Delinquency, FLGC.

21. I am building on Christopher Capozzola's concept of "a culture of coercive voluntarism" in reference to World War I. Capozzola, *Uncle Sam Wants You*, 8. I further explore the concept in Brooks, "Coercive Patriotism."

22. I am drawing on Melinda Chateauvert's concept of "sexually profiled" women to describe the women and girls whom police targeted for surveillance, as highlighted by Fischer, *Streets Belong to Us*, 9.

23. Browne, *One Righteous Man*, 380–462.

24. "Race Bias Denied as Rioting Factor," *New York Times*, August 3, 1943, 11; Llewelyn Ransom, "Racial Element Not Present in New York Riot," *People's Voice*, August 7, 1943, 3; Frank Crosswaith, "Wasn't Race Riot, but Could Have Been," *New York Amsterdam News*, August 14, 1943, 10.

25. "Gen. MacArthur Invites Valentine to Reorganize Japanese Police," *New York Times*, January 30, 1946, 1.

26. Fischer contends that New York and Chicago were ahead of the curve in implementing policing tactics that systematically targeted Black women and that would later be adopted by police leaders across the country. Fischer, *Streets Belong to Us*, 49.

27. Muhammad, *Condemnation of Blackness*; Clarence Taylor, *Fight the Power*; Balto, *Occupied Territory*; Suddler, *Presumed Criminal*; Vaz, *Running the Numbers*; Hinton, *America on Fire*; Hicks, *Talk with You*; Gross, *Colored Amazons*; Baer, *Beyond the Usual Beating*; Agyepong, *Criminalization of Black Children*. Though not exclusively about policing and criminalization, Purnell and Theoharis, *Strange Careers*, is an important intervention in this historiography.

28. Harris, "'Women and Girls'"; Harris, *Sex Workers*; Hicks, *Talk with You*; Gross, *Colored Amazons*; Fronc, *New York Undercover*; Agyepong, *Criminalization of Black Children*; Pliley, *Policing Sexuality*; Hartman, *Wayward Lives, Beautiful Experiments*; Flowe, *Uncontrollable Blackness*; Lindsay, *American Goddam*; Fischer, *Streets Belong to Us*; Lvovsky, *Vice Patrol*. Though they are not concerned with policing directly, LeFlouria's *Chained in Silence* and Haley's *No Mercy Here* are important interventions in historiographies on African American women, gender, the carceral state, labor history, and political and economic conceptions of "modernity" in the early twentieth-century United States.

29. Agee, *Streets of San Francisco*; Murakawa, *First Civil Right*; Felker-Kantor, *Policing Los Angeles*; Baer, *Beyond the Usual Beating*.

30. Bayor, *Fiorello La Guardia*, viii; Kessner, *Fiorello H. La Guardia*; Mason Williams, *City of Ambition*.

31. King, "Murder in Central Park," 43–66; and Johnson, *Street Justice*, 172–203, are important exceptions.

32. The mobilization for war created opportunities that activists successfully exploited to advance the Black freedom struggle, as scholars have convincingly argued. Lucander, *Winning the War*, 4; Lang, *Grassroots at the Gateway*, 43. Scholars of African American history and urban historians, however, have also shown the intense pressures put on Black Americans who pushed for equality or criticized the war mobilization during these years, as well as the complicated roles that military service played for Black Americans. For examples see Johnson, "Gender, Race, and Rumours"; Clarence Taylor, *Fight the Power*, 25–33; Delmont, *Half American*; and Phillips, *War!*, 48–55, 68–69. Historians of women and gender have examined the ways that women's sexuality was mobilized and criminalized at the federal level during the war. Winchell, *Good Girls*; Hegarty, *Victory Girls*; Littauer, *Bad Girls*; Escobedo, *Coveralls to Zoot Suits*, 6; Stern, *Trials of Nina McCall*. A small number of historians have considered the impact of the war on urban centers, and recent scholars have paid particular attention to policing. Escobar, *Race, Police*; Hendricks and Delgaudio, "'Vast War Establishment'"; Holloway, *Sexuality, Politics*; Strom "Controlling Venereal Disease"; Lee, "Hunting for

Sailors"; Beth Bailey and Farber, *First Strange Place*, 95–101; Johnson, *Second Gold Rush*; Hiltner, *Taking Leave, Taking Liberties*; Blower, "V-J Day, 1945"; Brooks, "'Rumor, Vicious Innuendo'"; Schrader, "Cops at War." Adam Hodges examines similar dynamics during World War I in Portland; *World War I*, 37–81.

33. Hiltner, *Taking Leave, Taking Liberties*, 143.

34. For more on war, militarization, and policing see, Go, "Imperial Origins"; and Kraska, "Militarization and Policing."

Chapter One

1. Hernandez, *City of Inmates*, 3.

2. Mosterman, *Spaces of Enslavement*, 58–59; Foote, *Black and White Manhattan*, 10, 27; Richardson, *New York Police*, 3.

3. Keller, *Triumph of Order*, 152.

4. Howe, *What Has God Wrought*, 118–20.

5. Keller, *Triumph of Order*, 152.

6. Wells, *Kidnapping Club*, 5.

7. Wells, 97.

8. Beckert, *Monied Metropolis*, 4–5.

9. Keller, *Triumph of Order*, 152.

10. Keller, 156.

11. Wells, *Kidnapping Club*, 35, 97.

12. Broeker, *Rural Disorder*; Vitale, *End of Policing*, 35.

13. "Correspondence of the Atlas," *Atlas*, March 31, 1844.

14. "The New Police Bill," *New-York Observer*, April 27, 1844.

15. "City Affairs," *New York Herald*, November 7, 1844.

16. "A Great Rush among the Natives," *New York Herald*, November 23, 1844.

17. Golway, *Machine Made*, 41.

18. Golway, 50–51.

19. Wilber Miller, *Cops and Bobbies*, 17.

20. Golway, *Machine Made*, 54.

21. Leslie Alexander, *African or American*, 168–73.

22. Golway, *Machine Made*, 72.

23. Wilber Miller, *Cops and Bobbies*, 18.

24. Golway, *Machine Made*, 54.

25. Stansell, *City of Women*, 171–73.

26. Stansell, 173.

27. Gilfoyle, *City of Eros*, 58–59.

28. *Herald*, July 6, 1857, as quoted in Keller, *Triumph of Order*, 159.

29. For more on the riots, see Bernstein, *New York City Draft*.

30. Harris, *In the Shadow*, 280.

31. "Junius," *Christian Records*, July 25, 1863, as quoted in Wellman, *Brooklyn's Promised Land*, 116–17.

32. Harris, *In the Shadow*, 286.

33. Keller, *Triumph of Order*, 160–64.

34. Beckert, *Monied Metropolis*, 274.

35. Beckert, 276.

36. Beckert, 287.

37. Thale, "Informal World," 200.

38. Thale, 201.

39. This dynamic can be seen as an illustration of a "social history of the state," as Margot Canaday describes in *Straight State*, 5.

40. King, *Whose Harlem?*, 7.

41. Vaz, "Tammany Hall," 105.

42. Czitrom, *New York Exposed*, 97.

43. Czitrom, 69.

44. Johnson, *Street Justice*, 51.

45. Johnson, 88.

46. King, *Whose Harlem?*, 23.

47. "Reminiscences of Samuel J. Battle," 1960, 20, 28, OHA.

48. David A. Goldberg notes that by the mid-1940s there were only ninety Black firemen in the FDNY. *Black Firefighters*, 97.

49. Czitrom, *New York Exposed*, 294.

50. Hicks, *Talk with You*, 55.

51. Johnson, *Street Justice*, 60–68.

52. King, *Whose Harlem?*, 154.

53. Fronc, *New York Undercover*, 3, 4.

54. Fronc, 96.

55. Evens, "Plainclothes Policewomen."

56. Go, "Imperial Origins," 1203–5.

57. Capozzola, *Uncle Sam Wants You*, 118.

58. "The Home Guard," *New York Times*, July 7, 1916, 10.

59. Allan Brandt, *No Magic Bullet*, 64; Stern, *Trials of Nina McColl*, 42–46.

60. Allan Brandt, *No Magic Bullet*, 74.

61. Brandt, 86.

62. Clement, *Love for Sale*, 125.

63. Clement, 127–31.

64. Czitrom, *New York Exposed*, 67–102; Golway, *Machine Made*.

65. Guariglia, "American Problem," 199–205, 213–14.

66. "Police Commissioner or Puppet?," *New York Times*, January 24, 1918, 8; "Commissioner Is Tammany Man," *Christian Science Monitor*, January 24, 1918, 7. For a discussion of the *New York Times* in the 1920s, see Brinkley, *Publisher*, 90–91.

67. "Hylan Forces Bugher Out; Names Enright," *New York Times*, January 24, 1918, 1.

68. "Reminiscences of August William Flath," 1958–1959, 21–22, OHA.

69. NYPD Annual Report, 1922, 240; "Reminiscences of August William Flath," 1958–1959, 22, OHA.

70. "Enright Admits Crime Wave in City; Adopts Woods Plan," *Brooklyn Daily Eagle*, December 19, 1920, 5.

71. Guariglia, "American Problem," 230.

72. NYPD Annual Report, 1922, 105.

73. Thale, "Assigned to Patrol," 1039, 1045.

74. Thale notes that merchants were an exception to this trend because they cultivated positive relationships with patrolmen from which both benefited. Thale, "Informal World," 196.

75. NYPD Annual Report, 1920, 25–26; NYPD Annual Report, 1922, 26–32.

76. NYPD Annual Report, 1922, 24–25.

77. For more on police violence and criminality during the mid-nineteenth century, see Wells, *Kidnapping Club*; Keller, *Triumph of Order*; Johnson, *Street Justice*; and Wilber Miller, *Cops and Bobbies*. Elizabeth Clement explores police involvement in the city's sex industries in the 1920s in *Love for Sale*, 193–98.

78. For a discussion of what Seabury's investigation revealed about police, magistrates, and women arrested for prostitution, see Hicks, *Talk with You*, 177–79. For more on police and alcohol prohibition, see Johnson, *Street Justice*, 114–22.

79. "Captain Beat Him, Prisoner Charges," *New York Times*, March 11, 1922, 3, quoted in Johnson, *Street Justice*, 115.

80. Johnson, *Street Justice*, 123–24.

81. Johnson, 134.

82. Hicks, *Talk with You*, 68–85; Flowe, *Uncontrollable Blackness*, 50–54.

83. Johnson, *Street Justice*, 136.

84. King, *Whose Harlem?*, 174.

85. Harris, "'Women and Girls.'"

86. King, *Whose Harlem?*, 174; T. R. Poston, "You Can't Win! The Law Made Luther Boddy a Killer—the Law Killed Him," *New York Amsterdam News*, May 19, 1934, 9.

87. Stephen Robertson, "Harlem Undercover," 500.

88. King, *Whose Harlem?*, 131–32.

89. Flowe, *Uncontrollable Blackness*, 60.

90. "Police Officer Tells Experiences Had with Harlem Citizens and Declares They Are among New York's Best Inhabitants," *New York Age*, September 26, 1925, 2.

91. "Police Now Stars in Pistol Practice," *New York Times*, February 1, 1925, 19; E. E. Hart, "The Negro and the Finest," *New York Amsterdam News*, September 9, 1925, 16.

92. Hart, "Negro and the Finest," 16.

93. Gallagher, *Black Women*, 18–29. Matthew Vaz argues that the important relationship between Black urbanites and Democratic machines like Tammany has been understudied and overlooked. "Tammany Hall."

94. "Hylan Charges Foes Seek an 'Open Town,'" *New York Times*, August 24, 1925, 1; Lerner, *Dry Manhattan*, 160–61.

95. Lerner, *Dry Manhattan*, 160–61.

96. "Northwest Sees Walker's Victory as Smith-Tammany Benefit," *Brooklyn Daily Eagle*, November 21, 1925, 6; Lerner, *Dry Manhattan*, 161.

97. Lerner, *Dry Manhattan*, 162, 168.

98. Binder, *All the Nations*, 161; David J. Goldberg, "Unmasking the Ku Klux Klan," 36.

99. Mitgang, *Once upon a Time*, 73–74.

100. "Hylan Says Enright Is Assured His Job While He Is Mayor," *Brooklyn Daily Eagle*, January 24, 1925, 3; "Alderman O'Reilly Scored Enright's 'Crazy Actions,'" *Brooklyn Daily Eagle*, May 27, 1925, 7; "Enright to Enter Business after Jan. 1, Is Report,"

Brooklyn Daily Eagle, September 17, 1925, 11; "Enright Heads List of Hylan's Followers to Go," *Brooklyn Daily Eagle*, November 4, 1925, 1.

101. "Enright Prefers La Guardia, He Says," *New York Times*, September 17, 1929, 5.

102. Martin Dickstein, "The Screen," *Brooklyn Daily Eagle*, January 7, 1933, 14.

103. Lerner, *Dry Manhattan*, 164–66; Chauncey, *Gay New York*, 294–95.

104. "Down to a 19-Hour Day," *New York Times*, October 23, 1926, 16.

105. Because it was so frequently violated, the law became a useful tool for NYPD officials to mobilize against ill-favored establishments, particularly after the NYPD took over the administration of cabaret licenses from the Department of Licenses in 1931. In 1940, the NYPD began requiring cabaret performers to undergo fingerprint checks to prove they had not been convicted of any crimes. This identity check constituted part of the city and the state's expanding regulation and criminalization of gay men and women, Black performers, and drug users. For more on the Cabaret Law and the regulation of gay men and women in New York City, see Chauncey, *Gay New York*, 352. Johann Hari discusses how Billie Holiday was stripped of her cabaret performer's license after Federal Bureau of Narcotics director Harry Anslinger's campaign against her resulted in her arrest for drug possession. Hari, *Chasing the Scream*, locations 482–503; "Billie's NY Nitery Jobs Seen Ended," *New York Age*, March 26, 1949, 2; Lerner, *Dry Manhattan*, 164–66. In an unlikely twist, the Cabaret Law became the Walker administration's longest-running legacy and served as a police weapon against nonwhite and working-class leisure until its repeal in 2017. "After 91 Years, New York Will Let Its People Boogie," *New York Times*, October 30, 2017.

106. James A. Hagerty, "New York City Election Brings Four Aspirants into the Field," *New York Times*, September 29, 1929, XX1.

107. "Walker Foes Score Rule at Luncheon," *New York Times*, May 19, 1929, 11.

108. "Text of La Guardia's Address, Pledging City Reorganization," *New York Times*, September 21, 1929, 10.

109. "Walker Scored for Rome 'Jim-Crowe,'" *New York Amsterdam News*, October 23, 1929, 3.

110. Hagerty, "New York City Election," XX1; J. A. Hagerty, "Rothstein Murder Still Big City Issue," *New York Times*, October 7, 1929, 3.

111. "Negroes Form Body to Support Walker," *New York Times*, October 8, 1929, 8; "Democrats to Speak in Harlem Monday Night," *New York Age*, November 2, 1929, 10.

112. Clinton L. Mosher, "497, 165 Plurality Hailed by Walker as a Vindication," *Brooklyn Daily Eagle*, November 6, 1929, 1.

113. Mosher, 1; "Big Vote Piled Up," *New York Times*, November 6, 1929, 1.

114. "Socialist Peak Set by Thomas's Vote," *New York Times*, November 6, 1929, 5.

115. King, *Whose Harlem?*, 108–18; "Harlem's Assemblymen-Elect: Will Seek Rent Relief, Court District and Harlem Senator," *New York Amsterdam News*, December 25, 1929, 1.

116. Editorial, "The Last Stand: Tammany Resorts to Race Prejudice in Attempt to Defeat Delaney," *New York Amsterdam News*, October 30, 1929, 1; "Delany Charges Tammany with Unfair Attacks," *Negro World*, November 9, 1929, 1.

117. "Major La Guardia," *New York Amsterdam News*, November 6, 1929, 20.

118. "Industry Fell Off Here in December," *New York Times*, January 21, 1930, 18.

119. Johnson, *Street Justice*, 152–65.

120. Mitgang, *Man Who Rode*, xv.

121. Mitgang, 176.

122. Mitgang, 180–88.

123. "Walker's Exit Dramatic," *New York Times*, October 7, 1932, 1.

124. "Big Vote for M'Kee," *New York Times*, November 9, 1932, 1.

125. Mitgang, *Man Who Rode*, 320.

126. Mitgang, 319.

127. Mitgang, 324.

Chapter Two

1. Mitgang, *Man Who Rode*, 326.

2. Mitgang, 357.

3. La Guardia, *Making of an Insurgent*, 30; Henry F. Pringle, "Pre-City Hall Days of Fiorello H. La Guardia," *New York Times*, May 23, 1948, BR3.

4. Mason Williams, *City of Ambition*, 19; Kessner, *Fiorello H. La Guardia*, 3–15.

5. La Guardia, *Making of an Insurgent*, 33; Mason Williams, *City of Ambition*, 20.

6. Mitgang, *Man Who Rode*, 326.

7. "Ready to Fight, He Warns," *New York Times*, December 20, 1933, 1.

8. La Guardia, *Making of an Insurgent*, 71.

9. La Guardia, 70–72.

10. La Guardia, 73.

11. The literature on the impact of New Deal programs is vast. Some particularly relevant examples of differential access to its programs include Katznelson, *When Affirmative Action*; and Deborah Gray White, *Too Heavy a Load*, 142–45. Mark Naison describes how Communists sought to capitalize on racism in New Deal programs to build their audience in Harlem in *Communists in Harlem*, 105. Cheryl Lynn Greenberg contends, however, that in New York City the dissemination of relief did not appear to be systemically racially discriminatory, though there were many individual examples of discrimination. Greenberg, *"Or Does It Explode?,"* 144–47. It is worth noting that in New York and at the federal level, some New Deal programs helped build the carceral state through working with local policing programs like the NYPD's Juvenile Aid Bureau. Suddler, *Presumed Criminal*, 25.

12. Theoharis and Cox, *Boss*, 121–32; Pliley, *Policing Sexuality*, 183–85.

13. Mills, "Liberalism," 32.

14. Muhammad, *Condemnation of Blackness*, 270–73.

15. Purnell and Theoharis, "Introduction," 2.

16. Karen Miller, *Managing Inequality*, 4. Naomi Murakawa shows that in the 1940s politicians at the federal level adopted an approach similar to La Guardia's, arguing that modernizing the state's carceral systems and removing individual racial bias from its ranks would advance the cause of civil rights. Murakawa, *First Civil Right*, 10, 29.

17. La Guardia to Miss Olsen, April 22, 1943, Folder 11, Roll 110, Subject Files: Juvenile Delinquency, FLGC.

18. McLeod, *Daughter*, xiii.

19. Kessner, *Fiorello H. La Guardia*, 536.

20. Capeci, "From Different Liberal Perspectives," 161.

21. Capeci; Haygood, *King of the Cats*, 40–43.

22. Office of Facts and Figures, *Negro Looks*, table 40.

23. Suddler, *Presumed Criminal*, 46–47.

24. Johnson, *Street Justice*, 168–72; "Valentine Named as Head of Police," *New York Times*, September 22, 1934, 1.

25. Lewis Valentine, "Editorially Speaking," *Spring 3100*, November 1934, 3.

26. "Valentine Named as Head of Police," *New York Times*, September 22, 1934, 1.

27. Valentine, *Night Stick*, 23–25.

28. William A. Turk, "Deportment and Morale," *Spring 3100*, October 1935, 23.

29. "Mayor Backs Police on 'Muss 'Em Up' Order; Finds City and Gangs in 'State of War,'" *New York Times*, January 27, 1935, 1.

30. "Army, Navy Spur Vice Drive Here," *New York Times*, August 11, 1942, 14.

31. Valentine, *Night Stick*, 12.

32. Valentine, 11.

33. Venereal Disease Control Conference, June 29, 1943, Roll 251, Folder 12, Subject Files: Venereal Disease, FLGC.

34. Police Department City of New York, Rules and Regulations, 1934, 9, Manuals of Procedure, JJCA.

35. Louis F. Costuma, "Police Procedure and Practice in Arrest and Apprehension," *Spring 3100*, April 1941, 14.

36. Police Department City of New York, Rules and Regulations, December 16, 1940, 391, 324–325, Manuals of Procedure, JJCA.

37. Police Department City of New York, 392.

38. Betty Brainered, "The Policewoman Is a Real Actress," *Brooklyn Daily Eagle*, February 17, 1935, 53.

39. John W. Harrington, "New York Policewomen Keen to Shoot Straight," *New York Times*, December 23, 1934, XX11.

40. "Policewoman's Kit: Has Two Kinds of Powder," *New York Times*, September 25, 1943, 12.

41. Freedman, *Their Sister's Keepers*, 58–64; "Nine More New Laws," *New York Times*, May 30, 1888; Odem, *Delinquent Daughters*, 96; Peiss, *Cheap Amusements*; Vapnek, *Breadwinners*; Ruth Alexander, *"Girl Problem"*; Hicks, "'In Danger.'"

42. Walker, *Critical History*, 55. Dorothy Schulz further explores women's roles in police departments in *Social Worker to Crimefighter*.

43. Police Department City of New York, Rules and Regulations, December 16, 1940, 23, Manuals of Procedure, JJCA.

44. Schulz, "Precinct of Their Own," 55.

45. "35 Years on Force, Woman to Retire," *New York Times*, April 3, 1946, 26; Sullivan, *My Double Life*, 280–81.

46. John H. Morris, "Programs for the Prevention of Juvenile Delinquency and Crime," *Spring 3100*, October 1940, 16, 17, 19.

47. John H. Morris, "Organization and Work of the Juvenile Aid Bureau," *Spring 3100*, November 1938, 15; Suddler, *Presumed Criminal*, 21–30. Agyepong explicates the

racialization of this narrative and the ways that it was put into practice in *Criminalization of Black Children*.

48. Hicks, *Talk with You*, 159–81; Deborah Gray White, *Too Heavy a Load*, 142–45.

49. "First Negro Policewoman Sworn in as Member of Bar," *New York Amsterdam News*, December 1, 1945, 9; "The Negro in the New York Fire and Police Departments," *New York Amsterdam News*, December 18, 1929, 12. There is no evidence that the department employed any Puerto Rican women in the 1940s. In 1988, "Hispanic officers" of all genders formed 11 percent of the force. "New York Cops Make Solid Citizens," *New York Times*, March 3, 1988, A30.

50. Darien, *Becoming New York's Finest*, 43.

51. King, *Whose Harlem?*, 176.

52. "Valentine Wants More Negro Police," *New York Times*, May 1, 1944, 23; "Raw Deal for Harlem," *People's Voice*, October 2, 1943.

53. "Policemen's Hostile Tactics Outlined by Mayor's Report," *New York Amsterdam News*, October 2, 1943, 5.

54. "Negroes on the N.Y. Police Force," *New York Amsterdam-Star News*, July 25, 1942, 6.

55. "Valentine Wants More Negro Police," 23.

56. "Harlemites Interested in Becoming Policemen," *New York Amsterdam News*, July 31, 1943, 10.

57. Darien, *Becoming New York's Finest*, 17–24.

58. "Denies Harlem Job 'Punishes' Police," *New York Times*, November 26, 1941, 48.

59. "Reminiscences of Samuel Battle," 1960, 46, OHA.

60. Darien, *Becoming New York's Finest*, 33.

61. Clarence Taylor, *Fight the Power*, 29.

62. Browne, *One Righteous Man*, 380–462.

63. "Reminiscences of Samuel Battle," 46.

64. Browne, *One Righteous Man*, 380–462; "Reminiscences of Samuel Battle," 46.

65. "Police Athletic League of All Nations," *Spring 3100*, April 1939, 27.

66. Lewis Valentine, "Juvenile Delinquency in Brooklyn," *Brooklyn Daily Eagle*, October 31, 1943, 1.

67. Tuttle, *Daddy's Gone to War*, 30.

68. "Municipal Civil Service Commission, New York City," *Spring 3100*, December 1939, 33.

69. Marsh, *Prostitutes in New York City*, 143. Scott Stern describes a provision similar to Article 17-B that was introduced in New York State in 1910 but was struck down by the state supreme court in 1911. Stern, *Trials of Nina McCall*, 25–26.

70. "Venereal Disease Control Conference," September 18, 1944, 32, Folder "New York," Box 7, Entry 40, NACP.

71. "Governor Lehman's Message to the Legislature Dealing Solely with Defense Problems in State," *New York Times*, January 9, 1941, 14.

72. "Big Steps to Be Taken to Build Up Defenses," *New York Times*, June 9, 1940, E7.

73. "State Guard Units to Begin Training," *New York Times*, June 13, 1943, 46.

74. "Governor Lehman's Message," 14.

75. "Harlem Is Orderly with Heavy Guard Ready for Trouble," *New York Times*, August 3, 1943, 1.

76. "Venereal Diseases," *New York Times*, October 14, 1939, 18; "Teamwork in Venereal Disease Prevention: A Report of the 1943 Activities to the Friends of the American Social Hygiene Association," 1, Box 231, Folder "ASHA Annual Reports," reprinted from *Journal of Social Hygiene*, March 1944, 11–12, SWHA.

77. "Venereal Disease Control Conference," 16.

78. Text of agreement in Hegarty, *Victory Girls*, appendix 1, 165–66.

79. "FWA Gives $1,717,080 for Venereal Care," *New York Times*, January 12, 1943, 15.

80. Charles Livermore to Tom Devine, May 10, 1945, Folder 6, Box 1, Entry 38, NACP. Date of creation of SPD from Hegarty, *Victory Girls*, 14.

81. Allan Brandt, *No Magic Bullet*, 169.

82. Meyer, *Creating GI Jane*, 103, 106.

83. "The Army Trained 'Tat' Terry for Job of Protecting New York," *New York Times*, June 4, 1942, 13.

84. "Conference Re: Prostitution and the Spread of Venereal Diseases among Our Armed Forces and Civilians," Office of the Commissioner of Health, August 5, 1942, Folder 23, Police Department—Venereal Conference on Prostitution, 1942, Box 2-1, City 24, Ernest Stebbins, HCR.

85. Allan Brandt, *No Magic Bullet*, 5.

86. "New York State Police Conference," *Spring 3100*, September 1940, 4.

87. "Mayor La Guardia to Ask Congress for Draft Revision," *Spring 3100*, December 1940, 4.

88. "New York State Police Conference," 4.

89. NYPD Annual Report, 1944, 2; "2D Policeman-Father Faces Yonkers Draft," *New York Times*, August 23, 1943, 8; "Draft of Policemen Will Decrease Here," *New York Times*, February 10, 1944, 10.

90. "Mayor La Guardia's Report on the City's Civilian Defense," *New York Times*, January 5, 1942, 8.

91. "Entire City Put on War Footing," *New York Times*, December 8, 1941, 1.

92. Lewis Valentine, "A Message from the Police Commissioner," *Spring 3100*, December 1941, 2.

93. R. M. Danford, "Final Report of the Commandant, City Patrol Corps to La Guardia," pt. 1, September 1945, 6, Folder 7, Roll 0152, Subject Files: City Patrol Corps, FLGC.

94. "Mayor Commissions Patrol Corps Aides," *New York Times*, October 6, 1942, 11.

95. Danford, "Final Report," pt. 1, p. 6; "As to Compulsory Drilling," *Brooklyn Daily Eagle*, December 19, 1920, 20; "Legion Heads to Seek Removal of Isaacs in Fight over Appointment of Gerson," *New York Times*, February 11, 1938, 7; "Patrol Corps Formed," *New York Times*, March 8, 1942, 28; "What's Going On in Lodge," *Brooklyn Daily Eagle*, May 19, 1935, 60.

96. NYPD Annual Report, 1942, 31, 1.

97. "La Guardia Threat Is Sent to 3-A Men," *New York Times*, June 27, 1942, 1. For more on the City Patrol Corps and the La Guardia administration, see Brooks, "Coercive Patriotism."

98. Danford, "Final Report," pt. 1, p. 7.

99. Marilynn Johnson's research on the San Francisco and Oakland area suggests that other auxiliary agencies did do police work informally, but it appears that the City

Patrol Corps had more official support for its policing work than other wartime auxiliary policing entities. Johnson, *Second Gold Rush*, 157–63.

100. Danford, "Final Report," pt. 1, p. 6.

101. Ozelious Clement to La Guardia, October 4, 1943; La Guardia to Valentine, October 19, 1943; La Guardia to Ozelious Clement, October 22, 1943, Folder 12, Roll 110, Subject Files: Juvenile Delinquency, FLGC.

102. Danford, "Final Report," pt. 1, p. 20.

103. "Heel a Group of Big Brothers! Company L of the City Patrol," *New York Amsterdam News*, December 25, 1943, 11_A.

104. "Join the City Patrol Corps," *New York Times*, September 23, 1943, 23.

105. "Final Report," HDQRS Bronx Division, City Patrol Corps, September 4, 1945, Folder 9, Roll 0152, Subject Files: City Patrol Corps, FLGC.

106. Lewis Valentine to Fiorello La Guardia, March 27, 1944, Folder 12, Roll 110, Subject Files: Juvenile Delinquency, FLGC.

107. Final Report, Supplement No.1, Headquarters Queens Division to Commandant City Patrol Corps, August 31, 1945, Folder 11, Roll 0152, Subject Files: City Patrol Corps, FLGC.

108. "Need Polise [*sic*] for Jamaica," *New York Amsterdam News*, July 29, 1944, 1B.

109. "Known Facts of Sunday Night's and Monday Morning's Disturbances," *People's Voice*, August 7, 1943, 2; "City Patrol Corps Dance to Feature Leading Stars," *People's Voice*, October 23, 1943, 6; Harlem riot of 1943 reports, Manuscripts, Archives, and Rare Books Division, Schomburg Center for Research in Black Culture, New York Public Library.

110. "City Patrol Corps Dance," 6; Walter White, *Man Called White*, 233–37.

111. Georgina W. Carson, "Final Report, Women's Division City Patrol Corps to Commandant City Patrols Corps," September 1, 1945, 31, Folder 12, Roll 0152, Subject Files: City Patrol Corps, FLGC.

112. R. M. Danford, "Final Report of the Commandant, City Patrol Corps to La Guardia," pt. 2, September 1945, Folder 8, Roll 152, Subject Files: City Patrol Corps, FLGC.

113. Sixth deputy police commissioner William M. Kent discusses the coordinating committees in relation to retrenchment in PAL budgets in his refutation of the report of the Mayor's Committee on Juvenile Delinquency. Kent to La Guardia, August 12, 1944, 7, Folder 37, Roll 111, Subject Files: Juvenile Delinquency, FLGC.

114. James B. Nolan to La Guardia, February 7, 1945, Folder 47, Roll 111, Subject Files: Juvenile Delinquency, FLGC.

115. Constitution of ___ Precinct Coordinating Council, Folder 18, Roll 110, Subject Files: Juvenile Delinquency, FLGC.

116. James B. Nolan to La Guardia, February 7, 1945, Folder 47, Roll 111, Subject Files: Juvenile Delinquency, FLGC.

117. Henry Grimmel to La Guardia, July 21, 1944, Folder 36, Roll 111, Subject Files: Juvenile Delinquency, FLGC.

118. NYPD Annual Report, 1942, 1; NYPD Annual Report, 1943, 3.

119. "12 Girls Start Training Today as Policewomen," *New York Herald-Tribune*, February 5, 1942, 16.

120. "First Negro Policewoman Sworn in as Member of Bar," *New York Amsterdam News*, December 1, 1945, 9; "New York Cops Make Solid Citizens," *New York Times*, March 3, 1988, A30.

121. "Strictly for the Girls!," *Spring 3100*, April 1944, 24.

122. "Fair, Fat and Forty," *Spring 3100*, April 1944, 25.

123. Schulz, *Social Worker to Crimefighter*, 5.

124. Darien, *Becoming New York's Finest*, 52–65.

125. Karen Anderson, *Wartime Women*; Hartmann, *Home Front and Beyond*.

126. Karen Anderson, "Last Hired, First Fired," 83–84.

127. Meyer, *Creating GI Jane*, 71–99.

128. Janann Sherman explores the postwar integration of women into the military in "They Either Need."

129. Valentine, *Night Stick*, 311, 316–17. Janis Appier argues that women in the LAPD faced a decline in status in the late 1930s and early 1940s as they became more fully integrated into the department and lost their policewoman-run advisory board. Appier contends that in these years the LAPD transitioned from a "crime prevention" model, in which women assisted with identifying and regulating behavior associated with morality, to a more masculine policy of "crime control," but she may overstate the divisions between these types of policing. She states, for example, that policewomen in the department continued to arrest large numbers of young women for sex delinquency in the 1940s, but she also argues that they lost their position as the "'natural' protectors of girls and women in public." Appier, *Policing Women*, 153–54. Dorothy Schulz argues that women were less central to policing during World War II than in World War I but notes than the NYPD, in which women played a "very definite part" in anti-vice policing, was an exception to this trend. Schulz, *Social Worker to Crimefighter*, 101–5.

130. John Sutter, "Police Responsibility for Social Protection in Wartime," 1943, Folder 15, Roll 251, Subject Files: Venereal Disease, FLGC; "Police to Safeguard Service Men in City," *New York Times*, February 5, 1942, 13; "Police Set Up a Roving Squad to Curb Vice," *New York Herald-Tribune*, February 5, 1942, 8.

131. "Police Department Adds a Division of Defense," *New York Times*, January 25, 1942, 32; "Mayor Bars Heavy Drinking as a Peril to Nation at War," *New York Times*, September 22, 1942, 1.

132. U.S. Census Bureau, 1940 Census, "Louis Costuma," Census Place: New York, New York, New York, Roll: m-t0627–02670, Page: 5B, Enumeration District: 31–1894, accessed through ancestry.com.

133. "Costuma Appointed to Parole Board Job," *New York Times*, July 25, 1945, 38.

134. "Police Honor Legion Elects David Salter," *New York Times*, December 17, 1940, 30; "Policemen Praised for War Sacrifices," *New York Times*, May 24, 1942, 41.

135. "Somewhere in the S.W. Pacific Combat Zone," *Spring 3100*, February 1943, 2.

136. Stanley Koutnick, letter to the editor, *Spring 3100*, April 1943, 6.

Chapter Three

1. "Tiger Chiefs at Bay, to Battle Seabury City Manager Plan," *Brooklyn Daily Eagle*, January 25, 1932, 1; Peretti, *Nightclub City*, 123–25. The quotation used for the title of

this chapter comes from Lewis Valentine, Conference on Matters Pertaining to Civilian Defense, February 11, 1942, Roll 7, Folder 2, Office of Civilian Defense Correspondence, FLGC.

2. Gilfoyle, *City of Eros*, 306.

3. Clement, *Love for Sale*, 193.

4. "Innocent Girls Arrested," *New York Times*, November 27, 1930, 1.

5. "Follow That Trail!," *New York Amsterdam News*, December 3, 1930, 20.

6. "The Truth Begins to Come Out," *Brooklyn Daily Eagle*, November 25, 1930, 20.

7. Clement, *Love for Sale*, 1.

8. D'Emilio and Freedman, *Intimate Matters*, 241, 233–74.

9. Littauer, *Bad Girls*, 19–23; Clement, *Love for Sale*, 2.

10. Simmons, *Making Marriage Modern*, 185.

11. Rupp, *Mobilizing Women for War*; Karen Anderson, *Wartime Women*; Hartmann, *Home Front and Beyond*. Rebecca Jo Plant provides a useful exploration of the antimaternalism that structured the family life of mothers, many of whom were working, in this period in *Mom*, 20–54, 77–85.

12. Seabury, *Investigation of the Magistrates' Courts*, 100.

13. Hartman, *Wayward Lives, Beautiful Experiments*, xiv.

14. Fischer, *Streets Belong to Us*, 67–75, 49.

15. Robinson, *Functioning of the Women's Court*, 24.

16. Hartman, *Wayward Lives, Beautiful Experiments*, 256.

17. Address by Police Commissioner Lewis J. Valentine, United States Conference of Mayors, Washington, D.C., November 16, 1936, 12, Folder 6, James Bolan Papers, JJCA.

18. This surveillance-based approach was not limited to New York; it was also embraced by the national Public Health Service and encouraged by Surgeon General Thomas Parran. Parran described his support of forced examination, treatment, and quarantine for the "socially irresponsible" as early as 1931. Stern, *Trials of Nina McCall*, 194–95. For more on Parran's career, see Snyder, "New York," 631.

19. Allan Brandt, *No Magic Bullet*, 138–40.

20. Robinson, *Functioning of the Women's Court*, 3.

21. NYPD Annual Report 1935, 2; Milton Bracker, "Streamlining the Policewoman: The New Policewoman," *New York Times*, March 26, 1939, 112.

22. Hutzel, *Policewoman's Handbook*, 20.

23. Robinson, *Functioning of the Women's Court*, 24.

24. Robinson, 28.

25. Robinson, 42.

26. "Arrest Activities in 1935," *Spring 3100*, June 1936, 7.

27. Marsh, *Prostitutes in New York City*, 26. For more on the history of this prison, see Ryan, *Woman's House of Detention*.

28. Senate Hearings before Subcommittee on Investigation and Control of Venereal Disease Hearings on S. 3290, February 14, 15, 1938, Folder 4, Roll 250, Subject Files: Venereal Disease, FLGC.

29. Conference Re: Prostitution and the Spread of Venereal Disease among Our Armed Forces and Civilians, Folder 11, Roll 251, Subject Files: Venereal Disease, FLGC.

30. Robinson, *Functioning of the Women's Court*, 3; John Rice to Henry Curran, July 2, 1940, Folder 21, Police (Venereal), Box 2-1, City 19, Rec 0050, John L. Rice, HCR.

31. Marsh, *Prostitutes in New York City*, 87.

32. Joan Cook, "Anna M. Kross Dies; An Ex-City Official," *New York Times*, August 29, 1979, 19.

33. "A Body Blow to Rackets," *Brooklyn Daily Eagle*, June 9, 1936, 18; "Crime Experts Blame Police for Vice Rings," *Brooklyn Daily Eagle*, June 14, 1936, 29.

34. "New Policy Set Up in Women's Court," *New York Times*, January 3, 1935, 24.

35. Marsh, *Prostitutes in New York City*, 143.

36. Stern, *Trials of Nina McCall*, 44–45; Allan Brandt, *No Magic Bullet*, 64.

37. John. L. Rice, "Medical and Educational Aspects of Venereal Disease Program for New York City," January 30, 1935, "Regional Conference on Social Hygiene" Folder 29, Box 2.59, Series 1, Subseries 2, John L. Rice, HCR.

38. Walter Clarke, "Development of the Bureau of Social Hygiene in 1936," December 16, 1935, Folder 10, 1935, Venereal (1 of 21), Box 2.59, Series 1, Subseries 2, John L. Rice, HCR.

39. "The Control of Venereal Diseases and the Problem of Prostitution in the City of N.Y.," report of Subcommittee of the Committee on Public Health Relations of the New York Academy of Medicine, from E. H. L. Corwin to John L. Rice, November 26, 1935, 4, Folder 11, 1935, Venereal (2 of 21), Series 1, Subseries 2, Box 2.59, John L. Rice, HCR.

40. Marsh, *Prostitutes in New York City*.

41. Chief, Division of Venereal Diseases, to deputy commissioner, April 5, 1935, Folder 17, Venereal (8 of 21), Series 1, Subseries 2, Box 2.59, John. L. Rice, HCR.

42. John L. Rice, Commissioner of Health, to Dr. E. H. L. Corwin, Executive Secretary, New York Academy of Medicine, November 30, 1935, Folder 11, Box 2.59, Series 1, Subseries 2, John L. Rice, HCR.

43. "Control of Venereal Diseases," 4.

44. "The Civil Service," *New York Times*, July 4, 1936, 28.

45. "Rockefeller Way to Deal with Vice," *New York Times*, January 27, 1913, 1.

46. For more on these transitions, see Fronc, *New York Undercover*, 145–88; and Pliley, *Policing Sexuality*, particularly 183–206.

47. Scott Stern notes that rapid treatment centers did not begin receiving penicillin for treatment until October 1943 and the drug remained scarce for civilian women throughout 1944. Stern, *Trials of Nina McCall*, 227–28. Interestingly, the first commercial plant for mass production of penicillin by submerged culture was in Williamsburg, Brooklyn. Parascandola, "John Mahoney," 5; "Men for Penicillin Plant," *Brooklyn Daily Eagle*, February 27, 1944, 27.

48. "Asks Courts to Aid Diseased Women," *New York Times*, June 5, 1938, 2.

49. La Guardia to Henry Morganthau Jr., June 22, 1938; La Guardia to Frances Perkins, June 22, 1938; La Guardia to Thomas Parran, July 7, 1938; acting secretary of the interior to La Guardia, August 30, 1938, Folder 6, Roll 251, Subject Files: Venereal Disease, FLGC.

50. Deputy mayor to William Hodson, May 23, 1938, Folder 05, Roll 251, Subject Files: Venereal Diseases, FLGC.

51. John Rice to William Hodson, June 3, 1938, Folder 05, Roll 251, Subject Files: Venereal Diseases, FLGC.

52. Briggs, *Reproducing Empire*, 100. The Rockefeller Foundation's work in Puerto Rico came under particular scrutiny in the 1930s after one of its doctors described his desire to "exterminate the population" in a letter that became public, as Daniel Immerwahr details in *How to Hide an Empire*, 144.

53. Eric von Wilkinson, "Gallivanting about Brooklyn," *New York Age*, February 2, 1935, 7.

54. Ebenezer Ray, "Dottings of a Paragrapher," *New York Age*, February 9, 1935, 6.

55. Fischer, *Streets Belong to Us*, 26–37.

56. Gallon, *Pleasure in the News*, 4. Jane Dailey describes how fear of interracial sexual and romantic relationships was at the center of many white supremacist campaigns throughout the twentieth century as well as how the right to choose romantic partners across races was a central civil rights demand of many Black activists. For how these dynamics played out in the 1930s and 1940s, see Dailey, *White Fright*, 55–131.

57. Gallon, *Pleasure in the News*, 114.

58. Theophilus Lewis, "Harlem Sketchbook: Police in Sheep's Clothing," *New York Amsterdam News*, March 16, 1935, 8.

59. "Prostitution Must Go," *New York Amsterdam News*, July 3, 1937, 14.

60. "Push Campaign on Vice District," *New York Amsterdam News*, July 30, 1938, 1.

61. "Police Deny Crime Increases in Harlem; Citizens Protest," *New York Amsterdam News*, October 8, 1938, 1, 5.

62. "Police Deny Crime Increases," 1, 5.

63. "Red Light Daisy Given 6 Months: Block Association in Cleanup Drive," *New York Amsterdam News*, November 23, 1935, 1; Harris, *Sex Workers*, 167–69.

64. "She Claims Police Tried Shakedown," *New York Amsterdam News*, November 19, 1938, 1.

65. "Valentine Ponders Brooklyn Appeal," *New York Amsterdam News*, August 20, 1938, A2.

66. King, *Whose Harlem?*, 154.

67. Many historians and scholars of African American studies have explored the diversity of Black material and political positions in twentieth-century urban America. Cheryl Hicks and Kali Gross consider experiences of working-class Black women, including when they came into conflict with their middle-class peers, in New York City and Philadelphia, respectively. See Hicks, *Talk with You*; and Gross, *Colored Amazons*. LaShawn Harris has explored experiences of working-class, Communist, and progressive Black women in New York City in much of her work. See Harris, "Running with the Reds," "Marvel Cooke," and *Sex Workers*. Robin Kelley's *Race Rebels* is an essential intervention in Black working-class cultural history. For more on the role that Black property owners played in twentieth-century American capitalism, see Connolly, *World More Concrete*. For more on the ideological positioning of middle-class Black women, see Higginbotham, *Righteous Discontent*, 15. Kim Gallon explores how the Black press created "sexual publics" that reflected and generated varied and sometimes conflicting notions about respectability, sex, and criminality. Gallon, *Pleasure in the News*.

68. Harris, *Sex Workers*, 167–200.

69. "Pastors to Support Anti-noise Crusade," *New York Amsterdam News*, November 30, 1935, 17; "See Post Offering Chance for Battle to Be of Greater Service to His People," *New York Amsterdam News*, August 30, 1941, 3.

70. "Negroes on the N.Y. Police Force," *New York Amsterdam News*, July 25, 1942, 6.

71. St. Clair Bourne and Marvel Cooke, "The Truth about Harlem Crime," *New York Amsterdam News*, April 8, 1939, 11.

72. Harris, "Marvel Cooke," 93.

73. "Asks Courts to Aid Diseased Women," *New York Times*, June 5, 1938, 2.

74. Last names have been removed to protect the privacy of the arrestees. Sarah, arrested April 25, 1940, Record Book, January 1–December 31, 1940, City Magistrates' Court and Court of Special Sessions, WCMA. U.S. Census Bureau, 1940 Census, "Sarah _____," Census Place: New York, New York, Sheet Number 62 A, Enumeration District: 31-1528, accessed on ancestry.com.

75. Bernice, arrested December 11, 1940, Record Book, January 1–December 31, 1940, City Magistrates' Court and Court of Special Sessions, WCMA. U.S. Census Bureau, 1940 Census, "Bernice _____," Census Place: New York, New York, Sheet Number 8A, Enumeration District: 31-886, accessed on ancestry.com.

76. Alice, arrested June 22, 1940, Record Book, January 1–December 31, 1940, City Magistrates' Court and Court of Special Sessions, WCMA. U.S. Census Bureau, 1940 Census, "Alice _____," Census Place: New York, Kings, New York, Sheet Number 3A, Enumeration District: 24-59, accessed on ancestry.com.

77. Rosetta, arrested May 14, 1941, Record Book, January 1–December 31, 1941, City Magistrates' Court and Court of Special Sessions, WCMA. U.S. Census Bureau, 1940 Census, "Rosetta _____," Census Place: New York, New York, Sheet Number 13 B, Enumeration District: 31-1838, accessed on ancestry.com.

78. Harris, *Sex Workers*, 125.

79. Marsh, *Prostitutes in New York City*, 175.

80. For more on prostitution in New York City in the eighteenth and nineteenth centuries, see Gilfoyle, *City of Eros*; Gilje, *Road to Mobocracy*; Stansell, *City of Women*; Wood, *Their Sisters' Keepers*; Srebnick, *Mysterious Death of Mary Rogers*; Crist, "Babies in the Privy"; Milne and Crabtree, "Prostitutes"; Yamin, "Wealthy, Free, and Female"; and Anbinder, *Five Points*.

81. For a discussion of the contradictory and controversial policies embraced toward prostitution by the U.S. military in France, see Roberts, "Price of Discretion" and *What Soldiers Do*. For a discussion of the conservatizing impact of U.S. military presence in postwar Germany in relation to prostitution and gender politics, see Höhn, *GIs and Frauleins*. John Dower discusses the Japanese Home Ministry's recruitment of Japanese women to sexually service American G.I.s during the American occupation in *Embracing Defeat*. For more on the reorganization of Japan's police force, see Aldous, *Police in Occupation Japan*, 148–53; Kuzmarov, *Modernizing Repression*, 57–78; Kramm, *Sanitized Sex*.

82. Winchell, *Good Girls*; Hegarty, *Victory Girls*; Littauer, *Bad Girls*; Rupp, *Mobilizing Women for War*; Karen Anderson, *Wartime Women*; Plant, *Mom*; Hartmann, *Home Front and Beyond*, Fischer, *Streets Belong to Us*, 50–58.

83. Fischer, *Streets Belong to Us*, 64.

84. Lewis Valentine, Conference on Matters Pertaining to Civilian Defense, February 11, 1942, Folder 2, Roll 7, Office of Civilian Defense Correspondence, FLGC; "Army, Navy Spur Vice Drive Here," *New York Times*, August 11, 1942, 14.

85. "Map Broad Drive on Social Disease," *New York Times*, October 7, 1940, 5.

86. For more on the Public Health Service campaign, see Allan Brandt, *No Magic Bullet*.

87. Press release, Mayor's Office, July 13, 1941, Folder 10, Roll 251, Subject Files: Venereal Disease, FLGC.

88. William Ringel to John Rice, March 10, 1941, Folder 16, Magistrates' Court, Box 2-1, City 21, Rec 0050, John L. Rice, HCR.

89. "To Prohibit Prostitution within Reasonable Distance of Military and Naval Establishments," hearing in the Committee on Military Affairs, House, Congress Session 77-1, March 11, 12, 18, 1941, 15–21, Hearing ID HRG-1941-MAH-0002; "La Guardia Backs Camp Zoning Bill," *New York Times*, March 12, 1941, 14.

90. Riley, "Caring for Rosie's Children," 660. For more on these treatment centers, see Hegarty, *Victory Girls*, 145–55; Stern, *Trials of Nina McCall*, 217–20; Parascandola, "Quarantining Women"; Holloway, *Sexuality*, *Politics*, 147–87.

91. Police Conferences, February 4, 1942, Folder 2, Box 4183, Roll 7, Office of Civilian Defense Correspondence, FLGC.

92. John Rice to Lewis Valentine, December 19, 1941, Folder 36, Police, Box 2-1, City 21, Rec 0050, John L. Rice, HCR.

93. "Venereal Disease Control Conference," September 18, 1944, 31, Folder "New York," Box 7, Entry 40, NACP; "Police to Safeguard Service Men in City," *New York Times*, February 5, 1942, 13; "New Vice Squad Formed to Protect Service Men," *Brooklyn Daily Eagle*, February 5, 1942, 19.

94. "Venereal Disease Control Conference," 31; "Police to Safeguard"; "Wholesale Raids Spur Another 'Wave' Smear," *People's Voice*, May 9, 1942, 3.

95. Marsh, *Prostitutes in New York City*, 19 (discussion of targeting of working-class women), 11 (pattern of prostitution arrests).

96. Office of the Commissioner of Health, Conference Re: Prostitution and the Spread of Venereal Disease among Our Armed Forces and Civilians, August 2, 1942, Roll 251, Folder 11, Subject Files: Venereal Disease, FLGC.

97. "Army, Navy Spur Vice Drive Here," *New York Times*, August 11, 1942, 14.

98. "800 Arrested in Drive on Vice, Hogan Says," *New York Times*, July 26, 1942, 34.

99. Bud Robbins, interview in Estes, *Ask and Tell*, 23.

100. Vining, *Gay Diary*, 245; "Of Local Origin," *New York Times*, November 17, 1942, 29; "Films of the Week," *New York Times*, June 28, 1942, X4.

101. Vining, *Gay Diary*, 257, also 260, 261.

102. John L. Rice to Lewis Valentine, May 9, 1941, Folder 3, Police Department—Venereal, Box 2-1, City 22, Rec 0050, John L. Rice, HCR.

103. Vining, *Gay Diary*, 374.

104. Bérubé, *Coming Out under Fire*, 98.

105. Bérubé, 107; C. M. Watson to Ernest Stebbins, December 9, 1942, Folder 1, Police (Venereal), 1942, Box 2-1, City 24; C. M. Watson to Ernest Stebbins, December 9, 1942, Folder 1, Police (Venereal), 1942, Box 2-1, City 24, Ernest Stebbins, HCR.

106. Major General Irving Phillipson to Mayor La Guardia, April 15, 1942; Major General Irving Phillipson to Mayor La Guardia, April 24, 1942, Folder 10, Roll 251, Subject Files: Venereal Disease, FLGC.

107. "Police to Round Up City's Prostitutes," *Brooklyn Daily Eagle*, August 10, 1945, 1.

108. Ruth Emilie Jaeger to Rachel Hopper Powell, March 27, 1943, 2, Folder: House of Detention, 1937–1947, Box 19, Directors' and Staff Correspondence and Reports, WPA.

109. Office of the Commissioner of Health, Conference Re: Prostitution and the Spread of Venereal Disease among Our Armed Forces and Civilians, August 2, 1942, Folder 11, Roll 251, Subject Files: Venereal Disease, FLGC.

110. Stebbins had taken over for John Rice in July 1942 when illness forced Rice to resign from the position. The new commissioner proved even more committed to controlling women than his predecessor. "Stebbins Is Named City Health Chief," *New York Times*, July 16, 1942, 21; "Venereal Disease and Youth," *New York Times*, November 6, 1943, 12; "Rise in Venereal Disease," *New York Times*, January 13, 1945, 10; "Stebbins Attacks City Sanitary Code," *New York Times*, October 5, 1943, 27.

111. Dr. Theodore Rosenthal to Lewis Valentine, September 5, 1942, Folder 1, Police (Venereal), Box 2-1, City 24, Rec 0050, John L. Rice, HCR.

112. Ernest L. Stebbins to Thomas Parran, February 2, 1943, Folder: Social Security, Detention Hospitals, Rapid Treatment Centers (3 of 5), Box 3-1-6, 9, Rec 0050, John L. Rice, HCR.

113. Venereal Disease Control Conference, June 19, 1943, Roll 251, Folder 12, Subject Files: Venereal Disease, FLGC; "Low-Income Families Become City Tenants," *New York Times*, July 15, 1940, 14; "Mayor Denounces Gambling in State," *New York Times*, April 16, 1940, 23.

114. Ernest Stebbins to Valentine, December 10, 1943; Ernest Stebbins to Valentine, December 15, 1943; Ernest Stebbins to Valentine, December 16, 1943; Ernest Stebbins to Valentine, December 23, 1943; Ernest Stebbins to Valentine, December 29, 1943, Folder 1 of 14, Police, Venereal, Box 3-1-2, 3, 1943, Rec 0050, Ernest Stebbins, HCR.

115. For a discussion of the American Social Hygiene Association and ideology of race in the Tuskegee experiment, see Sharma, "Diseased Race, Racialized Disease."

116. Wuebker, "Taking the Venereal Out," 241.

117. "Young Girls Found Menace to Troops," *New York Times*, February 3, 1943, 18.

118. Dr. Theodore Rosenthal to Lewis Valentine, September 5, 1942, Folder 1, Police (Venereal), Box 2-1, City 24, Rec 0050, John L. Rice, HCR. Stern, *Trials of Nina McCall*, documents the prolonged journey of incarceration and harassment experienced by one woman accused of having a venereal disease shortly after World War I.

119. "Stebbins Attacks City Sanitary Code," *New York Times*, October 5, 1943, 27.

120. "Mayor's Air Raid Fears Held Cause of Hospital's Freeing of Women," *New York Times*, October 6, 1943, 25; "Hart Investigates City Health Office," *New York Times*, September 5, 1943, 31.

121. "Army, Navy Set Up Disciplinary Board," *New York Times*, October 21, 1944, 8.

122. "Board Seeks Ban on 'Loose' Tavern," *New York Times*, November 4, 1944, 17.

123. "Venereal Disease Control Conference," September 18, 1944, 33, Folder "New York," Box 7, Entry 40, NACP.

124. "New Clinic Here Gets FWA Funds," *New York Times*, February 13, 1944, 44.

125. Minutes of meeting of Committee on Rapid Treatment Hospital, October 19, 1943, Folder: Social Security, Detention Hospitals, Rapid Treatment Centers (1 of 5), Box 3-1-6, 9, Rec 0050, Ernest Stebbins, HCR; "2,471 Venereal Cases Treated," *New York Times*, December 26, 1944, 10.

126. "Venereal Ills Cut in Armed Forces," *New York Times*, February 17, 1943, 17.

127. Stern, *Trials of Nina McCall*, 239.

128. "City Held Freest of Organized Vice," *New York Times*, November 15, 1948, 45.

Chapter Four

1. Valentine, *Night Stick*, 207.

2. Agyepong, *Criminalization of Black Children*, 2.

3. For more on the creation of youth courts and how they functioned, see Odem, *Delinquent Daughters*; Ruth Alexander, *"Girl Problem"*; Wolcott, *Cops and Kids*; Tanenhaus, *Juvenile Justice*, particularly 3–22; Schneider, *In the Web*; and Ward, *Black Child-Savers*.

4. Suddler, *Presumed Criminal*, 25.

5. Agyepong, *Criminalization of Black Children*, 52.

6. John J. O'Connell, "Nature and Extent of Juvenile Delinquency," *Spring 3100*, August 1935, 10.

7. Nasaw, *Children of the City*, 23–24; Stansell, "Women, Children"; Wolcott, *Cops and Kids*, 43–44.

8. "Humbert Moruzzi Youth Center Dedicated," *Spring 3100*, December 1941, 8.

9. Gold, *Jews without Money*, 28; Nasaw, *Children of the City*, 24.

10. Valentine, *Night Stick*, 207, 213.

11. Myers, *Youth Squad*, 4.

12. Valentine, *Night Stick*, 207, 213.

13. Charles Willis Thompson, "Woods to Bring Police Department into the Uplift," *New York Times*, April 12, 1914, SM1; "Enright 'Shakes Up' Police Department," *New York Times*, February 10, 1918, 5; Walker, *Critical History*, 55.

14. Thompson, "Woods to Bring"; "Enright 'Shakes Up'"; "Whalen Acts to Curb Juvenile Criminals," *New York Times*, October 4, 1929, 30; Virginia Pope, "New Police Bureau Aims at Prevention of Crime," *New York Times*, February 2, 1930, 131; Suddler, *Presumed Criminal*, 23.

15. Valentine, *Night Stick*, 207.

16. "Plan Reorganizing of Crime Bureau," *Brooklyn Daily Eagle*, December 14, 1934, 7; Suddler, *Presumed Criminal*, 24.

17. "New Name Sought for Crime Bureau," *New York Times*, April 29, 1934, 12.

18. "LaGuardia Hostile, Miss Additon Says," *New York Times*, September 29, 1934, 1; Suddler, *Presumed Criminal*, 24–25.

19. "Mayor's Reply Due Today on Additon Blast," *Brooklyn Daily Eagle*, September 29, 1934, 3.

20. "New Set-Up Given for Crime Bureau," *New York Times*, December 14, 1934, 8.

21. Report on the Juvenile Aid Bureau of the New York City Police Department and the Police Athletic League, sponsored by the Juvenile Aid Bureau, April 1, 1941, Folder 5, Roll 109, Subject Files: Juvenile Delinquency, FLGC.

22. John J. O'Connell, "Nature and Extent of Juvenile Delinquency," *Spring 3100*, August 1935, 11; Suddler, *Presumed Criminal*, 24.

23. "Director Byrnes Macdonald," *Spring 3100*, November 1935, 25; "MacDonald Sworn as Police Official," *Brooklyn Daily Eagle*, September 30, 1935, 1.

24. "Byrnes M'Donald Dead Here at 51," *New York Times*, October 11, 1959, 86.

25. "City Youth Centers to Aid Crime Fight," *New York Times*, December 9, 1935, 23.

26. NYPD Annual Report, 1934, 43.

27. Byrnes MacDonald, "Youth and Crime Today," *Spring 3100*, April 1936, 10.

28. Thelma Berlack-Boozer, "Broken-Home Children: Juvenile Aid Renders Other Forms of Service," *New York Amsterdam News*, October 9, 1937, 12.

29. "Ex-Police Deputy Returns to School," *Brooklyn Daily Eagle*, January 17, 1937, 27.

30. Suddler, *Presumed Criminal*, 26–27.

31. Arthur Wallander, "Annual PAL Boxing Show," *Spring 3100*, June, 1935, 25.

32. "City Youth Centres to Aid Crime Fight," *New York Times*, December 9, 1935, 23.

33. MacDonald, "Youth and Crime Today," 11.

34. John J. O'Connell, "Nature and Extent of Juvenile Delinquency," *Spring 3100*, August 1935, 16; "150 Police Issued for Honor Service," *New York Times*, December 30, 1933, 30.

35. In 1934, 45 percent of the 6,584 new juvenile cases investigated by the JAB were initiated by NYPD members. NYPD Annual Report 1934, 43.

36. Hicks, "'In Danger'"; Hicks, *Talk with You*, 184; Ruth Alexander, *"Girl Problem."*

37. O'Connell, "Nature and Extent," 26.

38. Clarke, *Wayward Minors' Court*, 4.

39. "Crime and the Police," *New York Amsterdam News*, July 18, 1936, 20; O'Connell, "Nature and Extent," 26.

40. "Man Held as Abductor," *New York Times*, May 28, 1935, 3.

41. "Krist Girl on Probation," *New York Times*, August 28, 1934, 24.

42. Earl Brown, "Drama in Blue," *New York Amsterdam News*, February 20, 1937, 13.

43. "First Negro Policewoman Sworn in as Member of Bar," *New York Amsterdam News*, December 1, 1945, 9; "The Negro in the New York Fire and Police Departments," *New York Amsterdam News*, December 18, 1929, 12.

44. For more on the history of this ideology, see Hicks, *Talk with You*, 186; Agyepong, *Criminalization of Black Children*, 16–19; and Muhammad, *Condemnation of Blackness*, 116–30.

45. Charles E. Grutzner, "Delinquency: Noted Jurist Blames City and State for High Negro Rate," *New York Amsterdam News*, August 4, 1934, 9. In Manhattan Black children were 25 percent of delinquency cases and Black residents were 12 percent of the population. In Brooklyn, the percentages were 8 percent of children in juvenile court and 3 percent of the population. In Queens, Black residents made up 2 percent of the population and Black children made up 7 percent of the delinquency cases.

46. As Carl Suddler and Jacqueline McLeod detail, Judge Jane Bolin, the first African American woman judge in the country, who fought against racial segregation in reformatories, was an important exception to this practice. Suddler, *Presumed Criminal*, 28–38; McLeod, *Daughter*, 63.

47. For a discussion of how young Black women were criminalized in the early twentieth century, see Hicks, *Talk with You*, particularly 182–204. For more on the horrific conditions and treatment Black girls experienced in these facilities, see "Find Girls' Prison Place of 'Horrors,'" *New York Times*, November 14, 1914, 9; and Hartman, *Wayward Lives, Beautiful Experiments*, 74–75, 265–67, 276–78. For the way that prison officials further criminalized Black girls at these facilities through their sexuality, see Kunzel, "Situating Sex," 262. For more on segregation and differential treatment at New York reformatories, see Ruth Alexander, *"Girl Problem,"* 69–101. A report published by Georgetown Law entitled *Girlhood Interrupted: The Erasure of Black Girls' Childhood*, explores how race affects the way adults perceive innocence among girls today. Epstein, Blake, and González, *Girlhood Interrupted*.

48. Thomas, *Puerto Rican Citizen*, 107.

49. Thomas, 203.

50. Thomas, 138.

51. "250 More Police in Harlem to Stamp Out Crime Wave," *New York Times*, November 8, 1941, 1.

52. Virginia McCormick, "Fair Morning," *Spring 3100*, September 1939, 6–8.

53. Alex Greenbaum, "Off Tackle," *Spring 3100*, April 1941, 23.

54. *Spring 3100*, June 1935, 28; *Spring 3100*, July 1935, 25; *Spring 3100*, August 1935, 31. For more on pickaninny depictions and how they harmed Black children, see Agyepong, *Criminalization of Black Children*, 13–15.

55. "Cop Accused of Brutal Attack on Boy," *New York Amsterdam News*, October 6, 1934, 3.

56. Commission on the Harlem Riot, *Complete Report*, 7–8.

57. Johnson, *Street Justice*, 186–87; Greenberg, "Politics of Disorder," 424.

58. Commission on the Harlem Riot, *Complete Report*, 14–15.

59. Edgar T. Rouzeau, "The Man in the Street," *New York Amsterdam News*, March 30, 1935, 9; "Mayor's Committee under Fire," *New York Amsterdam News*, March 30, 1935, 1.

60. Commission on the Harlem Riot, *Complete Report*, 115.

61. "Cop Accused of Brutal Attack," 3. Black activists in Jamaica, Queens, connected the uprising to their own experiences and sent a set of demands to La Guardia. "Mayor's Committee under Fire."

62. Commission on the Harlem Riot, *Complete Report*, 1.

63. "Cops to Stay, Is Valentine's Terse Decree," *New York Amsterdam News*, May 30, 1936, 1.

64. "Cops to Stay."

65. T. R. Poston, "One Year Ago," *New York Amsterdam News*, March 14, 1936, 13.

66. NYPD Annual Report, 1936, 15.

67. Marvel Cooke, "Crime Not Only Business of Crime Prevention Bureau," *New York Amsterdam News*, June 20, 1936, 15.

68. "Police Athletic League of All Nations," *Spring 3100*, April 1939, 27.

69. The uncritical acceptance of this idea among wide swaths of American society during this period can be understood through Antonio Gramsci's definition of common sense as a set of assumptions held widely across society and generally believed to be true in a particular moment in time. For Gramsci's discussion of this idea, see Hoare and Nowell-Smith, *Selections from the Prison Notebooks*, 321–77. For another example and discussion of this usage, see Kohler-Hausmann, *Getting Tough*, 12–19.

70. Ideas about the role of the family and social environment in creating or preventing juvenile delinquency, connections between criminality and race, and the construction of interracial interactions as a cause of crime had been developing throughout the twentieth century and helped inform the belief that because wartime mobilization exacerbated changes in these areas, juvenile delinquency would follow. For histories of these connections, see Wolcott, *Cops and Kids*, 9–27; Muhammad, *Condemnation of Blackness*, 88–146; Odem, *Delinquent Daughters*, 157–84; and Nasaw, *Children of the City*, 150–71.

71. La Guardia to Miss Olsen, April 22, 1943, Folder 11, Roll 110, Subject Files: Juvenile Delinquency, FLGC.

72. For more on the conditions underlying the Harlem uprising of 1935, see Greenberg, *"Or Does It Explode?,"* 13–91.

73. In the interwar period, societal norms around dating and premarital sex had been loosening. D'Emilio and Freedman, *Intimate Matters*, 256–65; Clement, *Love for Sale*, 212–39. Kim Gallon discusses how young Black women were represented in the Black press within this shifting sexual landscape in *Pleasure in the News*, 76–79.

74. Littauer, *Bad Girls*, 19–20, 30.

75. Henry Curran, "Youth as Seen from Bench," *New York Times*, March 26, 1944, SM8.

76. For more on the history of the Wayward Minor Law in Progressive Era New York City, see Hicks, "'In Danger'"; Ruth Alexander, *"Girl Problem."*

77. Curran, "Youth as Seen from Bench."

78. "Plan for the Prevention of Juvenile Delinquency in the City of New York," submitted to La Guardia by Stephen S. Jackson, no date; La Guardia to Judge Warren Hill, May 29, 1940, Folder 1, Roll 109, Subject Files: Juvenile Delinquency, FLGC; "New Child Aid Unit Formed by Mayor," *New York Times*, June 2, 1940, 4.

79. "New Child Aid Unit Formed by Mayor," *New York Times*, June 2, 1940, 4; La Guardia to Judge Warren Hill, May 29, 1940, Folder 1, Roll 109, Subject Files: Juvenile Delinquency, FLGC.

80. Joan Cook, "Dorris Clarke, 74, Dies in Queens," *New York Times*, December 11, 1980, D19.

81. Clarke, *Wayward Minors' Court*, 8.

82. Clarke, 4.

83. Clarke, 21.

84. Clarke, 19, caps in original.

85. Clarke, 52.

86. "Minority Resolution on Child Delinquency," *New York Post*, November 5, 1942.

87. Examples of the dozens of letters to La Guardia on this topic can be found in Folders 9, 10, Roll 109, Subject Files: Juvenile Delinquency, FLGC.

88. "Juvenile Delinquency and the Mayor," *New York Post*, December 12, 1942.

89. Mayor's Committee on Juvenile Delinquency, "Report on the Juvenile Bureau and the Prevention of Crime and Delinquency," June 5, 1944, Folder 2, Roll 112, Subject Files: Juvenile Delinquency, FLGC. Before La Guardia's cuts, the bureau's budget hovered around $500,000 per year. In 1942–43, this was cut to $440,046, but the following year the mayor increased the budget to $511,616.

90. Cooper, *Designs in Scarlet*; "F.B.I. Appeals to Police," *New York Times*, February 10, 1943, 21; "Female Arrests Rise 18.4 Per Cent," *New York Times*, September 17, 1943, 18; Pliley, *Policing Sexuality*, 122–51.

91. "Mayor Appeals for War-Time Curb on Liquor," *New York Herald-Tribune*, September 22, 1942, 1.

92. "Juvenile Cases Heard in City's Court," *New York Herald-Tribune*, October 28, 1942, 14.

93. "Text of Dewey's Message to the Legislature Outlining State's War-Time Program," *New York Herald-Tribune*, January 7, 1943, 10.

94. "The Proceedings of the National Conference of Juvenile Agencies," February 1943, Folder 11, Roll 109, Subject Files: Juvenile Delinquency, FLGC.

95. Meyer Berger, "Times Square Diary," *New York Times*, September 3, 1944, SM16.

96. John Sutter, "Police Responsibility for Social Protection in Wartime," *Spring 3100*, December 1943, 5.

97. "Venereal Disease Control Conference," September 18, 1944, 31, 32, Folder "New York," Box 7, Entry 40, NACP.

98. "Hearing Is Held to Seek Curbs in Delinquency," *New York Herald-Tribune*, December 15, 1942, 24.

99. William B. Herlands to Fiorello La Guardia, "Case of Lorraine Sorenson, A Juvenile Delinquent Report," May 24, 1943, Folder 11, Roll 109, Subject Files: Juvenile Delinquency, FLGC.

100. Herlands to La Guardia.

101. Herlands to La Guardia.

102. "The Juvenile Aid Bureau of the New York City Police Department and the Police Athletic League Sponsored by the Juvenile Aid Bureau," September 1, 1943, Folder 14, Roll 110, Subject Files: Juvenile Delinquency, FLGC.

103. Division Orders #4, June 15, 1943, Folder 12, Roll 109, Subject Files: Juvenile Delinquency, FLGC.

104. Sixth deputy police commissioner William M. Kent discusses the coordinating committees in relation to retrenchment in PAL budgets in his refutation of the report of the Mayor's Committee on Juvenile Delinquency. Kent to La Guardia, August 12, 1944, 7, Folder 37, Roll 111; Precinct Coordinating Committee Constitution and Bylaws, no date, Folder 18, Roll 110, Subject Files: Juvenile Delinquency, FLGC.

105. Valentine to La Guardia, June 5, 1943, Folder 12, Roll 110, Subject Files: Juvenile Delinquency, FLGC.

106. La Guardia to Valentine, February 28, 1944, Folder 24, Roll 110, Subject Files: Juvenile Delinquency, FLGC.

107. Ann Petry, "In Darkness and Confusion," 264. Farah Jasmine Griffin describes Annie May as one of the "too-too girls" who represented a possible female counterpart to young male zoot-suiters. Griffin, *Harlem Nocturne*, 122–23.

108. Domestic Relations Court—Children's Division, Allegedly Delinquent Children, March 3, 1944, Folder 24, Roll 110, Subject Files: Juvenile Delinquency, FLGC; U.S. Census Bureau, *1940 Census*, vol. 2, *Characteristics of the Population*, pt. 5, *New York* (Washington, D.C.: Government Printing Office, 1943), 137, 156, https://www2.census.gov/library/publications/decennial/1940/population-volume-2/33973538v2p5ch2.pdf.

109. "Police in Harlem to Stamp Out Crime Wave," *New York Times*, November 8, 1941, 1.

110. "Subway Policeman Beats Student Then Locks Her in Washroom," *People's Voice*, March 20, 1943, 3; "Minister Assails Police Brutality to Editor," *New York Amsterdam News*, April 3, 1943, 10.

111. "Suspend Subway Cop Who Beat High School Girl," *People's Voice*, April 3, 1943, 3; "Subway Cop Suspension Is Quick One," *People's Voice*, April 17, 1943, 3. For more on the *People's Voice* and organizing in Harlem during the war, see chapter 5.

112. Moya Bailey, *Misogynoir Transformed*.

113. "Extra Cops Won't Solve Harlem's Ills," *People's Voice*, March 27, 1943, 24.

114. "Letter to the Editor, This Letter Went to Butch," *People's Voice*, March 27, 1943.

115. "Subway Cop Suspension."

116. Elmer H. Robertson to La Guardia, March 2, 1944, Folder 25, Roll 110, Subject Files: Juvenile Delinquency, FLGC.

117. La Guardia to Elmer H. Robertson, March 10, 1944, Folder 25, Roll 110, Subject Files: Juvenile Delinquency, FLGC.

118. Wilson D. McKerrow to Bruce Cobb, acting presiding justice, Domestic Relations Court, Memo: Regarding Escape of Five Girls from the Shelter, August 8, 1944, Folder 37, Roll 111, Subject Files: Juvenile Delinquency, FLGC.

119. Truda Weil to La Guardia, Digest, Folder 40, Roll 111, Subject Files: Juvenile Delinquency, FLGC.

120. For more about the Midtown Civic League's intimidation of Black residents, see Woodsworth, *Battle for Bed-Stuy*, 52; "'Terrorism' Is Laid to Brooklyn Group," *New York Times*, December 17, 1937, 16; and "Boro Smear Amounts to Nasty Mess," *People's Voice*, November 27, 1943, 7.

121. "Tells Valentine to Get Facts on Bedford Crime," *Brooklyn Daily Eagle*, November 16, 1943, 1, 5.

122. Wilder, *Covenant with Color*, 184–85.

123. "Urge Caution in Use of Borough Youth Court," *New York Amsterdam News*, June 17, 1944, 2B; "Negro Operators Get Stiff Terms," *New York Amsterdam News*, December 23, 1944, 17; "'Nigger Haters' Go Wild on Trolley Car," *New York Amsterdam News*, January 20, 1945, 15; "Editorial: About the Trolley Car Incident," *New York Amsterdam News*, January 27, 1945, 2B; "Probe Jury Fears to Visit Bedford Area," *Brooklyn Daily Eagle*, September 19, 1943, 3.

124. While most grand juries in New York State hear evidence and issue indictments on felony criminal charges, a grand jury can also be empaneled to investigate a

particular accusation. These juries, sometimes known as special grand juries, call witnesses and hear testimony, often pertaining to government corruption. A number of high-profile grand jury investigations occurred in Brooklyn between 1938 and 1942 into charges of police corruption related to gambling, bail bonds, and criminal abortion. "Stolen Records Faked by Cops," *Brooklyn Daily Eagle*, December 14, 1938, 1; "Big Drum Gives Up Names of Amen's Jury," *Brooklyn Daily Eagle*, November 1, 1938; "1,000 in Graft by Police Charged," *New York Times*, April 9, 1942, 1.

125. Adam Clayton Powell Jr., "SoapBox," *People's Voice*, November 27, 1943, 5.

126. Names of jury members listed in "Text of Grand Jury Presentment on Bedford-Stuyvesant," *Brooklyn Daily Eagle*, November 15, 1943, 2, 10. Information about foreman Leon Alexander given in "Jury Flays Mayor in Bedford Crimes," *Brooklyn Daily Eagle*, November 15, 1943, 9. Demographic information about ten other jurors found in U.S. Census Bureau, 1940 Census, accessed on ancestry.com.

127. Powell, "SoapBox," 5.

128. Kings County Grand Jury, "Presentment," 1–4.

129. "Mayor Orders Probe of Jury's Charges," *Brooklyn Daily Eagle*, November 16, 1943, 1, 5.

130. Kings County Grand Jury, "Presentment," 3.

131. Kings County Grand Jury, 4.

132. Wilder, *Covenant with Color*, 196.

133. Kings County Grand Jury, "Presentment," 8–10. The Colored State Guard, which operated in Brooklyn and Queens, had first been formed after members of the Veterans of Foreign Wars petitioned Governor Lehman in 1942 to include African Americans in the state guard and engage "the entire combat manpower" available. "Brooklyn Wants Guard Regiment," *New York Amsterdam News*, August 8, 1942, 18; "Petition Seeks to Form Negro State Guard Unit," *Brooklyn Daily Eagle*, September 7, 1942, 4.

134. Kings County Grand Jury, "Presentment," 3.

135. Kings County Grand Jury, 18.

136. Kings County Grand Jury, 12.

137. Yvonne Gregory, "Bedford 'Civic' Meeting Not So Civic after All," *People's Voice*, November 27, 1943, 3; "Thugs Rule, No One Safe, Body Finds," *Brooklyn Daily Eagle*, November 15, 1943, 1.

138. "Valentine Acts to Punish Cop Critic of Mayor," *Brooklyn Daily Eagle*, November 22, 1943, 1, 3; "Today's Profile: Henry E. Ashcroft," *Brooklyn Daily Eagle*, January 18, 1945, 7.

139. Gregory, "Bedford 'Civic' Meeting," 3.

140. "Valentine Acts to Punish," 1, 3; "Jury Maps Presentment on Police," *Brooklyn Daily Eagle*, November 24, 1943, 1, 9.

141. "Jury Maps Presentment," 1, 9.

142. "Jury to Renew Bedford Quiz," *Brooklyn Daily Eagle*, November 26, 1943, 1.

143. Valentine, *Report of the Police Commissioner*, 13.

144. Valentine, 19.

145. "Negro Made Political Football, 'Y' Aide Says," *Brooklyn Daily Eagle*, November 23, 1943, 20.

146. "Labor, Radicals Charge Anti-Negro Conspiracy," *Brooklyn Daily Eagle*, November 24, 1943, 18. For a discussion of the New York Teachers Union's activism, see Taylor, *Reds at the Blackboard*, 75–99.

147. "'Hitler Tactics' in Bedford Hit at Academy Rally," *Brooklyn Daily Eagle*, November 26, 1943, 1, 11; "Boro Smear Amounts to Nasty Mess," *People's Voice*, November 27, 1943, 7.

148. "Police Minimize Crime in Brooklyn in Report to Mayor," *New York Times*, November 26, 1943, 1.

149. "Bedford Given New Police Setup," *Brooklyn Daily Eagle*, December 21, 1943, 3.

150. "Legislative Bill Jackets," Laws of 1945, Chapter 736, 2, 1945, New York Public Library.

151. MacNeil Mitchell to Thomas Dewey, April 7, 1945, "Legislative Bill Jackets," Laws of 1945, Chapter 736, 1945, New York Public Library.

152. Curran to Dewey, March 28, 1945, "Legislative Bill Jackets," Laws of 1945, Chapter 736, 1945, New York Public Library.

153. Curran to Dewey, March 28, 1945.

154. Curran to Dewey, March 28, 1945.

155. NYPD Annual Report, 1942, 22.

156. NYPD Annual Report, 1944, 18.

157. Clarke, *Wayward Minors' Court*, 8.

158. "Dewey Signs Bill on Delinquents," *New York Times*, April 17, 1945, 25.

159. "War News Summarized," *New York Times*, April 17, 1945, 1.

160. Suddler, *Presumed Criminal*, 68–95; Gilbert, *Cycle of Outrage*; Schneider, *Vampires*, 120–68.

161. "Supreme Court's Actions," *New York Times*, May 16, 1972, 22; "Youth Court Plan Assailed by Jury," *New York Times*, January 20, 1955, 33.

Chapter Five

1. Frank S. Hogan, "Law Enforcement . . . Then and Now," *Spring 3100*, May 1943, 10.

2. Shane White et al., *Playing the Numbers*, 32.

3. Lobel, "'Out to Eat,'" 214–18; Kaplan, "New York City," 598; Shane White, "'We Dwell in Safety,'" 467.

4. Flowe, *Uncontrollable Blackness*, 63.

5. Shane White et al., *Playing the Numbers*, 34.

6. Sacks, "'To Be a Man,'" 47.

7. Flowe, *Uncontrollable Blackness*, 60.

8. Shane White et al., *Playing the Numbers*, 18, 5, 40–44.

9. Harris, "Playing the Numbers," 57–58.

10. Harris, "Playing the Numbers," 57–58.

11. Shane White et al., *Playing the Numbers*, 22.

12. Harris, "Playing the Numbers," 66–69.

13. Shane White et al., *Playing the Numbers*, 5.

14. Seabury, *Investigation of the Magistrates' Courts*, 135–36.

15. Seabury, 146.

16. Harris, "Playing the Numbers," 53, 68.

17. Harris, 62.

18. Poston, "Numbers Racket," 921.

19. Harris, "Playing the Numbers," 53, 68.

20. Harris, 68; "Display Ad 70—No Title," *New York Amsterdam News*, September 4, 1929, 12.

21. Harris, "Playing the Numbers," 68.

22. Shane White et al., *Playing the Numbers*, 5–6.

23. Kessner, *Fiorello H. La Guardia*, 351–52.

24. Harris, "Playing the Numbers," 53–76; Stolberg, *Fighting Organized Crime*, 94; "Arrest of Hines Worries 11th A.D.: 'Squealer'?," *New York Amsterdam News*, June 4, 1938, 4.

25. Harris, "Playing the Numbers," 61–62.

26. Stolberg, *Fighting Organized Crime*, 227; "Hines Name Linked to Café Gangsters," *New York Times*, January 30, 1937, 1.

27. "Hines, Numbers," *New York Amsterdam News*, June 4, 1938, 12.

28. Stolberg, *Fighting Organized Crime*, 94.

29. Stolberg, 232–33, 246.

30. Stolberg, 232–33, 246.

31. "Arrest Activities in 1934," *Spring 3100*, June 1935, 14.

32. "New Method of Slot Machine Destruction," *New York Times*, August 18, 1938, 3.

33. "Text of Mayor La Guardia's Report on 1934 Administration," *New York Times*, January 11, 1935, 2.

34. Valentine, *Night Stick*, 30–31.

35. Valentine, 35–36.

36. Valentine, 189.

37. Commission on the Harlem Riot, *Complete Report*, 115–16.

38. "Precinct Shifts," 42.

39. "Mayor's Voice on Record Advises Sailors to 'Call a City Cop' If SP Gets in Their Way," *New York Times*, September 26, 1944, 25.

40. "Mayor Cites Law on Vagrancy," *Spring 3100*, February 1940, 18.

41. Harris, *Sex Workers*, 61.

42. Robin Kelley discusses the ways that working-class Black New Yorkers like Malcolm X constructed an alternative masculinity performed through the zoot suit and leisure culture that challenged a wartime masculinity predicated on productivity and military service. Kelley, *Race Rebels*, 161–81.

43. Brooks, "'Rumor, Vicious Innuendo,'" 1033.

44. Blum, "Work or Fight"; William Taylor, *Military Service*, 7–33; Kotlowski, *Paul V. McNutt*, 341–74.

45. Goldstein, *Helluva Town*, 60.

46. Whalen, *Murder Inc.*, 124.

47. Valentine, *Night Stick*, 196.

48. Goldstein, *Helluva Town*, 58.

49. "M'Nutt Made Head of New Board to Rule Manpower," *New York Times*, April 19, 1942, 1.

50. Kotlowski, *Paul V. McNutt*, 342–48; "M'Nutt Proposes Man-Power Board," *New York Times*, January 27, 1942, 15.

51. La Guardia speech, Police Academy graduation, September 20, 1942, emphasis added, La Guardia Speech Collection, NYPR Archive Collections, New York Public Radio, New York City Municipal Archives WNYC Collection, https://www.wnyc.org /story/police-academy-graduation.

52. "'Tip' Sheets Barred from Newsstands," *New York Times*, October 4, 1942, 54.

53. "55 Seized in 3 Raids for Betting on Races," *New York Times*, October 25, 1942, 31.

54. "Valentine Speeds Drive on Gambling," *New York Times*, October 31, 1942, 17.

55. "Rhine City Ablaze," *New York Times*, September 12, 1942, 1; "R.A.F. Bombs Blast Cologne," *New York Times*, October 17, 1942, 1; "First Daytime Air Raid Drill Ties Up City for 24 Minutes," *New York Times*, October 23, 1942, 1.

56. Symon Gould to La Guardia, April 14, 1942, Folder 9, Roll 70, Subject Files: Gambling, FLGC.

57. Marie Franconi to La Guardia, September 22, 1942. Folder 9, Roll 70, Subject Files: Gambling, FLGC.

58. For Release, Morning Papers, Sunday, September 20, 1942, Folder 9, Roll 70, Subject Files: Gambling, FLGC.

59. Symon Gould to La Guardia, April 14, 1942, Folder 9, Roll 70, Subject Files: Gambling, FLGC.

60. "Preaching to Mayor on Father's Gambling Held Perilous to Family Relationship," *New York Times*, September 16, 1942, 25; "Mayor Says Press Aids BookMakers," *New York Times*, September 20, 1942, 1.

61. Commanding Officer, Investigating Squad, to Police Commissioner, Subject: Investigation of One Henry G. Hoffman, June 22, 1943, Folder 10, Roll 70, Subject Files: Gambling, FLGC.

62. To Inspector Murphy, June 15, 1943, Folder 10, Roll 70, Subject Files: Gambling, FLGC.

63. To Local Bd. #250, no date, Folder 10, Roll 70, Subject Files: Gambling, FLGC.

64. Blum, "Work or Fight," 367.

65. Blum, 367.

66. Blum, 368–80.

67. For a discussion of the development of these debates in the urban North, see Muhammad, *Condemnation of Blackness*, particularly 88–145.

68. Dan Burley, "'Social Dregs' Slur Hit by Citizens," *New York Amsterdam News*, September 18, 1943, 1.

69. "Tavern Topics," *New York Amsterdam News*, October 23, 1943, 21.

70. Carolyn Dixon, "What's Happened to the Numbers Game?," *New York Amsterdam News*, December 18, 1943, 24.

71. W. E. B. Du Bois, "As the Crow Flies," *New York Amsterdam News*, October 9, 1943, 10.

72. For more on Du Bois's perspectives on race and Marxism in the 1930s and 1940s, see Lewis, *W.E.B. Du Bois*, 546–646.

73. "Check on Cars Near Race Tracks by Police Ordered by La Guardia," *New York Times*, May 10, 1943, 21.

74. "James Byrnes Dies at 92," *New York Times*, April 10, 1972, 1. For more on Byrnes, see David Robertson, *Sly and Able*.

75. "All Racing Banned on Call of Byrnes to Aid War Effort," *New York Times*, December 24, 1944, 1.

76. "La Guardia Acclaims Ban Put on Race Tracks," *New York Times*, December 24, 1944, 18; "Mayor Sees End of 'Bookies,'" *New York Times*, December 25, 1944.

77. "5 Women Landed in Court on Tinhorn Charges," *Brooklyn Daily Eagle*, December 7, 1942, 5.

78. "Scolds Women Gamblers," *New York Herald-Tribune*, March 19, 1943, 21.

79. "Court Flays Facing oBokie [*sic*] Count," *New York Amsterdam News*, October 2, 1943, 18.

80. Fiorello La Guardia, "Sunday Broadcast to the People of New York," WNYC, New York, New York, January 21, 1945, the NYPR Archive Collections.

81. "Mayor Orders Draft Check in Gaming Arrests," *New York Herald-Tribune*, January 22, 1945, 22.

82. "Gamblers Warned to Work or Fight," *New York Times*, January 22, 1945, 19.

83. "2,100 Attend St. George Breakfast," *Spring 3100*, April 1943, 2.

84. Frank S. Hogan, "Law Enforcement . . . Then and Now," *Spring 3100*, May 1943, 10.

85. Helen G. H. Estelle to La Guardia, October 2, 1942, Folder 9, Roll 70, Subject Files: Gambling, FLGC.

86. "A Resident" to Mayor La Guardia, January 18, 1945, Folder 13, Roll 70, Subject Files: Gambling, FLGC.

87. Commanding Officer, Third Division, to Borough Commander, Manhattan-West, March 16, 1945, Folder 13, Roll 70, Subject Files: Gambling, FLGC.

88. Field Instructions, All Regional Manpower Directions, Folder 18, Roll 32, Subject Files: Curfew, FLGC.

89. James Byrnes to La Guardia, no date, Folder 20, Roll 32, Subject Files: Curfew, FLGC.

90. "164 Arrested in Curfew Raids: 7 of 30 Women Jailed 2 Days," *New York Herald-Tribune*, March 11, 1945, 1; "12 Speakeasy Customers Jailed; 2 Homes Raided," *New York Times*, March 11, 1945, 1.

91. Veteran World War II to Mayor, no date [likely August 1945], Folder 18, Roll 71, Subject Files: Gambling, FLGC.

92. La Guardia broadcast, August 26, 1945, Folder 18, Roll 71, Subject Files: Gambling, FLGC.

93. Sporting Women's Moral Club to La Guardia, August 15, 1945, Folder 19, Roll 71, Subject Files: Gambling, FLGC.

94. Mrs. W. H. Bush to La Guardia, no date, Folder 12, Roll 70, Subject Files: Gambling, FLGC.

95. "Sailor and Waitress Held as Bookmakers," *New York Times*, August 30, 1945, 32.

96. "180 Guards Patrol Staten Island Problem Area, 60 in M.P. Detail," *New York Herald-Tribune*, March 16, 1945, 19.

97. "200 Police, MPS's Guard Vicinity of Fox Hills," *Staten Island Advance*, March 16, 1945, 1.

98. Operative S.J., "General Report," no date, Folder 12, Box II B-193, NAACP.

99. Operative S.J., "General Report."

100. Brooks, "'Rumor, Vicious Innuendo.'"

101. Biondi, *To Stand and Fight*, 13; Nat Brandt, *Harlem at War*, 100–101.

102. Phillips, *War!*, 22.

103. Phillips, 48–55, 68–70.

104. Scholars have explored the history of Black men in the military and their roles in Black communities. David F. Krugler discusses the leadership role that Black veterans played in self-defense campaigns against white mob attacks in *1919*, 3, 6, 16. Chad L. Williams has argued that in the World War I era, Black soldiers and supporters often viewed serving in the military as a means of laying claim to masculine citizenship, while white Americans perceived Black soldiers as a particular threat to the preservation of white supremacy in the country. Williams, *Torchbearers of Democracy*, 3–7.

105. Jackson, *WWII & NYC*, 23.

106. Nat Brandt, *Harlem at War*, 166.

107. Office of Facts and Figures, *Negro Looks*, iv, 8.

108. Nat Brandt, *Harlem at War*, 93–95; Office of Facts and Figures, *Negro Looks*, 4–5. For more on Black attitudes toward Japan during the 1930s and 1940s, see Horne, *Facing the Rising Sun*. Nikhil Pal Singh argues that during the war, many Black Americans rejected American exceptionalism in favor of a global politics built on antiracism and anti-imperialism in *Black Is a Country*, 114–19.

109. Goldstein, *Helluva Town*, 117–18.

110. Mayor's Committee on Unity, "Draft of Report to the Mayor on Staten Island Situation," April 27, 1945, Folder 9, Box 3, NDP.

111. Carl Dunbar Lawrence, "Inquiry Unearths Scheme to 'Frame' Negro Soldiers," *New York Amsterdam News*, March 24, 1945, 1A.

112. Mayor's Committee on Unity, "Staten Island," March 28, 1945, Folder 9, Box 3, NDP. For more on Italian service units and Italian prisoners of war, see Worrall, "Reflections on Italian Prisoners."

113. Mayor's Committee on Unity, "Staten Island."

114. Biondi, *To Stand and Fight*, 13.

115. "Kane, Military Authorities to Study Rise in Crime," *Staten Island Advance*, February 24, 1945, 1.

116. "Kane Asks Army Aid in Soldier Crime Rise," *New York Times*, February 25, 1945, 13.

117. "U.S. Jury Probes S.I. Crime Wave," *Brooklyn Daily Eagle*, March 20, 1945, 2; "Army Heads Join in Rapist Hunt," *Brooklyn Daily Eagle*, March 15, 1945, 2; "Troop Transfer Follows Assault," *Brooklyn Daily Eagle*, March 16, 1945, 2; "2 Soldiers Face 20-Year Terms on Attack Convictions," *Brooklyn Daily Eagle*, June 27, 1945, 1; "Special Police and Army Join Hunt for Staten Island Attacker," *New York Herald-Tribune*, March 15, 1945, 21A; "180 Guards Patrol Staten Island Problem Area, 60 in M.P. Detail," *New York Herald-Tribune*, March 16, 1945, 19; "S.I. Grand Jury Criticizes Lack of Army Curbs," *New York Herald-Tribune*, April 4, 1945, 14.

118. "Negro Soldiers Stationed in Staten Island under Stricter Discipline after Stabbing," *New York Age*, March 10, 1945, 1; "Trouble in Staten Island," *New York Age*,

March 24, 1945, 6; "Military Authorities Insist on Right to Try Negro Soldiers in Staten Island," *New York Age*, April 14, 1945, 2; "2 Negro Soldiers Held by Staten Island Judge," *New York Age*, April 28, 1945, 11.

119. Jackson, *Encyclopedia of New York City*, 1237.

120. "Staten Island Widow of Hero Is Attacked," *New York Times*, March 14, 1945, 10; "Staten Island 'Crime' Wave Experts Falter," *People's Voice*, April 14, 1945, 4; Llewellyn Ransom, "PV Reporter Visits Staten Island Base to Probe Rape Charges," *People's Voice*, March 31, 1945, 2; Llewellyn Ransom, "GI 'Crime Wave' Is Propaganda," *People's Voice*, March 24, 1945, 2.

121. "City, Army Police Patrols Increased on East Shore," *Staten Island Advance*, March 6, 1945, 1.

122. "Man Beaten, Robbed by Soldiers in Concord," *Staten Island Advance*, March 17, 1945, 1.

123. "250 Ask More Police for East Shore Patrols," *Staten Island Advance*, March 13, 1945, 1.

124. Ransom, "GI 'Crime Wave.'"

125. Lawrence, "Inquiry Unearths Scheme," 1A; "Soldiers Beat, Rob, Staten Island Man," *New York Times*, March 17, 1945, 15; "Fox Hills Area Quiet: Police Patrols Continue," *Staten Island Advance*, March 19, 1945, 1.

126. Lawrence, "Inquiry Unearths Scheme," 1A.

127. "Staten Island Acts to End Crime Wave," *New York Times*, March 15, 1945.

128. Commanding Officer, Staten Island Terminal, and Commanding General, New York Port of Embarkation, to the Chief of Transportation, "Report on Racial Conditions at Fox Hills Terminal," March 21, 1945, Folder 1, Box 17, ASF.

129. "200 Police, MPS's Guard," 1.

130. "Fox Hills Area Quiet," 1.

131. Dodson, "Mayor's Committee on Unity."

132. Dodson, 292; "Staten Island," March 28, 1945, Folder 9, Box 3, NDP.

133. Mayor's Committee on Unity, "Report to the Mayor on Fox Hills, Staten Island, Situation," no date, 4, Folder 9, Box 3, NDP.

134. Wilkins to Marshall, March 26, 1945, Folder 12, Box II B-193, NAACP. For more on the activities of the Staten Island NAACP during the war, see Brooks, "'Rumor, Vicious Innuendo,'" 1037–42.

135. Wilkins to Marshall, March 26, 1945.

136. Roy Wilkins to Fiorello La Guardia, March 15, 1945, Folder 12, Box II B-193, NAACP.

137. "Report on Racial Conditions at Fox Hills Terminal, Stapleton and Vicinity, Staten Island, New York," March 21, 1945, Folder 1, Box 17, ASF.

138. "Case No. 114, Re: Stapleton, Staten Island," April 2, 1945, 12, Folder 12, Box II B-193, NAACP.

139. Dodson, "Mayor's Committee on Unity," 292.

140. "Staten Island Begins Crime Study Today," *New York Times*, March 20, 1945, 21.

141. Richard Rovere, "Good Citizen—I," *New Yorker*, October 28, 1944, 28.

142. "Fox Hills Grand Jury Summons Army Aids," *Staten Island Advance*, March 21, 1945, 1.

143. "Fox Hills Grand Jury."

144. "Army Shifts 600 from Fox Hills, Patrols Increased," *Staten Island Advance*, March 15, 1945, 1, 2; "Servicemen's Club, Fence to Be Built at Fox Hills," *Staten Island Advance*, March 28, 1945, 1.

145. "200 Police, MPS's Guard," 1; "Fox Hills Area Quiet," 1.

146. "City Voters to Fill 38 Vacant Offices," *New York Times*, November 2, 1947, 2; "R.E. Johnson Named as Successor to Kane," *New York Times*, August 14, 1947, 3; "Kathleen Leddy Bride of Farrell M. Kane Jr.," *New York Times*, August 20, 1961, 92.

147. "Board Votes Police Rise," *New York Times*, May 19, 1948, 55; Charles Bennett, "7 Councilmen Act to Curb New Taxes as Protests Mount," *New York Times*, April 4, 1952, 1.

148. "2 Negro Soldiers Guilty of Assault," June 27, 1945, Folder 12, Box II B-193, NAACP.

149. "Two Soldiers Sentenced: Sing Sing Terms Imposed for Staten Island Attack," *New York Times*, July 28, 1945, 13; "2 Negro Soldiers Guilty of Assault."

150. NYPD Annual Report, 1940, 4, 13.

Chapter Six

1. A rich field of scholarship exists that explores the dynamic and heterogeneous world of urban nightlife culture in the early to mid-twentieth century. Chad Heap examines the interconnected racial, class, geographic, sexual, and cultural politics implicated in the practice of slumming in *Slumming*. Kevin Mumford considers interracial vice districts in Chicago and New York as spaces of cultural and social marginalization and production in *Interzones*. Robin Kelley explores the role of spaces like the Savoy Ballroom in Harlem in the production of Black working-class culture in *Race Rebels*. Dominic J. Capeci Jr. uses the closure of the Savoy Ballroom and other episodes of conflict between Black New Yorkers and La Guardia as a means to analyze the relationship between Black political leaders and the mayor in "Walter F. White" and "From Different Liberal Perspectives." Elizabeth Clement considers how the practice of "treating," in which young working-class women exchanged nights out for sexual favors, reshaped sexual and gender politics in the early twentieth century in *Love for Sale*. George Chauncey's *Gay New York* depicts the city's nightlife and leisure spaces as a key part of gay male subcultures. Stephen Robertson examines the role Black investigators played in the work of private vice associations like the Committee of Fourteen in policing vice in "Harlem Undercover."

2. Douglas Flowe discusses how Tammany permitted illicit venues to operate for a price. He contends that this dynamic created opportunities for venue owners, but also made them vulnerable to extortion. Flowe, *Uncontrollable Blackness*, 79–80. For more on the role of saloons in Tammany's power structure and the way that the Democratic club permitted brothel and pool hall owners to operate with regular payoffs, see Golway, *Machine Made*, 65, 153, 162. For a detailed discussion of the systems of police bribery and extortion that were revealed in the 1894 Lexow investigation, see Czitrom, *New York Exposed*, 175–99. Timothy Gilfoyle argues that police operated a system of "de facto regulation" of sex work in the city in the early twentieth century, which was

hyperlocalized, like Tammany's system of political organization. Gilfoyle, *City of Eros*, 251–70. Clement discusses the system of higher and less predictable bribes and extortion that emerged for sex workers during alcohol prohibition in *Love for Sale*, 193–96.

3. "Moss Talks on the Theatre," *New York Times*, June 18, 1937, 25; "Burlesque Shows of City Are Shut as Public Menace," *New York Times*, May 2, 1937, 1.

4. Clinton Seymour, "The Age of Minsky," *Brooklyn Daily Eagle*, March 21, 1937, 79–80. For more on Moss and La Guardia's efforts to close burlesque theaters, see Friedman, "'Habits of Sex-Crazed Perverts,'" 208. For a discussion of the regulation of leisure in Times Square, see Chronopoulos, "Morality, Social Disorder," 6–10. For a history of burlesque, see Minsky, *Minsky's Burlesque*; and Zeidman, *American Burlesque Show*.

5. Anne Gray Fischer argues that in many cities across the country, white women were the focus of police anti-prostitution crackdowns, while Black women and Black neighborhoods received more violent and sporadic attention but less systematic surveillance. In New York, however, Valentine and La Guardia embraced a different approach, which would become more common across the country after the war. Fischer, *Streets Belong to Us*, 67–75.

6. La Guardia to General Thomas A. Terry and Edward J. Marquart, January 24, 1944, Folder 2, Roll 0150, Subject Files: Out of Bounds Prostitution, FLGC. In her discussion of gender, race, and the 1943 riots, Marilynn Johnson frames the conflict that precipitated the Harlem uprising as a "mother/child atrocity story" because the victim was shot while defending his mother. Johnson, "Gender, Race, and Rumours." This chapter will explore how the drive to keep white enlisted men safe from disorderly venues justified the presence of police officers like James Collins in venues like the Braddock Hotel and focused their attention on Black women like Margie Polite.

7. Valentine, *Night Stick*, 305.

8. "Police Seize 333 in Crime Round-Up Test of Law Seen," *New York Times*, February 8, 1935, 1.

9. "Valentine Orders Clean-Up of City," *New York Times*, January 12, 1938, 1; "50 Top Patrolmen Put on Vice Study," *New York Times*, January 25, 1938, 1.

10. Lvovsky, *Vice Patrol*, 24.

11. Chauncey, *Gay New York*, 346–47; Lvovsky, *Vice Patrol*, 30.

12. Police Department City of New York, Rules and Regulations, December 16, 1940, 292–96, Manuals of Procedure, JJCA.

13. Wilkerson, *Warmth of Other Suns*, 45.

14. Mumford, *Interzones*, xviii.

15. For more on conditions of housing in Harlem and tenant activism in the early twentieth century, see King, *Whose Harlem?*, 93–119; and Flowe, *Uncontrollable Blackness*, 36–43. For discussion of why Black Manhattanites moved to Harlem from interracial communities farther south in Manhattan, see King, *Whose Harlem?*, 17–23; and Nat Brandt, *Harlem at War*, 22–23.

16. Ann Petry, *Street*, 206.

17. Petry, 57–58.

18. For more on Black men's experiences of employment discrimination, crime, and work in the underground economy, see Flowe, *Uncontrollable Blackness*, 43–50, 63–67.

For more on Black women's experiences of employment discrimination and work in the underground economy, see Harris, *Sex Workers*, 30–53. For more on policing gambling and Black employment, see Vaz, *Running the Numbers*, 12–15; Harris, "Playing the Numbers," 57–58; and Shane White et al., *Playing the Numbers*, 22.

19. Greenberg, *"Or Does It Explode?,"* 66.

20. Mumford argues that white reformers drove prostitution into Black neighborhoods in the 1910s in *Interzones*, 23–26. For more on reformers segregating leisure spaces, see Fronc, *New York Undercover*, 96. For a discussion of white progressives who excluded Black urbanites from reform projects, see Muhammad, *Condemnation of Blackness*, 117–45. Heap explores the complex and generative interactions between white and Black urbanites in early twentieth-century nightlife in *Slumming*, 8–9. Mumford considers exoticized cultural depictions of Harlem in the early twentieth century as well as how white tourism changed the neighborhood in *Interzones*, 133–56.

21. For discussions of varied attempts by middle- and working-class Black residents to protect and control Black women in the early twentieth century and the relationships between these efforts and the state, see Hicks, *Talk with You*, particularly 91–121, 159–204. LaShawn Harris explicates the complex conflicts and negotiations around morality and labor expressed through working-class anti-vice campaigns in 1930s New York City in *Sex Workers*, 167–200. Fischer discusses these dynamics of the racialization of vice and morals law enforcement in *Streets Belong to Us*, 26–49.

22. "Police Seize 333," 1.

23. "250 More Police in Harlem to Stamp Out Crime Wave," *New York Times*, November 8, 1941, 1.

24. Venereal Disease Control Conference, June 29, 1943, Headquarters, Second Service Command, Governors Island, New York, Folder 12, Roll 251, Subject Files: Venereal Disease, FLGC.

25. Historians of policing have described how the different forms of racialized violence in policing worked together in various ways. Harris discusses the many ways in which these dynamics made Black women vulnerable and how they fought back in "'Women and Girls.'" Shannon King describes Black New Yorkers as "overpoliced *and* underprotected" in "Murder in Central Park," 44. Simon Balto uses the framing "overpatrolled" and "underprotected" in *Occupied Territory*, 1. Fischer dubs this dynamic "violent neglect" and "violent action" in *Streets Belong to Us*, 27–28. Micol Siegel contends that policing is itself "work that relies upon violence or the threat thereof. Violence work." Siegel, *Violence Work*, 9.

26. Commission on the Harlem Riot, *Complete Report*, 22, 23.

27. Commission on the Harlem Riot, 13.

28. Commission on the Harlem Riot, 133–34.

29. The Civilian Complaint Review Board has been a major mobilizing issue in police and city politics since before it was formally created. Clarence Taylor tracks its importance to Black activists and police from the 1940s through the 2010s in *Fight the Power*, 84–254.

30. Fischer discusses how policing of morals laws contributed to mass uprisings in 1960s Los Angeles in "'Land of the White Hunter.'"

31. Clarence Taylor, *Fight the Power*, 87.

32. Commission on the Harlem Riot, *Complete Report*, 120.

33. "Denies Harlem Job 'Punishes' Police," *New York Times*, November 26, 1941, 48.

34. King describes a horrific attack against a Black woman in 1939 that the NYPD took weeks to follow up on. King, "Murder in Central Park," 49–50.

35. Harris, *Sex Workers*, 167–86.

36. Commission on the Harlem Riot, *Complete Report*, 110–11.

37. Commissioner John L. Rice to Lewis Valentine, March 9, 1939; Commissioner John Rice to Lewis Valentine, December 23, 1938; Commissioner John Rice to Lewis Valentine, June 21, 1939, Folder 22, Box 2.173, Series 1, Subseries 4, Sub-subgroup 2: John L. Rice, HCR.

38. Operative S.J., "General Report," no date, Folder 12, Box II B-193, NAACP.

39. "6 Dance Halls Shut on Police Charges," *New York Times*, September 11, 1943, 15; Hegarty, *Victory Girls*, 12–41, 128–55. For more on military efforts to thwart interracial relationships between Black soldiers and white women during the war, see Dailey, *White Fright*, 77–115.

40. Venereal Disease Control Conference, June 29, 1943.

41. "Gambling Drive Traps 100," *New York Times*, September 28, 1942, 1; Lloyd Shearer, "A Night with an M.P.: Roaming the Town with a Military Policeman," *New York Times*, December 6, 1942, SM23.

42. Dailey, *White Fright*, 112–14.

43. R. M. Danford, "Final Report of the Commandant, City Patrol Corps to La Guardia," pt. 1, September 1945, Folder 7, Roll 0152, Subject Files: City Patrol Corps, FLGC; "La Guardia Threat Is Sent to 3-A Men," *New York Times*, June 27, 1942, 1; Brooks, "Coercive Patriotism."

44. Lewis Valentine, Venereal Disease Control Conference, June 29, 1943, Headquarters Second Service Command, Governors Island, Folder 11, Roll 251. Subject Files: Venereal Disease, FLGC; Danford, "Final Report," pt. 1; "6 Dance Halls Shut," 15.

45. Seymour, "Age of Minsky," 79–80.

46. "Star Theater Closes in Drive on Burlesque," *Brooklyn Daily Eagle*, March 17, 1942, 2.

47. "Burlesque Scored in New Affidavits," *New York Times*, March 22, 1942, 50; "Moss Is Upheld on Burlesque Ban," *New York Times*, April 12, 1942, 46.

48. John Martin and Neal Patterson, "Harlem Barred to Service Men in Vice Cleanup," *New York Daily News*, August 11, 1942, 2.

49. "Conference Re: Prostitution and the Spread of Venereal Disease among Our Armed Forces and Civilians," August 2, 1942, Folder 11, Roll 251, Subject Files: Venereal Disease, FLGC.

50. "Ask Police Rulings on Army-Navy Ban," *Chicago Defender*, August 22, 1942, 8.

51. La Guardia to General Thomas A. Terry and Edward J. Marquart, January 24, 1944, Folder 2, Roll 0150, Subject Files: Out of Bounds Prostitution, FLGC.

52. Joe Bostic, "Police Commissioner Denies Press Stories," *People's Voice*, August 15, 1942, 3; "Ask Police Rulings."

53. John Martin and Neal Patterson, "Valentine Defends City's Reputation on Vice," *New York Daily News*, August 12, 1942, 8.

54. Bostic, "Police Commissioner Denies," 3. The *Voice*'s backers included Moe Gale, one of the two owners of the Savoy, who contributed financial support to the paper, while the Savoy's other owner-manager, Charles Buchanan, served as its editor. The newspaper would take a central role in defending the Savoy in 1943.

55. For more on Cooke's work and activism, see Harris, "Marvel Cooke"; and "Crime Smear So Bad Even Dixie Puzzled," *People's Voice*, April 3, 1943, 3. For a discussion of the literary careers and politics of the contributors and publishers of the *People's Voice*, see Wald, *Trinity of Passion*, 108–45; Clarence Taylor, *Fight the Power*, 11; and "Editorial Policy of the Voice," *People's Voice*, February 14, 1942.

56. For examples, see "Extra Cops Won't Solve Harlem's Ills," *People's Voice*, March 27, 1943, 24; "Only the People Can Save New York," *People's Voice*, April 10, 1943; "Hunter College Students Finish 'Mugging' Study," *People's Voice*, July 17, 1943, 13; "Negro Boy Killed by Hoodlums," *People's Voice*, March 20, 1943, 3; and Clarence Taylor, *Fight the Power*, 9–33. For more on police brutality during the war, see Johnson, *Street Justice*, 191–203; and Darien, *Becoming New York's Finest*, 19.

57. Office of Facts and Figures, *Negro Looks*, table 45, 18.

58. Bostic, "Police Commissioner Denies," 3.

59. "Protesting 'News' Smear Campaign," *People's Voice*, August 15, 1942, 1.

60. Ann Petry, "Harlem Women Wax Indignant over Latest 'Crime' Campaign," *People's Voice*, August 15, 1942, 3.

61. "Protesting 'News' Smear Campaign," 1.

62. King, "Murder in Central Park," 52.

63. For a discussion of policing and the vulnerability of Black women in New York in the 1920s, see Harris, "'Women and Girls.'"

64. Ann Petry, "Harlem Urged to Attend First Meeting of 'Women, Inc.,'" *People's Voice*, May 2, 1942, 17.

65. Deborah White, *Too Heavy a Load*, 145–75.

66. Griffin, *Harlem Nocturne*, 99; King, "Murder in Central Park," 58.

67. Quoted in Elisabeth Petry, *At Home Inside*, 74.

68. Griffin, *Harlem Nocturne*, 99–100.

69. Ann Petry to "girls," January 25, 1943, Folder 1, Box 15, APP.

70. Negro Women, Incorporated, newsletter, November 1944, Folder 3, Box 13; Negro Women Inc. newsletter, no date, Folder 1, Box 14, APP.

71. Ann Petry to "girls," October 9, 1944, Folder 1, Box 15, APP.

72. December 1944–January 1944 Negro Women Incorporated newsletter, Folder 2, Box 15, APP.

73. Negro Women Inc. newsletter, no date, Folder 1, Box 14, APP.

74. Ann Petry, "Harlem Women Wax Indignant," 3.

75. Joe Bostic, "What's Behind the Savoy Closing," *People's Voice*, May 1, 1943, 1–2. For quotes, see Jervis Anderson, *This Was Harlem*, 307; and "Savoy Ballroom Closed by Police as 'Base for Vice,'" *New York Age*, May 1, 1943, 1.

76. Quote from Engelbrecht, "Swinging at the Savoy," 3; Jervis Anderson, *This Was Harlem*, 309–10.

77. "Who Says Harlem Has No Heart? The Service Men Say She Has!," *New York Amsterdam News*, January 24, 1942, 8; "Harlem Center for Service Men to Be For-

mally Opened Saturday with Gala Dedicatory Program," *New York Age*, November 29, 1941, 1.

78. Many scholars have explored the particular role that the Savoy played in the city's nightlife. Heap argues that in the 1940s it was Harlem's last interracial venue. Heap, *Slumming*, 280. For discussions of the venue's popularity and importance among zoot-suit-wearing young people, see Peiss, *Zoot Suit*, 59; and Alvarez, *Power of the Zoot*, 116. For a discussion of the venue's importance to working-class Black youth, see Kelley, *Race Rebels*, 169. For more on the complicated and productive relationship between marginality, exclusion, and creativity, see Mumford, *Interzones*, xiii.

79. Anderson, Jervis *This Was Harlem*, 313–14. Russell Gold also emphasizes the interracial makeup of the Savoy's patrons, though he describes the clientele as two-thirds African American and one-third white in the early 1940s in "Guilty of Syncopation," 52. For a discussion of collaborations between Puerto Rican and African American bandleaders who played at the Savoy, see Glasser, *My Music*, 65–76.

80. Ann Petry to "Girls," February 8, 1943, Folder 1, Box 15, APP.

81. Jervis Anderson, *This Was Harlem*, 313–14.

82. "Review of Activities between Health Department, Bureau of Social Hygiene, and Police Department Covering 1942, May 23," Folder 8: Police (Venereal), Box 2-1, City 24, HCR.

83. Savoy Associates, Inc. v. Lewis Valentine, 6016, 39–40, 1943, Supreme Court, Appellate Division, New York County Lawyer's Association Archives.

84. "Interim Report—New York City (Venereal Disease Repression and Control Activities in Harlem)," January 20, 1945, Folder "New York," Box 7, Entry 40, NACP.

85. "Brown, Eunice," June 17, 1943, Box 68, WPA.

86. Savoy Associates, Inc. v. Lewis Valentine, 6016, 25–31.

87. Savoy Associates, Inc. v. Lewis Valentine, 23.

88. Savoy Associates, Inc. v. Lewis Valentine, 47.

89. "Mixed Dancing Closed Savoy Ballroom," *New York Amsterdam News*, May 1, 1943, 1; "Assignment New York," *New York Age*, May 15, 1943, 10.

90. Bostic, "What's Behind," 1, 3.

91. Peter Dana, "Harlem in the Spring of 1943," *New York Age*, June 19, 1943, 7; "Army Didn't Close Savoy," *New York Amsterdam News*, May 8, 1943, 2.

92. "Indignation Grows over Savoy Case," *New York Amsterdam News*, May 15, 1943, 1.

93. "Harlem to Fight for Reopening of Dance Hall," *New York Herald-Tribune*, April 28, 1943, 14; "Mayor Says He Can't Act in Savoy Ballroom Case," *New York Herald-Tribune*, April 29, 1943, 10A; Capeci, "Walter F. White."

94. Adam Clayton Powell Jr., "Savoy Closing Step Backward in Race Relations," *People's Voice*, May 8, 1943, 16.

95. Capeci, "From Different Liberal Perspectives," 164.

96. PV Special Reporter, "Savoy Still Closed: PV Exposes Vice and Filth in Downtown Dance Halls," *People's Voice*, May 8, 1943, 1, 3.

97. Powell, "Savoy Closing Step Backward," 16.

98. Andy Razaf, "'Guilty' Savoy," *People's Voice*, May 22, 1943, 26.

99. Ann Petry, "An Open Letter to Mayor LaGuardia," *People's Voice*, May 22, 1943, 4.

100. Petry, "Open Letter."

101. Vivian Wenham, "Calls for Savoy Closing Protest," *People's Voice*, May 29, 1943; Negro Women Incorporated newsletter, November 1944, Folder 3, Box 13, APP.

102. "Ballroom Regains Permit," *New York Times*, October 16, 1943, 10; Dan Burley, "Dan Burley's Back Door Stuff," *New York Amsterdam News*, October 30, 1943, B8.

103. "Indignation Grows over Savoy Case," 1.

104. Russell Gold, "Guilty of Syncopation," 50–60.

105. "6 Dance Halls Shut on Police Charges," *New York Times*, September 11, 1943, 15.

106. Capeci, *Harlem Riot of 1943*, 116–18; Walter White and Thurgood Marshall, *What Caused the Detroit Riot?* National Association for the Advancement of Colored People, July 1943, New York City; Browne, *One Righteous Man*, 380–462.

107. "Valentine Willing to Add More Negroes to Police Force," *People's Voice*, July 17, 1943, 3.

108. "Twenty-Two Sign at League for Police Officer Training," *People's Voice*, July 24, 1943, 3.

109. Capeci, *Harlem Riot of 1943*, 124; "Harlem Riot at a Glance," *Baltimore Afro-American*, August 7, 1943, 1; James Collins entry in U.S. Bureau of Census, 1940 Census, accessed through ancestry.com.

110. Malcolm X, *Autobiography*, 74.

111. Marjaie Polite entry in U.S. Bureau of Census, 1940 Census, accessed through ancestry.com.

112. Capeci, *Harlem Riot of 1943*, 99.

113. "Rumors of Soldier's 'Killing' Caused Frenzied Mob to Riot," *New York Amsterdam News*, August 7, 1943, 4; "Shooting of Negro Soldier Stirs Trouble in Harlem," *Baltimore Sun*, August 2 1943, 9.

114. Baldwin, "Me and My House . . . ," 60.

115. Ann Petry to "mother," August 3, 1943, Folder 3, Box 13, APP.

116. Walter White, *Man Called White*, 233–37.

117. Harlem riot reports, 1943, Sc MG193, Schomburg Center for Research in Black Culture, Manuscripts, Archives and Rare Brooks Division, the New York Public Library.

118. Baldwin, "Me and My House . . . ," 57–58.

119. Farah Jasmine Griffin notes that Petry wrote the story immediately following the uprising but could not find a publisher until 1946. Griffin, *Harlem Nocturne*, 127.

120. Ann Petry, "In Darkness and Confusion."

121. "Execute Negro Sergeant for Killing," *New York Amsterdam News*, July 31, 1943, 1.

122. Ann Petry to "Girls," August 11, 1943, Folder 1, Box 15, APP.

123. Griffin, *Harlem Nocturne*, 88.

124. For a thorough account of the uprising, see Capeci, *Harlem Riot of 1943*. Both Capeci and Janet L. Abu-Lughod, in *Race, Space, and Riots*, argue that Harlem's 1943 uprising bore similarities to the urban uprisings of the 1960s in the way it unfolded as a "commodity riot" and in the response from police and city officials. For a discussion of the role of rumor in motivating people to participate in the theft and vandalism, the participation of women in these actions, and other urban conflicts in 1943, see Johnson, "Gender, Race, and Rumours." Laurie Leach explores different ways that city and police officials, the city's Black newspapers, and participants in the uprising

discussed Margie Polite's role in the conflict in "Margie Polite, the Riot Starter." Luis Alvarez explores the role of the zoot suit and youth culture in racial conflicts in New York and Los Angeles during the war in *Power of the Zoot*, 200–234. Cheryl Lynn Greenberg links the riots to efforts and failures of grassroots politics in "Politics of Disorder."

125. Capeci, *Harlem Riot of 1943*, 127.

126. Ted Yates, "I've Been Around," *New York Age*, October 30, 1943, 10; Dan Burley, "Dan Burley's Back Door Stuff," *New York Amsterdam News*, October 23, 1943, 21.

127. "Savoy Ballroom Opens Friday Night," *New York Amsterdam News*, October 23, 1943, 21.

128. "Interim Report—New York City (Venereal Disease Repression and Control Activities in Harlem)," January 20, 1945, Folder "New York," Box 7, Entry 40, NACP.

129. La Guardia to General Thomas A. Terry and Edward J. Marquart, January 24, 1944, Folder 2, Roll 0150, Subject Files: Out of Bounds Prostitution, FLGC.

130. "Venereal Disease Control Conference," September 18, 1944, 33, Folder "New York," Box 7, Entry 40, NACP.

Conclusion

1. Sam Zolotow, "'On the Town' Set for Debut Tonight," *New York Times*, December 28, 1944, 25.

2. Lewis Nichols, "The Play," *New York Times*, December 29, 1944, 11.

3. The young woman who played Ivy Smith's character in the Broadway show, Japanese American dancer Sono Osato, would likely have been perceived as a threat for both her race and her gender. Her father was arrested by the FBI and imprisoned while she was headlining the show, and she performed under her mother's name, Fitzpatrick, during the war. For more on Osato's career and experience in *On the Town*, see Baber, "'Manhattan Women,'" 76; and Oja, *Bernstein Meets Broadway*, 133–50.

4. "Ushers Picket City Hall," *New York Times*, February 28, 1942, 19.

5. This casting was extremely progressive for its time, and performers cast in these roles remembered experiencing equitable and integrated treatment backstage. The show also hired violinist Everett Lee as conductor and musical director, and Lee became the first African American to occupy that position. "Everett Lee Sets Musical Precedent," *New York Amsterdam News*, September 22, 1945, 14; Oja, *Bernstein Meets Broadway*, 155, 178.

6. For more on African American integration into the navy, see Drane, "Role of African-American Musicians," 64; and Nalty, *Strength for the Fight*, 184–204.

7. "Venereal Disease Control Conference," September 18, 1944, 36, Folder "New York," Box 7, Entry 40, NACP.

8. Hinton, *From the War on Poverty to the War on Crime*; "150 Policewomen Up for Sergeant's Test," *New York Times*, April 11, 1964, 8.

9. National Advisory Police Committee on Social Protection of the Federal Security Agency, "Techniques of Law Enforcement in the Use of Policewomen with Special Reference to Social Protection," 1945, 2, 55, JJCA.

10. Fischer, *Streets Belong to Us*, 76.

11. Ann Petry, "Harlem Women Wax Indignant over Latest 'Crime' Campaign," *People's Voice*, August 15, 1942, 3.

12. "Salutations, Commissioner Wallander! Farewell, Commissioner Valentine!," *Spring 3100*, September–October 1945, 5; Gilbert, *Cycle of Outrage*, 37.

13. "Rise of Juvenile Crime," *New York Times*, March 21, 1946, 24.

14. "Senators Start Morals Hearings," *New York Times*, May 25, 1955, 1.

15. For more on delinquency and popular culture, see Gilbert, *Cycle of Outrage*; and Hajdu, *Ten-Cent Plague*. For discussions of the politics of gangs, drug use, and delinquency in postwar New York City, see Woodsworth, *Battle for Bed-Stuy*, 16–42; and Schneider, *Vampires*, 120–68. For federal responses to juvenile delinquency, see Barnosky, "Violent Years." Elizabeth Hinton considers the role of the federal government in criminalizing African American youth in the 1960s in "Creating Crime."

16. Carl Dunbar Lawrence, "V-E Day Finds Harlem Quiet, Broadway Loud," *New York Amsterdam News*, May 12, 1945, A1.

17. Dan Gardner, "V-J Day Rejoicing, but What Did American Negroes Gain?," *New York Amsterdam News*, September 8, 1945, 7A.

18. Clarence Taylor, *Fight the Power*, 87. Harlem riot reports, 1943.

19. "Police War Urged on the Pick-Up Girl," *New York Times*, July 27, 1944, 19; Calkin, "Military Police Replacements," 20.

20. Murray Trilling, "Letter to the Editor," *Spring 3100*, August 1945, 12.

21. Edward T. Lynch, "Letter to the Editor," *Spring 3100*, August 1945, 13.

22. "Mayor Opens Fight on Rise in Crime," *New York Times*, November 20, 1945, 1.

23. Charles Harruld, *Spring 3100*, January 1946, cover art.

24. "Gen. MacArthur Invites Valentine to Reorganize Japanese Police," *New York Times*, January 30, 1946, 1; "Valentine Is Back after Tokyo Work," *New York Times*, June 1, 1946, 8. For more on the reorganization of Japan's police force, see Aldous, *Police in Occupation Japan*, 148–53; Kuzmarov, *Modernizing Repression*, 57–78; and Kramm, *Sanitized Sex*.

25. Valentine, *Night Stick*, 305.

26. "Salutations, Commissioner Wallander!," 5.

27. John G. Rogers, "The La Guardia Era at an End after 12 Color-Packed Years," *New York Herald-Tribune*, December 31, 1945, 11.

28. Isaac Siegel to La Guardia, July 28, 1942, Folder 7, Roll 109, Subject Files: Juvenile Delinquency, FLGC.

Bibliography

Archival Collections

Center for Jewish History, American Jewish Historical Society Collection,
   New York, N.Y.
   Nathan D. Pearlman Collection
Columbia University, Rare Book and Manuscript Library
   Reminiscences of Samuel J. Battle, 1960
John Jay College, Lloyd Sealy Library, Manuscripts and Special Collections,
   New York, N.Y.
   Manuals of Procedure, NYPD Collection
Library of Congress, Manuscript Division, Washington, D.C.
   Records of the National Association for the Advancement of Colored People
National Archives, Record Groups 215 and 160, College Park, Md.
   Records of the Army Service Forces
   Records of the Office of Community War Services
New York City Municipal Archives, New York, N.Y.
   Health Commissioner's Records, John L. Rice and Ernest Stebbins Subgroups
   Mayor Fiorello H. La Guardia Records
   Women's Court Record Book, Manhattan 9th District, Criminal Court
New York County Lawyer's Association Archives, New York, N.Y.
   Supreme Court, Appellate Division
New York Public Library, Manuscripts and Archives Division, Astor, Lenox, and
   Tilden Foundations, New York, N.Y.
   Vito Marcantonio Papers
   Women's Prison Association of New York Records
New York State Archives, State of New York Department of Corrections,
   Albany, N.Y.
   Sing Sing Prison Admission Registers
Schomburg Center for Research in Black Culture, Manuscripts, Archives, and
   Rare Books Division, New York Public Library, New York, N.Y.
   Ann Petry Papers
   Harlem Riot of 1943 Reports
Staten Island Institute of Arts and Sciences Archives, Staten Island, N.Y.
   History Pamphlets
University of Minnesota Libraries, Social Welfare History Archives, Migration and
   Social Services in the Archives and Special Collections Department,
   Minneapolis
   American Social Health Association Collection

Newspapers and Magazines

Atlas
Brooklyn Daily Eagle
Chicago Defender
New York Age
New York Amsterdam News

New York Herald
New York Herald-Tribune
New-York Observer
New York Post
New York Times

People's Voice
Spring 3100
Staten Island Advance

Government Reports

Clarke, Dorris. *The Wayward Minors' Court: An Evaluative Review of Procedures and Purposes, 1936–1941*. New York: Magistrates' Courts, 1941.

Commission on the Harlem Riot. *The Complete Report of Mayor LaGuardia's Commission on the Harlem Riot of March 19, 1935*. New York: Arno Press and *New York Times*, 1969.

Kings County Grand Jury. "Presentment of the August, 1943 Grand Jury of Kings County to Hon. Louis Goldstein Country Judge, Kings County." November 15, 1943.

Marsh, Marguerite. *Prostitutes in New York City: Their Apprehension, Trial, and Treatment, July 1939–June 1940*. New York: Research Bureau, Welfare Council of New York City, 1941.

Office of Facts and Figures. *The Negro Looks at the War: Attitudes of New York Negroes toward Discrimination against Negroes and a Comparison of Negro and Poor White Attitudes toward War-Related Issues*. Extensive Surveys Division, Bureau of Intelligence, 1942.

New York City Police Department. *Annual Reports*.

Robinson, Sophia M. *An Inquiry into the Present Functioning of the Women's Court in Relation to the Problem of Prostitution in New York City*. Welfare Council of New York City Research Bureau, May 1935.

Seabury, Samuel, referee. *The Investigation of the Magistrates' Courts in the First Judicial Department and the Magistrates Thereof, and of Attorneys-at-Law Practicing in Said Courts*. New York, March 28, 1932.

Valentine, Lewis. *Report of the Police Commissioner to the Mayor*. November 20, 1943.

Published Books and Articles

Abu-Lughod, Janet L. *Race, Space, and Riots in Chicago, New York, and Los Angeles*. Oxford: Oxford University Press, 2007.

Agee, Christopher Lowen. *The Streets of San Francisco: Policing and the Creation of a Cosmopolitan Liberal Politics, 1950–1972*. Chicago: University of Chicago Press, 2014.

Agyepong, Tera Eva. *The Criminalization of Black Children: Race, Gender, and Delinquency in Chicago's Juvenile Justice System, 1899–1945*. Chapel Hill: University of North Carolina Press, 2018.

Aldous, Christopher. *The Police in Occupation Japan: Control, Corruption and Resistance to Reform*. New York: Routledge, 1997.

Alexander, Leslie. *African or American: Black Identity and Political Activism in New York City, 1784-1861*. Urbana: University of Illinois Press, 2008.

Alexander, Ruth. *The "Girl Problem": Female Sexual Delinquency in New York, 1900-1930*. Ithaca, N.Y.: Cornell University Press, 1995.

Alvarez, Luis. *The Power of the Zoot: Youth Culture and Resistance during World War II*. Berkeley: University of California Press, 2008.

Anbinder, Tyler. *Five Points: The Nineteenth-Century New York City Neighborhood That Invented Tap Dance, Stole Elections, and Became the World's Most Notorious Slum*. New York: Free Press, 2001.

Anderson, Jervis. *This Was Harlem: A Cultural Portrait, 1900-1950*. New York: NoonDay, 1981.

Anderson, Karen. "Last Hired, First Fired: Black Women Workers during World War II." *Journal of American History* 69, no. 1 (June 1982): 82-97.

————. *Wartime Women: Sex Roles, Family Relations, and the Status of Women during World War II*. Westport, Conn.: Praeger, 1981.

Appier, Janis. *Policing Women: The Sexual Politics of Law Enforcement and the LAPD*. Philadelphia: Temple University Press, 1998.

Baber, Katherine. "'Manhattan Women': Jazz, Blues, and Gender in *On the Town* and *Wonderful Town*." *American Music* 31, no. 1 (Spring 2013): 73-105.

Baer, Andrew S. *Beyond the Usual Beating: The Jon Burge Police Torture Scandal and Social Movements for Police Accountability in Chicago*. Chicago: University of Chicago Press, 2020.

Bailey, Beth, and David Farber. *The First Strange Place: Race and Sex in World War II Hawaii*. Baltimore: Johns Hopkins University Press, 1992.

Bailey, Moya. *Misogynoir Transformed: Black Women's Digital Resistance*. New York: New York University Press, 2021.

Baldwin, James. "Me and My House . . ." *Harper's*, November 1, 1955, 54-61.

Balto, Simon. *Occupied Territory: Policing Black Chicago from Red Summer to Black Power*. Chapel Hill: University of North Carolina Press, 2019.

Barnosky, Jason. "The Violent Years: Responses to Juvenile Crime in the 1950s." *Polity* 38, no. 3 (July 2006): 314-44.

Bayor, Ronald H. *Fiorello La Guardia: Ethnicity, Reform, and Urban Development*. Hoboken, N.J.: Wiley Blackwell, 2018.

Beckert, Sven. *The Monied Metropolis: New York City and the Consolidation of the American Bourgeoisie, 1850-1896*. Cambridge: Cambridge University Press, 2001.

Bernstein, Iver. *The New York City Draft Riots: Their Significance for American Society and Politics in the Age of the Civil War*. New York: Oxford University Press, 1990.

Bérubé, Allan. *Coming Out under Fire: The History of Gay Men and Women in World War II*. Chapel Hill: University of North Carolina Press, 2010.

Binder, Frederick. *All the Nations under Heaven: An Ethnic and Racial History of New York City*. New York: Columbia University Press, 1995.

Biondi, Martha. *To Stand and Fight: The Struggle for Civil Rights in Postwar New York*. Cambridge, Mass.: Harvard University Press, 2006.

Blower, Brooke. "V-J Day, 1945, Times Square." In *The Familiar Made Strange: American Icons and Artifacts after the Transnational Turn*, edited by Brooke L. Blower and Mark P. Bradley, 70–87. Ithaca, N.Y.: Cornell University Press, 2015.

Blum, Albert A. "Work or Fight: The Use of the Draft as a Manpower Sanction during the Second World War." *ILR Review* 16, no. 3 (April 1963): 366–80.

Brandt, Allan. *No Magic Bullet: A Social History of Venereal Disease in the United States since 1880*. New York: Oxford University Press, 1985.

Brandt, Nat. *Harlem at War: The Black Experience in World War II*. Syracuse: Syracuse University Press, 1996.

Briggs, Laura. *Reproducing Empire: Race, Sex, Science, and U.S. Imperialism in Puerto Rico*. Berkeley: University of California Press, 2002.

Brinkley, Alan. *The Publisher: Henry Luce and His American Century*. New York: Alfred A. Knopf, 2010.

Broeker, Galen. *Rural Disorder and Police Reform in Ireland, 1812–36*. Abingdon, U.K.: Routledge, 2015.

Brooks, Emily. "Coercive Patriotism: Gender, Militarism, and Auxiliary Police in New York City during World War II." *Labor History*, 2022. https://doi.org/10.1080/0023656X.2022.2147912.

———. "'Rumor, Vicious Innuendo, and False Reports': Policing Black Soldiers in Wartime Staten Island." *Journal of Urban History* 47, no. 5 (2021): 1032–49.

Browne, Arthur. *One Righteous Man: Samuel Battle and the Shattering of the Color Line in New York*. New York: Beacon, 2015.

Calkin, Homer L. "Military Police Replacements in World War II." *Social Science* 27, no. 1 (January 1952): 17–22.

Canaday, Margot. *The Straight State: Sexuality and Citizenship in Twentieth-Century America*. Princeton, N.J.: Princeton University Press, 2009.

Capeci, Dominic J., Jr. "From Different Liberal Perspectives: Fiorello H. La Guardia, Adam Clayton Powell, Jr., and Civil Rights in New York City, 1941–1943." *Journal of Negro History* 62, no. 2 (April 1977): 160–73.

———. *The Harlem Riot of 1943*. Philadelphia: Temple University Press, 1977.

———. "Walter F. White and the Savoy Ballroom Controversy of 1943." *Afro-Americans in New York Life and History* 5, no. 2 (July 1981): 1–13.

Capozzola, Christopher. *Uncle Sam Wants You: World War I and the Making of the Modern American Citizen*. Oxford: Oxford University Press, 2008.

Chauncey, George. *Gay New York: Gender, Urban Culture, and the Making of the Gay Male World, 1890–1940*. New York: Basic Books, 1994.

Chronopoulos, Themis. "Morality, Social Disorder, and the Working Class in Times Square, 1892–1954." *Australasian Journal of American Studies* 30, no. 1 (July 2011): 1–19.

Clement, Elizabeth. *Love for Sale: Courting, Treating, and Prostitution in New York City, 1900–1945*. Chapel Hill: University of North Carolina Press, 2006.

Connolly, Nathan. *A World More Concrete: Real Estate and the Remaking of Jim Crow South Florida*. Chicago: University of Chicago Press, 2014.

Cooper, Courtney Ryley. *Designs in Scarlet*. Boston: Little Brown, 1939.

Crist, Thomas A. "Babies in the Privy: Prostitution, Infanticide, and Abortion in New York City's Five Points District." *Historical Archaeology* 39, no. 1 (2005): 19–46.

Czitrom, Daniel. *New York Exposed: The Gilded Age Police Scandal That Launched the Progressive Era*. Oxford: Oxford University Press, 2016.

Dailey, Jane. *White Fright: The Sexual Panic at the Heart of America's Racist History*. New York: Basic Books, 2020.

Darien, Andrew. *Becoming New York's Finest: Race, Gender, and the Integration of the NYPD, 1935-1980*. New York: Palgrave MacMillan, 2003.

Delmont, Matthew F. *Half American: The Epic Story of African Americans Fighting World War II at Home and Abroad*. New York: Viking, 2022.

D'Emilio, John, and Estelle Freedman. *Intimate Matters: A History of Sexuality in America*. 3rd ed. Chicago: University of Chicago Press, 2012. Originally published 1988.

Dodson, Dan W. "The Mayor's Committee on Unity of New York City." *Journal of Educational Sociology* 19, no. 5 (January 1946): 289–98.

Dower, John. *Embracing Defeat: Japan in the Wake of World War II*. New York: W. W. Norton, 1999.

Drane, Gregory. "The Role of African-American Musicians in the Integration of the United States Navy." *Music Educators Journal* 101, no. 3 (March 2015): 63–67.

Engelbrecht, Barbara. "Swinging at the Savoy." *Dance Research Journal* 15, no. 2 (Spring 1983): 3–10.

Epstein, Rebecca, Jamilia J. Blake, and Thalia González. *Girlhood Interrupted: The Erasure of Black Girls' Childhood*. Center on Poverty and Inequality, Georgetown Law, 2017.

Escobar, Edward. *Race, Police, and the Making of a Political Identity: Mexican Americans and the Los Angeles Police Department, 1900-1945*. Berkeley: University of California Press, 1999.

Escobedo, Elizabeth Rachel. *From Coveralls to Zoot Suits: The Lives of Mexican American Women on the World War II Home Front*. Chapel Hill: University of North Carolina Press, 2013.

Estes, Steve. *Ask and Tell: Gay and Lesbian Veterans Speak Out*. Chapel Hill: University of North Carolina Press, 2009.

Evens, Elizabeth. "Plainclothes Policewomen on the Trail: NYPD Undercover Investigations of Abortionists and Queer Women, 1913-1926." *Modern American History* 4, no. 1. Published ahead of print, December 22, 2020. https://doi.org/10.1017/mah.2020.22.

Felker-Kantor, Max. *Policing Los Angeles: Race, Resistance, and the Rise of the LAPD*. Chapel Hill: University of North Carolina Press, 2018.

Fischer, Anne Gray. "'Land of the White Hunter': Legal Liberalism and the Racial Politics of Morals Enforcement in Midcentury Los Angeles." *Journal of American History* 105, no. 4 (March 2019): 868–84.

———. *The Streets Belong to Us: Sex, Race, and Police Power from Segregation to Gentrification*. Chapel Hill: University of North Carolina Press, 2022.

Flowe, Douglas J. *Uncontrollable Blackness: African American Men and Criminality in Jim Crow New York*. Chapel Hill: University of North Carolina Press, 2020.

Foner, Nancy. "Introduction: West Indian Migration to New York: An Overview." In *Islands in the City: West Indian Migration to New York*, edited by Nancy Foner, 1–22. Berkeley: University of California Press, 2001.

Foote, Thelma Wills. *Black and White Manhattan: The History of Racial Formation in Colonial New York City*. New York: Oxford University Press, 2004.

Freedman, Estelle. *Their Sister's Keepers: Women's Prison Reform in America, 1830–1930*. Ann Arbor: University of Michigan Press, 1981.

Friedman, Andrea. "'The Habits of Sex-Crazed Perverts': Campaigns against Burlesque in Depression-Era New York City." *Journal of the History of Sexuality* 7, no. 2 (October 1996): 203–38.

Fronc, Jennifer. *New York Undercover: Private Surveillance in the Progressive Era*. Chicago: University of Chicago Press, 2009.

Gallagher, Julie. *Black Women and Politics in New York City*. Champaign: University of Illinois Press, 2012.

Gallon, Kim. *Pleasure in the News: African American Readership and Sexuality in the Black Press*. Chicago: University of Illinois Press, 2020.

Gilbert, James. *A Cycle of Outrage: America's Reaction to the Juvenile Delinquent in the 1950s*. New York: Oxford University Press, 1986.

Gilfoyle, Timothy. *City of Eros: New York City, Prostitution, and the Commercialization of Sex, 1790–1920*. New York: W. W. Norton, 1994.

Gilje, Paul A. *The Road to Mobocracy: Popular Disorder in New York City, 1763–1834*. Chapel Hill: University of North Carolina Press, 1987.

Glasser, Ruth. *My Music Is My Flag: Puerto Rican Musicians and Their New York Communities, 1917–1940*. Berkeley: University of California Press, 1995.

Go, Julian. "The Imperial Origins of American Policing: Militarization and Imperial Feedback in the Early 20th Century." *American Journal of Sociology* 125, no. 5 (March 2020): 1193–254.

Gold, Michael. *Jews without Money*. 1930; repr., New York: Avon Books, 1965.

Gold, Russell. "Guilty of Syncopation, Joy, and Animation: The Closing of Harlem's Savoy Ballroom." *Studies in Dance History* 5, no. 1 (Spring 1994): 50–64.

Goldberg, David A. *Black Firefighters and the FDNY: The Struggle for Jobs, Justice, and Equity in New York City*. Chapel Hill: University of North Carolina Press, 2017.

Goldberg, David J. "Unmasking the Ku Klux Klan: The Northern Movement against the KKK, 1920–1925." *Journal of American Ethnic History* 15, no. 4 (Summer 1996): 32–48.

Goldstein, Richard. *Helluva Town: The Story of New York City during World War II*. New York: Free Press, 2010.

Golway, Terry. *Machine Made: Tammany Hall and the Creation of Modern American Politics*. New York: Liveright, 2014.

Greenberg, Cheryl Lynn. *"Or Does It Explode?": Black Harlem in the Great Depression*. New York: Oxford University Press, 1991.

———. "The Politics of Disorder: Reexamining Harlem's Riots of 1935 and 1943." *Journal of Urban History* 18, no. 4 (August 1992): 395–441.

Griffin, Farah Jasmine. *Harlem Nocturne: Women Artists and Progressive Politics during World War II*. New York: Basic Civitas, 2013.

Gross, Kali. *Colored Amazons: Crime Violence, and Black Women in the City of Brotherly Love*. Durham, N.C.: Duke University Press, 2006.

Guariglia, Matthew. "The American Problem: Race, Empire and Policing in New York City, 1840–1930." PhD diss., University of Connecticut, 2019.

Hajdu, David. *The Ten-Cent Plague: The Great Comic-Book Scare and How It Changed America*. New York: Farrar, Straus and Giroux, 2009.

Haley, Sarah. *No Mercy Here: Gender, Punishment, and the Making of Jim Crow Modernity*. Chapel Hill: University of North Carolina Press, 2016.

Hari, Johann. *Chasing the Scream: The First and Last Days of the War on Drugs*. New York: Bloomsbury, 2015. Ebook.

Harris, LaShawn. "Marvel Cooke: Investigative Journalist, Communist and Black Radical Subject." *Journal for the Study of Radicalism* 6, no. 2 (Fall 2012): 91–126.

———. "Playing the Numbers: Madame Stephanie St. Clair and African American Policy Culture in Harlem." *Black Women, Gender + Families* 2, no. 2 (Fall 2008): 53–76.

———. "Running with the Reds: African American Women and the Communist Party during the Depression." *Journal of African American History* 94, no. 1 (Winter 2009): 21–43.

———. *Sex Workers, Psychics, and Number Runners: Black Women in New York City's Underground Economy*. Urbana: University of Illinois Press, 2016.

———. "'Women and Girls in Jeopardy by His False Testimony': Charles Dancy, Urban Policing, and Black Women in New York City during the 1920s." *Journal of Urban History* 44, no. 3 (May 2018): 457–75.

Harris, Leslie M. *In the Shadow of Slavery: African Americans in New York City, 1626–1863*. Chicago: University of Chicago Press, 2003.

Hartman, Saidiya. *Wayward Lives, Beautiful Experiments: Intimate Histories of Riotous Black Girls, Troublesome Women, and Queer Radicals*. New York: W. W. Norton, 2019.

Hartmann, Susan. *The Home Front and Beyond: American Women in the 1940s*. Boston: Twayne, 1984.

Haygood, Wil. *King of the Cats: The Life and Times of Adam Clayton Powell, Jr*. New York: Amistad, 1993.

Heap, Chad. *Slumming: Sexual and Racial Encounters in American Nightlife, 1885–1940*. Chicago: University of Chicago Press, 2009.

Hegarty, Marilyn. *Victory Girls, Khaki-Wackies, and Patriotutes: The Regulation of Female Sexuality during World War II*. New York: New York University Press, 2008.

Hendricks, Craig, and Julian Delgaudio. "'A Vast War Establishment': World War II Comes to Long Beach." *Southern California Quarterly* 99, no. 4 (2017): 443–74.

Hernandez, Kelly Lytle. *City of Inmates: Conquest, Rebellion, and the Rise of Human Caging in Los Angeles, 1771–1965*. Chapel Hill: University of North Carolina Press, 2017.

Hicks, Cheryl. "'In Danger of Becoming Morally Depraved': Single Black Women, Working-Class Black Families, and New York State's Wayward Minor Laws, 1917–1928." *University of Pennsylvania Law Review* 151, no. 6 (June 2003): 2077–121.

———. *Talk with You like a Woman: African American Women, Justice, and Reform in New York, 1890–1935*. Chapel Hill: University of North Carolina Press, 2010.

Higginbotham, Evelyn Brooks. *Righteous Discontent: The Women's Movement in the Black Baptist Church, 1880–1920*. Cambridge, Mass.: Harvard University Press, 1993.

Hiltner, Aaron. *Taking Leave, Taking Liberties: American Troops on the World War II Home Front*. Chicago: University of Chicago Press, 2020.

Hinton, Elizabeth. *America on Fire: The Untold History of Police Violence and Black Rebellion since the 1960s*. New York: Liveright, 2021.

———. "Creating Crime: The Rise and Impact of National Juvenile Delinquency Programs in Black Urban Neighborhoods." *Journal of Urban History* 41, no. 5 (September 2015): 808–24.

———. *From the War on Poverty to the War on Crime: The Making of Mass Incarceration in America*. Cambridge: Harvard University Press, 2017.

Hoare, Quintin, and Geoffrey Nowell-Smith, eds. *Selections from the Prison Notebooks of Antonio Gramsci*. New York: International Publishers, 1971.

Hodges, Adam J. *World War I and Urban Order: The Local Class Politics of National Mobilization*. New York: Palgrave Macmillan, 2016.

Höhn, Maria. *GIs and Frauleins: The German-American Encounter in 1950s West Germany*. Chapel Hill: University of North Carolina Press, 2002.

Holloway, Pippa. *Sexuality, Politics, and Social Control in Virginia, 1920–1945*. Chapel Hill: University of North Carolina Press, 2006.

Horne, Gerald. *Facing the Rising Sun: African Americans, Japan, and the Rise of Afro-Asian Solidarity*. New York: New York University Press, 2018.

Howe, Daniel Walker. *What Has God Wrought: The Transformation of America, 1815–1848*. Oxford: Oxford University Press, 2007.

Hutzel, Eleonore L. *The Policewoman's Handbook*. New York: Columbia University Press, 1933.

Immerwahr, Daniel. *How to Hide an Empire: A History of the Greater United States*. New York: Picador, 2019.

Jackson, Kenneth T., ed. *The Encyclopedia of New York City*. 2nd ed. New Haven, C.T.: Yale University Press, 2010.

———. *WWII & NYC*. New York: New York Historical Society, 2013.

Johnson, Marilynn S. "Gender, Race, and Rumours: Re-examining the 1943 Race Riots." *Gender and History* 10, no. 2 (August 1998): 252–77.

———. *The Second Gold Rush: Oakland and the East Bay in World War II*. Berkeley: University of California Press, 1993.

———. *Street Justice: A History of Police Violence in New York City*. Boston: Beacon, 2003.

Kaplan, Michael. "New York City Tavern Violence and the Creation of a Working-Class Male Identity." *Journal of the Early Republic* 15, no. 4 (Winter 1995): 591–617.

Katznelson, Ira. *When Affirmative Action Was White: An Untold History of Racial Inequality in Twentieth-Century America*. New York: W. W. Norton, 2006.

Keller, Lisa. *Triumph of Order: Democracy and Public Space in New York and London*. New York: Columbia University Press, 2010.

Kelley, Robin. *Race Rebels: Culture, Politics, and the Black Working Class*. New York: Free Press, 1996.

Kessner, Thomas. *Fiorello H. La Guardia and the Making of Modern New York*. New York: Penguin Books, 1989.

King, Shannon. "A Murder in Central Park: Racial Violence and the Crime Wave in New York during the 1930s and 1940s." In *The Strange Careers of the Jim Crow North:*

Segregation and Struggle outside of the South, edited by Brian Purnell and Jeanne Theoharis with Komozi Woodard, 43–66. New York: New York University Press, 2019.

——. *Whose Harlem Is This, Anyway? Community Politics and Grassroots Activism during the New Negro Era*. New York: New York University Press, 2015.

Kohler-Hausmann, Julilly. *Getting Tough: Welfare and Imprisonment in 1970s America*. Princeton, N.J.: Princeton University Press, 2017.

Kotlowski, Dean J. *Paul V. McNutt and the Age of FDR*. Bloomington: Indiana University Press, 2015.

Kramm, Robert. *Sanitized Sex: Regulating Prostitution, Venereal Disease, and Intimacy in Occupied Japan*. Berkeley: University of California Press, 2017.

Kraska, Peter. "Militarization and Policing: Its Relevance to 21st Century Police." *Policing: A Journal of Policy and Practice* 1, no. 4 (2007): 501–13.

Krugler, David F. *1919, the Year of Racial Violence: How African Americans Fought Back*. New York: Cambridge University Press, 2015.

Kunzel, Regina G. "Situating Sex: Prison Sexual Culture in the Mid-Twentieth-Century United States." *GLQ: A Journal of Lesbian and Gay Studies* 8, no. 3 (2002): 253–70.

Kuzmarov, Jeremy. *Modernizing Repression: Police Training and Nation Building in American Century*. Amherst: University of Massachusetts Press, 2012.

La Guardia, Fiorello. *The Making of an Insurgent*. Philadelphia: Lippincott, 1948.

Lang, Clarence. *Grassroots at the Gateway: Class Politics and Black Freedom Struggle in St. Louis, 1936–75*. Ann Arbor: University of Michigan Press, 2009.

Leach, Laurie F. "Margie Polite, the Riot Starter: Harlem, 1943." *Studies in the Literary Imagination* 40, no. 2 (Fall 2007): 25–48.

Lee, Heather. "Hunting for Sailors: Restaurant Raids and Conscription of Laborers during World War II." In *A Nation of Immigrants Reconsidered: US Society in an Age of Restriction, 1924–1965*, edited by Maddalena Marinari, Madeline Y. Hsu, and Maria Cristina Garcia, 107–22. Urbana: University of Illinois Press, 2019.

LeFlouria, Talitha L. *Chained in Silence: Black Women and Convict Labor in the New South*. Chapel Hill: University of North Carolina Press, 2015.

Lerner, Michael. *Dry Manhattan: Prohibition in New York City*. Cambridge, Mass.: Harvard University Press, 2008.

Lewis, David Levering. *W. E. B. Du Bois: A Biography*. New York: Henry Holt, 2009.

Lindsay, Treva B. *American Goddam: Violence, Black Women, and the Struggle for Justice*. Oakland: University of California Press, 2022.

Littauer, Amanda. *Bad Girls: Young Women, Sex, and Rebellion before the Sixties*. Chapel Hill: University of North Carolina Press, 2015.

Lobel, Cindy R. "'Out to Eat': The Emergence and Evolution of the Restaurant in Nineteenth-Century New York City." *Winterthur Portfolio* 44, no. 2/3 (Summer/Autumn 2010): 193–220.

Lucander, David. *Winning the War for Democracy: The March on Washington Movement, 1941–1946*. Urbana: University of Illinois Press, 2014.

Lvovsky, Anna. *Vice Patrol: Cops, Courts and the Struggle over Urban Gay Life before Stonewall*. Chicago: University of Chicago Press, 2021.

Malcolm X. *The Autobiography of Malcolm X*. New York: Grove, 1964.

Massoni, Kelly. *Fashioning Teenagers: A Cultural History of "Seventeen" Magazine*. Walnut Creek, Calif.: Left Coast, 2010.

McKay, Nellie. Afterword to *Daddy Was a Number Runner*, by Louise Meriwether, 314–63. New York: Feminist Press, 1970.

McLeod, Jacqueline A. *Daughter of the Empire State: The Life of Judge Jane Bolin*. Urbana: University of Illinois Press, 2011.

Meriwether, Louise. *Daddy Was a Number Runner*. New York: Feminist Press, 1970.

Meyer, Leisa D. *Creating GI Jane: Sexuality and Power in the Women's Army Corps during World War II*. New York: Columbia University Press, 1997.

Miller, Karen. *Managing Inequality: Northern Racial Liberalism in Interwar Detroit*. New York: New York University Press, 2015.

Miller, Wilber. *Cops and Bobbies: Police Authority in New York and London, 1830–1870*. Chicago: University of Chicago Press, 1977.

Mills, Charles. "Liberalism and the Racial State." In *State of White Supremacy: Racism, Governance, and the United States*, edited by Moon-Kie Jung, João H. Costa Vargas, and Eduardo Bonilla-Silva, 27–46. Palo Alto, Calif.: Stanford University Press, 2011.

Milne, C., and Pamela J. Crabtree. "Prostitutes, a Rabbi, and Carpenter—Dinner at the Five Points in the 1830s." *Historical Archeology* 35, no. 3 (2001): 31–48.

Minsky, Morton. *Minsky's Burlesque: A Fast and Funny Look at America's Bawdiest Era*. New York: Arbor House, 1986.

Mitgang, Herbert. *The Man Who Rode the Tiger: The Life and Times of Samuel Seabury*. New York: Fordham University Press, 1996.

———. *Once upon a Time in New York: Jimmy Walker, Franklin Roosevelt, and the Last Great Battle of the Jazz Age*. New York: Free Press, 2000.

Mosterman, Andrea. *Spaces of Enslavement: A History of Slavery and Resistance in Dutch New York*. Ithaca, N.Y.: Cornell University Press, 2021.

Muhammad, Khalil Gibran. *Condemnation of Blackness: Race, Crime, and the Making of Modern Urban America*. Cambridge, Mass.: Harvard University Press, 2010.

Mumford, Kevin. *Interzones: Black/White Sex Districts in Chicago and New York in the Early Twentieth Century*. New York: Columbia University Press, 1997.

Murakawa, Naomi. *The First Civil Right: How Liberals Built Prison America*. Oxford: Oxford University Press, 2014.

Myers, Tamara Gene. *Youth Squad: Policing Children in the Twentieth Century*. Montreal: McGill-Queen's University Press, 2019.

Naison, Mark. *Communists in Harlem during the Depression*. Champaign: University of Illinois Press, 1983.

Nalty, Bernard C. *Strength for the Fight: A History of Black Americans in the Military*. New York: Free Press, 1986.

Nasaw, David. *Children of the City: At Work and at Play*. New York: Anchor Books, 1985.

Odem, Mary. *Delinquent Daughters: Protecting and Policing Adolescent Female Sexuality in the United States, 1885–1920*. Chapel Hill: University of North Carolina Press, 1995.

Oja, Carol J. *Bernstein Meets Broadway: Collaborative Art in a Time of War*. Oxford: Oxford University Press, 2014.

Parascandola, John. "John Mahoney and the Introduction of Penicillin to Treat Syphilis." *Pharmacy in History* 43, no.1 (2001): 3–13.

———. "Quarantining Women: Venereal Disease Rapid Treatment Centers in World War II America." *Bulletin of the History of Medicine* 83, no. 3 (Fall 2009): 431–59.

Peiss, Kathy. *Cheap Amusements: Working Women and Leisure in Turn-of-the-Century New York*. Philadelphia: Temple University Press, 1986.

———. *Zoot Suit: The Enigmatic Career of an Extreme Style*. Philadelphia: University of Pennsylvania Press, 2011.

Peretti, Burton W. *Nightclub City: Politics and Amusement in Manhattan*. Philadelphia: University of Pennsylvania Press, 2007.

Petry, Ann. "In Darkness and Confusion." In *Miss Muriel and Other Stories*, 238–279. New York: Mariner Classics, 2023.

———. *The Street*. Boston: Houghton Mifflin, 1946.

Petry, Elisabeth. *At Home Inside: A Daughter's Tribute to Ann Petry*. Jackson: University Press of Mississippi, 2009.

Phillips, Kimberley L. *War! What Is It Good For? Black Freedom Struggles and the U.S. Military from World War II to Iraq*. Chapel Hill: University of North Carolina Press, 2012.

Plant, Rebecca Jo. *Mom: The Transformation of Motherhood in Modern America*. Chicago: University of Chicago Press, 2010.

Pliley, Jessica. *Policing Sexuality: The Mann Act and the Making of the FBI*. Cambridge, Mass.: Harvard University Press, 2014.

Poston, Ted. "The Numbers Racket." In *Delinquency, Crime, and Social Process*, edited by Donald R. Cressey, 920–934. New York: Harper and Row, 1969.

Purnell, Brian, and Jeanne Theoharis. "Introduction: Histories of Racism and Resistance, Seen and Unseen: How and Why to Think about the Jim Crow North." In *The Strange Careers of the Jim Crow North: Segregation and Struggle outside of the South*, edited by Brian Purnell and Jeanne Theoharis with Komozi Woodard, 1–42. New York: New York University Press, 2019.

———, eds. *The Strange Careers of the Jim Crow North: Segregation and Struggle outside of the South*. With Komozi Woodard. New York: New York University Press, 2019.

Richardson, James F. *The New York Police: Colonial Times to 1901*. New York: Oxford University Press, 1970.

Riley, Susan E. "Caring for Rosie's Children: Federal Child Care Policies in the World War II Era." *Polity* 26, no. 4 (Summer 1994): 655–75.

Roberts, Mary Louise. "The Price of Discretion: Prostitution, Venereal Disease, and the American Military in France." *American Historical Review* 115, no. 4 (October 2010): 1002–30.

———. *What Soldiers Do: Sex and the American GI in World War II France*. Chicago: University of Chicago Press, 2013.

Robertson, David. *Sly and Able: A Political Biography of James F. Byrnes*. New York: W. W. Norton, 1994.

Robertson, Stephen. "Harlem Undercover: Vice Investigators, Race, and Prostitution, 1910–1930." *Journal of Urban History* 35, no. 4 (May 2009): 486–504.

Robertson, Stephen, Shane White, Stephen Garton, and Graham White. "Disorderly Houses: Residences, Privacy, and the Surveillance of Sexuality in 1920s Harlem." *Journal of the History of Sexuality* 21, no. 3 (September 2012): 443–66.

Rupp, Leila. *Mobilizing Women for War: German and American Propaganda, 1939–1945.* Princeton, N.J.: Princeton University Press, 1978.

Ryan, Hugh. *The Woman's House of Detention: A Queer History of a Forgotten Prison.* New York: Bold Type Books, 2022.

Sacks, Marcy. *Before Harlem: The Black Experience in New York City before World War I.* Philadelphia: University of Pennsylvania Press, 2006.

———. "'To Be a Man and Not a Lackey': Black Men, Work, and the Construction of Manhood in Gilded Age New York City." *American Studies* 45, no. 1 (Spring 2004): 39–63.

Sanchez-Korrol, Virginia. *From Colonia to Community: The History of Puerto Ricans in New York City.* Berkeley: University of California Press, 1983.

Schneider, Eric. *In the Web of Class: Delinquents and Reformers in Boston, 1810s–1930s.* New York: New York University Press, 1993.

———. *Vampires, Dragons, and Egyptian Kings: Youth Gangs in Postwar New York.* Princeton, N.J.: Princeton University Press, 1999.

Schrader, Stuart. "Cops at War: How World War II Transformed U.S. Policing." *Modern American History* 4, no. 2 (2021): 159–79.

Schulz, Dorothy. *From Social Worker to Crimefighter: Women in United States Municipal Policing.* Westport, Conn.: Praeger, 1995.

———. "A Precinct of Their Own: The New York City Women's Precinct, 1921–1923." *New York History* 85, no. 1 (Winter 2004): 39–64.

Sharma, Alankaar. "Diseased Race, Racialized Disease: The Story of the Negro Project of American Social Hygiene Association against the Backdrop of the Tuskegee Syphilis Experiment." *Journal of African American Studies* 14, no. 2 (June 2010): 247–62.

Sherman, Janann. "They Either Need These Women or They Do Not." *Journal of Military History* 54, no. 1 (January 1990): 47–78.

Siegel, Micol. *Violence Work: State Power and the Limits of Police.* Durham, N.C.: Duke University Press, 2018.

Simmons, Christina. *Making Marriage Modern: Women's Sexuality from the Progressive Era to World War II.* Oxford: Oxford University Press, 2009.

Singh, Nikhil Pal. *Black Is a Country: Race and the Unfinished Struggle for Democracy.* Cambridge, Mass.: Harvard University Press, 2004.

Snyder, Lynne Page. "New York, the Nation, the World: The Career of Surgeon General Thomas J. Parran Jr., MD, 1892–1968." *Public Health Reports* 119, no. 5 (September–October 1995): 630–32.

Srebnick, Amy Gilman. *The Mysterious Death of Mary Rogers: Sex and Culture in Nineteenth Century New York.* Oxford: Oxford University Press, 1995.

Stansell, Christine. *City of Women: Sex and Class in New York, 1789–1860.* Champaign: University of Illinois Press, 1987.

———. "Women, Children, and the Uses of the Streets, 1850–1860." *Feminist Studies* 8, no. 2 (Summer 1982): 309–35.

Stern, Scott. *The Trials of Nina McCall: Sex, Surveillance, and the Decades-Long Government Plan to Imprison "Promiscuous" Women*. New York: Beacon, 2018.

Stolberg, Mary M. *Fighting Organized Crime: Politics, Justice, and the Legacy of Thomas E. Dewey*. Boston: Northeastern University Press, 1995.

Strom, Claire. "Controlling Venereal Disease in Orlando during World War II." *Florida Historical Quarterly* 91, no. 1 (2012): 86–117.

Suddler, Carl. *Presumed Criminal: Black Youth and the Justice System in Postwar New York*. New York: New York University Press, 2019.

Sullivan, Mary. *My Double Life: The Story of a New York Policewoman*. New York: Farrar and Rinehart, 1938.

Tanenhaus, David S. *Juvenile Justice in the Making*. Oxford: Oxford University Press, 2005.

Taylor, Clarence. *Fight the Power: African Americans and the Long History of Police Brutality in New York City*. New York: New York University Press, 2019.

———. *Reds at the Blackboard: Communism, Civil Rights, and the New York City Teachers Union*. New York: Columbia University Press, 2011.

Taylor, William A. *Military Service and American Democracy: From World War II to the Iraq and Afghanistan Wars*. Lawrence: University Press of Kansas, 2016.

Thale, Christopher. "Assigned to Patrol: Neighborhoods, Police, and Changing Deployment Practices in New York City before 1930." *Journal of Social History* 37, no. 4 (Summer 2004): 1037–64.

———. "The Informal World of Police Patrol: New York City in the Early Twentieth Century." *Journal of Urban History* 33, no. 2 (January 2007): 183–216.

Theoharis, Athan, and John Stuart Cox. *The Boss: J. Edgar Hoover and the Great American Inquisition*. Philadelphia: Temple University Press, 1988.

Thomas, Lorrin. *Puerto Rican Citizen: History and Political Identity in Twentieth-Century New York City*. Chicago: University of Chicago Press, 2010.

Tuttle, William. *Daddy's Gone to War: The Second World War in the Lives of America's Children*. Oxford: Oxford University Press, 1993.

Valentine, Lewis. *Night Stick: The Autobiography of Lewis J. Valentine, Former Police Commissioner of New York*. New York: Dial, 1947.

Vapnek, Lara. *Breadwinners: Working Women and Economic Independence, 1865–1920*. Champaign: University of Illinois Press, 2009.

Vaz, Matthew. *Running the Numbers: Race, Police and the History of Urban Gambling*. Chicago: University of Chicago Press, 2020.

———. "Tammany Hall and the Machine Style in Black Politics." *Modern American History* 4 (2021): 103–7.

Vining, Donald. *A Gay Diary, 1933–1946*. New York: Pepys, 1979.

Vitale, Alex. *The End of Policing*. New York: Verso, 2017.

Wald, Alan. *Trinity of Passion: The Literary Left and the Antifascist Crusade*. Chapel Hill: University of North Carolina Press, 2007.

Walker, Samuel. *A Critical History of Police Reform: The Emergence of Professionalism*. Lexington, Mass.: Lexington Books, 1977.

Wallace, Mike. *Greater Gotham: A History of New York City from 1898 to 1919*. Oxford: Oxford University Press, 2017.

Ward, Geoff K. *The Black Child-Savers: Racial Democracy and Juvenile Justice*. Chicago: University of Chicago Press, 2012.

Wellman, Judith. *Brooklyn's Promised Land: The Free Black Community of Weeksville, New York*. New York: New York University Press, 2014.

Wells, Jonathan Daniel. *The Kidnapping Club: Wall Street, Slavery, and Resistance*. New York: Bold Type Books, 2020.

Whalen, Robert Weldon. *Murder Inc., and the Moral Life: Gangster and Gangbusters in La Guardia's New York*. New York: Fordham University Press, 2018.

White, Deborah Gray. *Too Heavy a Load: Black Women in Defense of Themselves, 1894-1994*. New York: W. W. Norton, 1999.

White, Shane. "'We Dwell in Safety and Pursue Our Honest Callings': Free Blacks in New York City, 1783–1810." *Journal of American History* 75, no. 2 (September 1988): 445–70.

White, Shane, Stephen Garton, Stephen Robertson, and Graham White. *Playing the Numbers: Gambling in Harlem between the Wars*. Cambridge, Mass.: Harvard University Press, 2010.

White, Walter. *A Man Called White*. New York: Arno Press and *New York Times*, 1969.

White, Walter, and Thurgood Marshall. *What Caused the Detroit Riot?* New York: National Association for the Advancement of Colored People, July 1943.

Wilder, Craig Steven. *A Covenant with Color: Race and Social Power in Brooklyn*. New York: Columbia University Press, 2001.

Wilkerson, Isabel. *The Warmth of Other Suns: The Epic Story of America's Great Migration*. New York: Vintage Books 2010.

Williams, Chad L. *Torchbearers of Democracy: African American Soldiers in the World War I Era*. Chapel Hill: University of North Carolina Press, 2013.

Williams, Mason. *City of Ambition: FDR, La Guardia, and the Making of Modern New York*. New York: W. W. Norton, 2013.

Winchell, Megan. *Good Girls, Good Food, Good Fun: The Story of USO Hostesses during World War II*. Chapel Hill: University of North Carolina Press, 2008.

Wolcott, David. *Cops and Kids: Policing Juvenile Delinquency in Urban America, 1890-1940*. Columbus: Ohio State University Press, 2006.

Wood, Marilynn Hill. *Their Sisters' Keepers: Prostitution in New York City, 1830-1870*. Berkeley: University of California Press, 1993.

Woodsworth, Michael. *Battle for Bed-Stuy: The Long War on Poverty in New York City*. Cambridge, Mass.: Harvard University Press, 2016.

Worrall, Janet E. "Reflections on Italian Prisoners of War: Fort Wadsworth, 1943–46." *Italian Americana* 10, no. 2 (Spring/Summer 1992): 147–55.

Wright, Nazeera Sadiq. *Black Girlhood in the Nineteenth Century*. Urbana: University of Illinois Press, 2016.

Wuebker, Erin. "Taking the Venereal Out of Venereal Disease: The Public Health Campaign against Syphilis, 1934–1945." PhD diss., Graduate Center, City University of New York, 2015.

Yamin, Rebecca. "Wealthy, Free, and Female: Prostitution in Nineteenth-Century New York." *Historical Archaeology* 39, no. 1 (2005): 4–18.

Zeidman, Irving. *The American Burlesque Show*. New York: Hawthorne Books, 1967.

Index

Page numbers appearing in italics refer to illustrations.

Biondi, Martha, 138
birth control, 56
Black children: criminalization of, 95–96, 99, 195n45 (*See also* juvenile delinquency); as females, 102, 106–7 (*See also* young women); *Spring 3100* and, 96–97
Blackness, 34
Black New Yorkers: anti-prostitution campaign and, 64–69; Bedford-Stuyvesant and, 109–14; City Patrol Corps and, 49; civil rights and, 5; as Democrats, 17; Draft Riots and, 15; as firefighters, 18, 179n48; gambling and, 118–19, 120, 143; housing and, 148–49; labor and, 130, 202n42; La Guardia and, 35; as migrants, 148; in military, 137; in nineteenth century, 12, 13; in NYPD, 18, 35, 40–41, 57, 67, *81, 88,* 163; police disregard for, 16–17, 97, 107, 149, 151; police misconduct and, 24–25, 150, 167; as political candidates, 25, 28; population of, 3, 18, 148; as property owners, 66–67; Valentine and, 38, 149; as voters, 17, 25, 156; Walker and, 27; white mobs and, 18–19. *See also* Black children; Black women; discrimination
Black servicemen, 170, 171–72; on Staten Island, 125, 136–37, 138–43, 144, 205n104
Black women: nightlife policing and, 152, 155–56, 161–62; in NYPD, 40, 95; prostitution and, 5, 59–60, 68–69, 76–77, 146, 208n5; targeting of, 57–58, 69, 171, 177n26; as victims, 18; wartime employment of, 52
Boddy, Luther, 24
Bolin, Jane, 196n46
Bostic, Joe, 155, 160
Bourne, St. Clair, 68
Bowery Boys, 15
boycotts, 5, 16, 157
Boyle, Edward, 95

Braddock Hotel incident, 138, 163–64, 166
Braham, Belle, 131
Brandt, Allan, 46
Brandt, Nat, 137
bridge generation, 51–52
Briggs, Laura, 64
Brooklyn Academy of Music event, 113
Brooklyn Daily Eagle: on crime, 139; on election of 1929, 27; on juvenile delinquency, 42–43, 110; on nightlife policing, 153; on prostitution, 55–56, 73, 74
Buchanan, Bessie, 157–58
Buchanan, Charles, 158, 159–60, 162, 167, 211n54
Bureau for the Prevention of Juvenile Delinquency, 101
Bureau of Education, 92–93
Bureau of Social Hygiene, 61–62, 63, 75–76
Burkard, Joseph, 46
burlesque performers, 5, 169
burlesque theaters, 153
Burley, Dan, 130
Butler, Edward, 163
Byrnes, James F., 131, 133

Cabaret Law of 1926, 26–27, 181n105
Cacchione, Peter, 113
Campbell, Grace, 25
Capeci, Dominic, 35
Capodici, Albert, 50
carceral track for juvenile delinquency, 90
cartoons of NYPD, 23
Chase, William, 97
Chicago, 154, 177n26
Chicago Defender, 154
citizen-police relationship, 16–17, 23, 106–7, 180n74
Citizens' Home Defense League, 20
Citizen's Protective League, 18
City College Division of Public Service Training, 51

City Patrol Corps, 42, 47–50, 109, 153, 185–86n99
civilian complaint review board, 150, 209n29
Civil Rights Act of 1873, 19
Clarke, Dorris, 101–2, 104, 115
class: Blacks and, 18, 57, 66–68; criminality and, 5, 37, 57, 63, 110; juvenile delinquency and, 102; policing nightlife and, 145, 151, 157–58; prostitution and, 57–59, 66, 67–68; reform and, 19–20, 39, 51; women and, 3, 5, 58–59. *See also* middle class; working class
Clement, Elizabeth, 20
clubhouses, Police Athletic League, 93
Coast Guard, 138
Code of Criminal Procedure, 24
coercive patriotism, 6, 48
Collins, James, 163–64, 166
Colored State Guard, 111, 200n133
command system of NYPD, 38
Commission on the Harlem Riot, 149–52
Commission on Training Camp Activities, 20, 61
Committee of Fourteen, 19, 24, 61, 80, 147
Committee on Unity, 141–42
common sense, 197n69
community-police relations, 16–17, 23, 106–7, 180n74
Comstock Law, 56
Conference on Child Health and Protection, 90–91
confidential squad, 36, 122
Congress of Industrial Organizations, 56, 113
conscription, 15, 45–46, 48, 71, 118, 124–25, 129, 132
Conscription Act of 1863, 15
contact tracing, 43, 46, 58, 76–77, 167
contraception, 56
Cooke, Marvel, 68, 155
Corrigan, Joseph, 23

corruption, police: background and overview of, 1–2, 3, 17; Costigan and, 36; gambling and, 119–20, 121, 122; grand juries and, 200n124; investigation of, 28–30; La Guardia and, 2, 32–33; prostitution and, 55–56; Tammany Hall and, 1, 21, 22, 23, 25–26; under Walker, 22, 26–27, 28–29
Costello, Frank, 121, 125–26
Costello, John, 71–72
Costigan, Dan "Honest Dan," 36, 37
Costuma, Louis F., 52–53
Council for Democracy, 141
Council of National Defense, 61
crime-consciousness, 90
Crime Prevention Bureau, 91–92, 98
crime wave, postwar, 171
Crowley, Francis "Two Gun," 37
curfew, national, 134
Curran, Henry, 101, 114–15
Czitrom, Daniel, 17

Dailey, Jane, 190n56
Daily News, 139, 154–56, 157
Darien, Andrew, 40, 41
Davis, Ben, 142
Dead Rabbits, 15
Defense Housing Act, 72
deferment, 6, 48, 129, 132
De Hart, Clarence, 141
Delaney, Hubert, 28
D'Emilio, John, 56
demobilization, 115, 170–71, 173
Democratic Party: Black voters and, 25; in nineteenth century, 12, 13, 17; Tammany Hall and, 1, 13, 17, 21, 27, 30
demographic shifts, 3, 11, 71, 96
Department of Health. *See* Health Department
detention facilities for women, 72, 78, 87
Detroit uprisings, 162–63
Dewey, Thomas E., 44, 103, 115, 121, 125–26

intersection of police with city politics, 7

investigations: grand jury, 110–13, 199–200n124; of Harlem uprisings, 97–98, 149–50, 172; by Lexow Committee, 17; of prostitution arrests, 55–57; by Seabury, 23, 28–30, 55–57, 120, 121; of Staten Island's "crime wave," 139, 140–42; of Tammany Hall, 1

investment, municipal, 2, 11

Irish, the, 13, 26

Italian prisoners of war, 138

JAB (Juvenile Aid Bureau). *See* Juvenile Aid Bureau (JAB)

JAB2 cards, 92

Jackson, Stephen, 101, 103, 170

Japan, 6, 47, 137, 173

Japanese Americans, 47

"Jim Crow North, the," 35

jobs, police, 12, 13, 21. *See also specific jobs*

Johnson, Marilynn, 24

Joint Army-Navy Disciplinary Control Board, 77

Jones, J. Raymond, 17

Journal of Educational Sociology, 142

Juvenile Aid Bureau (JAB): about, 53, 92–93; in Bedford-Stuyvesant, 113; budget of, 102–3, 198n89; cases of, 94, 195n35; neighborhood councils and, 98; requesting services of, 107; surveillance and, 101, 104; wartime services of, 105; Wayward Minor Law and, 115; women and, 39–40

juvenile delinquency: arrests for, 104, 105, 106; background and overview of, 90–93; City Patrol Corps and, 49; crime in Bedford-Stuyvesant and, 109–14; gender and, 60–61, 93–95, 103–9, 114–15; PAL and, 42–43; postwar, 171; race and, 90–91, 93, 95–100, 102, 106–7; rates of, 95, 195n45; surveillance for, 40, 50, 90, 92–93, 100–104, 107–8, 116; wartime concern

for rise of, 99–103, 197nn69–70; wartime policing of girls and, 103–9

juvenile justice system, 90, 103

Kane, Farrell M., 136, 138–39, 141–43

Kaplon, Evelyn, 104

Katz, Max, 132

Kay, Harold, 49

Keller, Lisa, 12

Kelley, Gene, 169

King, Shannon, 19, 24, 67

Kingston Avenue Hospital for Communicable Diseases, 63, 75

Kline, Emanuel, 67, 163

Knights of Labor, 16

Koenig, Raphael, 114–15

Koutnick, Stanley, 53

Kresel, Isidor, 55–56

Kross, Anna, 60–61

labor: at Fox Hills Army Facility, 138; gambling and, 117–18, 123–24, 129–30, 131; movements of, 12, 15–16, 19; women and, 50–51, 52, 56

La Guardia, Fiorello, 83–84; background and overview of, 1–6, 7; Battle and, 42; Bedford-Stuyvesant and, 111, 112, 114; as a candidate, 27, 28, 30–31; curfew and, 134; gambling and, 117–18, 121–28, 131, 132, 135, 143–44; ideology of, 32–36, 37, 58, 170; juveniles and, 91–92, 98, 99–100, 102–3, 105, 108, 109; nightlife policing and, 145–46, 154, 160–61, 167; postwar, 173; prostitution and, 57, 71–72, 79; race and, 34–36, 140, 141, 149, 162–63; uprisings and, 151, 164; war mobilization and, 44, 46, 47, 53

Lanham Act, 44, 72, 78, 79

Lansky, Meyer, 125–26

Lanza, Socks, 125–26

LAPD (Los Angeles Police Department), 187n129

presentment of Bedford-Stuyvesant grand jury, 110–11, 112–14
preventative juvenile delinquency policing, 90–93, 101, 116, 171, 197n70
prisoners of war, 138, 166
prisons: for juveniles, 95–96; for women, 63, 72, 78, 87
procession regulation law, 15
production, wartime, 52, 123, 126, 130–32, 153, 176n15
profiling: of juveniles, 96; of prostitutes, 37, 45, 58–59, 64–65, 74–75, 77–79, 170
promotions for Black NYPD members, 40, 41
propaganda, anti-prostitution, 45, 71
prostitution: in Bradford-Stuyvesant, 110; campaign against (See anti-prostitution campaign); framing for, 23, 29, 55, 56; juvenile delinquency and, 100–101, 104; La Guardia and, 33; men as prostitutes and, 60; nightlife policing and, 152–53, 158–59; in nineteenth century, 14; postwar, 78, 170–71; as a psychiatric problem, 60–61; race and, 59–60, 146, 171, 208n5; Valentine and, 36, 37; venereal disease and, 43, 44–46; during WWI, 20–21; WWII mobilization and, 43–45
protection: campaigns for by Black New Yorkers 18–19, 25, 119, 125, 139, 144, 149–50
protection of juveniles, 95, 97
protection of property, 11, 12, 15, 16
protection of servicemen: anti-prostitution campaign and, 71–74, 79; from gambling, 118, 123–27, 133–36, 144; juveniles and, 99–100; nightlife policing and, 152–54, 156, 162, 167, 168; race and, 125, 139–40, 142, 144; reform and, 44–46, 52
protection payments, 23
Public Health Law, 43–44, 61

Public Health Service, U.S., 62, 71, 72, 188n18
public relations campaign, police, 25
public sanitary facilities, 72.
Puerto Rican New Yorkers, 3, 40, 59, 76, 96, 106, 184n49

Rabinowitz, Mary, 131
race: Bedford-Stuyvesant and, 109–14; consumption and production and, 130–31; criminality and, 5, 7, 34–35; gambling and, 118–19, 120, 123, 129–30; girls' sexuality and, 95; hierarchies of, 2, 3, 35, 172; housing and employment and, 148–49; juvenile delinquency and, 90–91, 93, 95–100, 102, 106–7; La Guardia and, 34–36, 140, 141, 149, 162–63; liberalism and, 2, 34, 176n5; mobilization for WWII and, 50–52, 57, 125; New Deal and, 182n11; nightlife policing and, 148; policing servicemen and, 125, 136–43, 144, 202n104; prostitution and, 59–60, 146, 171, 208n5; solidarity of, 67, 137; Valentine and, 37–38, 40–43, 149, 162–63; venereal diseases and, 76–77; war mobilization and, 50–52, 57, 125
racial liberalism, 2, 176n5
"raided premises," 77, 148, 154, 163, 166, 167
Raided Premises Squad, 38
raids: for gambling, 127, 132; in Harlem, 65, 73, 121; on Japanese, 47; on nightclubs and theaters, 73, 146–47; Valentine and, 36, 67
Randolph, Philip, 160
Ransom, Llewellyn, 140
Ray, Ebenezer, 65
Razaf, Andy, 161
Recovery Party, 30
Reed, Edmund, 165
reform, police: class and, 19–20, 39, 51, 124; of early twentieth century, 19–20, 22; in nineteenth century,